Christian Spirituality
in Context

Christian Spirituality
in Context

—

지은이 이주형
펴낸곳 도서출판 케노시스

등 록 제2011-24호(2011. 5. 23)
전 화 02) 453-2208, 450-5435-6
팩 스 02) 2201-6953
주 소 서울시 광진구 광장로 5길 25-1

인 쇄 2019년 5월 7일
발 행 2019년 5월 13일

I S B N 979-11-85698-24-3 (93230)

값 15,000원 (*파본은 바꿔드립니다)

Christian Spirituality in Context

이주형 지음

Co ntext

도서출판 케노시스

　　이주형 교수님의 "Christian Spirituality in Context"의 출판을 마음 깊이 환영하며 감사하는 마음을 전한다. 다음과 같은 세 가지 이유 때문이다. 첫째는 한국적 상황의 영성을 소개한다는 의미에서 환영하고 감사한다. 한국교회의 역사가 서양 기독교에 비하면 미천하기에 그 동안 영성을 학문으로 추구하는 학자들은 그 자료들이나 주제들을 주로 서양영성의 전통에 의존해 왔다. 새로운 분야를 이 땅에 소개하는 과정에서 그러한 일들은 불가피하다고 할 수 있다. 그러나 우리 교회 환경 안에서 비평적 성찰이 없이 단순히 답습하고 소개하는 일에 머물러 있다면, 우리가 그 동안 입고 있는 옷을 모조리 발가벗기고 새로운 옷을 입히고자 하는 시도와 같다. 그러한 일은 가능하지도 않을 뿐만 아니라, 가능하다 할지라도 상당한 상처와 부작용을 남길 수밖에 없다. 더욱이 발전적으로 영성학이 이 땅에 뿌리를 내릴 수 없다. 그런데 본 저서는 그 서양전통의 뿌리를 잘 소화시켜서 한국교회 영성에 접목시켜 더 풍성한 영적인 전통을 이어주려는 시도를 하고 있다.

　　두 번째는 실천적이고 현장적인 주제를 다양하게 펼치고 있는 저서라는 의미에서 축하하고 환영한다. 영성이 다분히 이론적인 담론에만 머물면, 그것이 여타 다른 신학분야와 차별성을 두기가 쉽지 않다. 때로 그것은 실천신학이나 역사신학, 심지어는 조직신학의 분야처럼 보이기도 한다. 그런데 본 저서에서 다루고 있는 논제들은 언 듯 보아도 전문적인 영성학에서 다루어야

할 주제라는 확신을 주고 있다. 본 저서가 다루고 있는 영적지도, 분별, 영성 훈련, 기도 등이 그렇다. 이러한 주제들은 한국교회의 상황에서는 그렇게 익숙한 분야라 할 수 없다. 그래서 저자는 낯선 실천적 주제들을 격조 높은 이론적 배경과 전통들을 소개하면서, 우리 교회 안에서 그러한 영성의 분야들이 어떻게 이해되어지고 활용되어야 하는지에 대한 치열한 고민 담겨져 있는 저서이다. 그러므로 본 저서는 상아탑 안의 학문적 자료뿐만 아니라, 교회 현장을 살찌울 수 있는 지침서로도 손색이 없을 만큼 생동력이 넘치는 책이다.

셋째는 한국 교회에 걸맞는 상황적이고 토착적인 영성의 주제를 영문으로 출판한 것에 대해서 환영과 감사를 보낸다. 이 땅의 영성학이 걸음마 수준이기에, 우리가 다루는 영성의 주제들과 자료들은 거의 대부분이 서양 기독교 전통에 의존하고 있다. 그렇기에 영성학을 전공으로 하는 모든 이들은 서양 기독교 전통에 많은 빚을 지고 있다고 할 수 있다. 그런데 본 저서가 영문으로 펼쳐짐으로서 미약하나마 빚을 갚을 수 있게 되었다는 의미에서 감사가 있다.

한 가지 부언하자면, 단행본들은 보통 뒷장은 전장을 전제로 해서 읽어야 더 잘 이해가 되며, 또 전체를 잃어야 저자가 전해주고자 하는 메시지를 제대로 받을 수 있다. 그러나 본 저서는 각 장 자체서로 완전한 학문적 가치를 지니고 있는 논문에 해당되는 것이기에, 필요한 만큼 읽을 수 있는 좋은 참고서적이 될 수도 있다. 이 책이 학문을 하는 사람이나, 현장의 목회자들이나 그리고 해외에서 연구하는 이들 모두에게 널리 널리 읽혀지기를 기대하며 추천합니다.

유해룡 (전 장신대 영성신학 교수, 현 모새골 교회 담임목사)

근대시대에 분리되었던 마음과 영혼이 현대에 와서 다시 만나기 시작하였습니다. 정신의학과 심리치료가 현대에 들어서 영성과의 대화를 통해 새로운 인간 치유를 지향해가고 있음을 목도합니다. 인간 정신 문제를 다루며 영혼을 다루지 못하는 심리치료는 전인적인 치유를 지향하는 현대사회에서 그 설자리를 점점 잃어갈 것입니다. 이주형 박사는 심리학과 영성, 목회상담과 영성지도를 두루 수련 받으며, 현대사회가 요청하는 기독교 영성치유의 학문적이고 전문적인 영역을 구축하고 있는 학자이자 영성지도자입니다. 기독영성상담의 이론적 기틀을 다지고 있는 이주형 박사의 기독교 영성적 토대를 보여주는 전문서적이 출간되어 반갑게 생각합니다. 기독교 영성이 지닌 인간 변화의 근원성에 믿음을 갖고 있는 목회자, 상담가, 심리치료사 및 영혼돌봄 사역자들에게 훌륭한 학문적 토대를 제공하리라 확신하기에 기쁜 마음으로 추천합니다.

이만홍

(전 연세대 의대 정신과 교수, 전 한국기독교상담심리학회장, 현 한국영성지도 · 영성상담협회 공동회장)

영성은 더 이상 특정한 종교의 테두리 안에 갇혀있지 않습니다. 다양한 정신병리 현상으로 고통 받고 있는 현대인들이 명상과 영성을 통해 치유와 회복을 경험하고 있습니다. 이주형 교수는 종교심리학/목회상담과 영성 분야에서 다년간 수련을 받으며 이론과 실제를 겸비한 기독교영성지도 전문가입니다. 그의 첫 연구서적 출간이 반가운 이유는 학문으로서 영성이 지니는 이론적인 체계와 공고한 합리성을 증명하고 있기 때문입니다. 인간 변화와 치유를 이끄는 기독교 영성이 초월적이고 신비적이지만, 결코 모호하거나

애매하지 않습니다. 오히려 학문적 체계 속에서 확고한 자리매김을 하고 있다는 사실을 이주형 교수의 저서가 증명하고 있습니다. 영성에 대한 학문적이고 이론적인 체계에 도움을 받고자 하는 상담가, 심리치료사, 교육가, 목회자와 사역자들에게 이 책은 반가운 소식이 될 것입니다.

윤종모 (대한성공회 주교, 전 한국기독교상담심리학회장, 〈치유명상〉 저자)

우리는 요즘 영성이란 주제가 들어간 다양한 책들을 접하고 있습니다. 그러나 영성을 전공한 전문가의 글은 많지 않습니다. 이주형 교수는 영성신학의 이론과 실천을 전공하고 그동안 국내외에 주목할만한 연구논문과 글들을 발표하며 영성분야 발전에 기여해왔습니다. 그의 글의 장점은 이론과 실천의 균형이 있고, 전문적인 내용을 누구든 이해하기 쉽게 쓰며, 특히 그에게는 나다나엘같은 담백한 마음으로 단순한 삶을 사랑하는 진정한 영성가의 향기가 있습니다. 그의 이런 장점이 잘 담긴 이 책 역시 이 분야의 단비가 되리라 믿으며, 일독을 적극 권하는 바입니다.

구제홍 (명지대 인문교양학부 교수, 교목실장)

이 책은 기독교영성 관련 영어 논문 모음집이다. 국내에서 출판된 최초의 기독교영성학 영어논문집이라고 할 수 있다. 먼저 영성지도자인 이주형 교수는 이 책에서 영성훈련, 영성지도, 영적분별, 그리고 영성형성 등 기독교영성의 실천적이고 목회적인 주제들을 개인적인 경험과 함께 폭넓고 다양하게 다루고 있다. 다음으로 기독교영성학자인 저자는 대표적인 영성가들 ― 닛사의 그레고리, 이냐시오 로욜라, 조나단 에드워즈, 그리고 토마스 머튼 등―을 깊이 있게 분석하고 인용한다. 또한 이 논문들은 기독교영성학의 간학문적(interdisciplinary) 방법론의 예를 잘 보여주고 있다. 여성신학, 토착심리학, 뇌과학, 그리고 생태학 등 신학과 일반 학문의 성과를 차용하여 기독교인의 경험을 해석하는데 유용한 새로운 관점들을 제시하고 있다. 마지막으로 대학교 교목인 저자는 기독교영성의 주제들을 대학 교육 현장에 적용하려고 시도하고 있다: "N세대를 위한 향심기도"와 "대학생의 소명을 위한 영성형성" 등. 이 책을 기독교영성학을 전공하는 석사 및 박사 과정 학생들을 비롯해서 기독교영성학 및 영성지도에 관심 있는 학자들과 일반 신자들에게 적극 추천한다.

이강학 (횃불트리니티신학대학원대학교, 기독교영성학 부교수)

기독교 영성과 영성지도에 깊은 학문적 조예와 풍부한 경험이 있으신 이주형 박사님의 옥고들을 만나게 되어 더 없는 기쁨입니다.

홍영택 (감리교신학대학교 목회상담학 교수)

　　새로운 세기가 시작될 무렵부터 인류 문명은 영성에 대한 관심을 고조시
켜 왔다. 세 번째 밀레니엄에 대한 문명적 호기심과 두려움, 낯선 여정에 대
한 불안과 기대가 혼재하는 상황에서 초월과 신비를 향한 역설적 소망이 투
영된 역사적 현상이라 분석할 수 있을 것이다. 인간과 사회에 대한 새로운
패러다임을 영성이란 용어와 개념을 통해 새로운 돌파구를 찾으려는 학문
탐구는 심리학과 사회학을 비롯한 학계 전반에 걸쳐 지금도 지속되어 왔다.
서구사회는 NRBS(Not Religious, But Spiritual!), SBNR(Spiritual, but not Religious!)라
는 종교사회학적 표현 하에, 영성에 대한 탐구와 갈망이 젊은 세대 중심으로
정착되고 있는 형국이다. 한국사회도 문명적 흐름과 크게 다르지 않아 영성
에 대한 갈급함은 사회전반에 걸쳐 증가하고 있지만, 제도권 교회는 젊은이
들로부터 외면당하는 와중에도 뚜렷한 대안을 찾지 못하고 있는 상황이다.
그 와중에 영성수련과 영성지도를 중심으로 기독교 영성의 고귀한 지혜와
역사 깊은 전통이 현대사회와 한국사회 곳곳에서 새롭게 재발견되고 있는
것 같아 반가운 마음이다. 한국 기독교와 한국 교회는 기독교 영성의 심오한
지혜와 통찰을 통해, 한국인의 영적 목마름을 해갈할 수 있을까? 이 궁극적
질문에 대해 미력이나마 응답하고 싶은 소박한 열망에서 이 책의 연구가 출
발되었다.

기독교 영성학(Christian Spirituality as Academic Discipline)은 해석학적 접근을 통해 인간 경험을 주요 탐구 대상으로 삼는다. 인간의 개별적 상황에서 하나님을 새롭게 만나고, 그 초월적이며 영적인 경험의 의미를 발견하여 오늘 삶의 자리에서 영적 변화와 성장을 추구한다. 본 저작은 인간 경험의 필수적 구성요소로 문화를 지목하여 주요 대화자로 삼았다. 경험을 구성하는 모든 요소들이 문화의 테두리, 혹은 문화적 프레임 안에서 형성되기 때문이다. 먹고, 자고, 기도하고 예배하는 행위로부터, 관계를 맺고 사회 구조에 참여하여 체계를 구축하는 행위, 자연생태계를 대하는 태도 등 모든 경험에는 문화적 요소가 영향을 미친다. 그래서 인간의 개별적 상황에서 심층적인 하나님 경험을 탐구하기 위해서는 문화에 대한 이해가 우선되어야 한다는 저자의 확신이 각 장마다 담겨 있다. 하나님은 지금 이 순간에 문화의 옷을 입고 우리 안에 임재하여 계신다. 그런 의미에서, 기독교 영성학은 문화 안에 임재하여 계신 하나님(culturally incarnated God)에 대한 철저한 이해와 탐구가 필요한 시점이다.

저자의 영적인 여정과 학문적 탐구 여행은 기독교영성의 거대한 해양에서 태생하였고, 유영하였으며, 목표를 향해 지금도 항해하고 있다. 기독교 영성은 이론과 실천, 학문과 사역 현장사이에 일치와 통합을 요청하기에 실존적으로 어려운 학문이다. 스승님들과 선배님들의 영적 순례를 닮아가고자 노력하고 있지만, 여전히 내 인격과 삶은 학문적 지식을 따라가지 못해 쉽게 실망감에 휩싸인다. 그럼에도 항상 다시 일어날 수 있는 이유는 영적 여정을 통해 연단시키셨던 하나님의 은혜에 대한 믿음 때문이다. 날마다 나의 부족함을 인식하지만 다시금 주님의 은혜에 의지하여서 새롭게 시작할 용기를 얻는다.

　여기 모은 논문들은 짧게는 박사과정 후 한국에서 적응하는 3년 동안, 길게는 학문수련을 한 15년여 동안, 한국적 상황에서 기독교 영성의 가치가 온전히 발견되길 기도하는 마음으로 연구해 온 결과물이다. 기독교 영성의 학문적인 수준을 담보하기 위해 세계영성지도자협회 저널지(Presence)에 수록된 논문과 한국연구재단 등재지에 게재된 논문만을 수록하였다. 영어 논문을 작성해온 이유는 첫째, 박사과정 중 연구한 주제들을 확장하여 다루었기 때문이며, 둘째는 저자의 학문적 언어가 부족했기 때문이다. 신학 입문을 유학으로부터 시작하였기에 저자에게 용이한 언어로 연구하였다. 물론, 한국 기독교 영성 연구가 세계 곳곳에 소개되길 바라는 작은 소망도 담겨있다. 저자는 이 논문들을 게재하는 과정에서 기독교 영성에 대한 한국 기독교 학계의 적극적 관심과 호기심을 몸소 체험하여왔다. 이 책을 통해 한국 기독교 영성학의 학문적 발전에 조금이나마 기여하고, 한국적 상황에서 적실한 기독교 영성연구와 학문적 대화에 미력이나마 보탬이 되길 소망한다.

　영성지도와 영성수련을 담고 있는 Part 1의 Chapter 1은 향심기도가 지닌 심리치료적 특징과 영적 역동이 현대 청춘들의 영성생활에 유의미한 변화와 성장을 이끈다는 사실을 기독교 영성 방법론을 이용하여 증명하고자 했다. Chapter 2는 이냐시오 영신수련 원문을 분석한 연구로서, 영신수련의 궁극적 목표 중에 하나인 거룩한 선택에 이르는 수련 방법이 거룩한 상상력을 기반으로 한다는 사실을 증명하고자 했다. Chapter 3은 생태여성주의 신학자인 Rosemary Reuther의 조직신학적 프레임을 영성지도의 영성형성에 적용하고 구체화한 연구이다. Chapter 4는 세계 영성지도협회의 유일한 학술지인 Presence: The International Journal of Spiritual Direction에 기고한 논문으로, 아시아(한국)인 남성의 정체성을 지닌 영성지도자가 사역에 참여했을 때 갖추어야한 문화사회적 자의식에 관한 문화영성 연구이다.

Part 2는 필자의 주요 탐구 영역인 영적 분별에 관한 연구를 담고 있다. Chapter 5는 Jonathan Edwards의 영적 분별 전통을 현대 사회에서 인간에 대한 가장 최선의 정보를 제공하고 있는 신경과학적 근거를 통해 재개념화하고 분석한 연구이다. 종교와 과학간의 대립과 갈등이 고조되고 있는 한국 개신교 상황 속에서 영적 경험을 최신의 과학적 근거를 통해 분석함으로써, 전통적인 기독교 영성을 현대적 상황에서 최적화시키기 위해 시도한 연구 결과물이다. Chapter 6은 영적 분별에 있어 욕망의 중심성을 주장하면서, Gregory of Nyssa의 설교에 녹아 있는 인간 욕망에 대한 영적 이해를 통해 현대 기독인들의 욕망의 정화의 필요성과 영적 분별을 통한 영적 성숙을 제시한 연구이다. Chapter 7은 한국 기독교회 리더십의 문제와 한계를 분석하면서 공동체 분별을 통해 공동체 리더십의 영적 변화와 성장을 위한 꾀하고 있다.

기독교 영성형성을 다루고 있는 Part 3는 저자의 사역 현장이 던지는 목회적 도전과 질문에 대한 학문적 응답이 담겨 있다. Chapter 8은 기독교 영성의 존재론적 지식을 대학 교육 현장에서 어떻게 적용할지에 대한 연구이다. 기술과 정보 위주의 인식론적 지식에서 존재론적 만남을 통한 배움의 과정이 인간 변화와 성장에 필수적 요소라는 사실을 탐구하고 있다. Chapter

9는 대학생의 인생 과업을 정체성 탐구로 규정하고, 성찰기도를 중심으로 한 영성수련을 통해 기독교 영성 형성의 필요성과 구체적 방안을 연구하고 있다. Chapter 10은 20세기 이후 가장 영향력 있는 기독교 영성가인 Thomas Merton의 영성 속에서 긍휼의 영성을 발굴하여 폭력적 문명과 사회 속에 비폭력적 영성을 실천하는 학문적 방안을 모색하였다. Chapter 11 이면서 마지막 장은 자연과학과 조직신학적 개념을 통해 자연과 인간 본성을 성화시키는 하나님 은혜의 주도성을 탐구하고 있다. 이는 영성수련과 영성지도 사역에 있어 하나님 임재와 현존에 대한 경험과 영성형성을 위한 기독교 영성형성적 탐구의 일환이다.

지면을 통해서 감사의 인사를 드리고 싶은 분들은 헤아릴 수 없이 많다. 여기에 언급된 분들보다 언급되지 못하신 분들은, 보이는 곳에서 또는 보이지 않는 곳에서 저자의 부족한 인격과 학문적 단점에도 불구하고, 저와 제 가족에게 하나님의 사랑을 부족함 없이 나눠주셨습니다. 제 학문적 여정의 산파 역할을 해주신 GTU의 Lieberts 교수님, Rambo 교수님, CST의 Dreitcer 교수님과 Rogers 교수님께 존경을 담아 감사드립니다. 귀국 후, 인생의 새로운 터전을 잡을 수 있도록 길을 열어주신 명지대 구제홍 교목실장님, 숭실대 조은식 교목실장님, 연세대 정용한 교목님께 진심을 담아 감사 인사드립니다. 한국 사회와 교회 상황 속에서 기독교 영성지도와 영성사역을 실천할 수 있도록 학문적인 기틀과 전문적인 안내를 제공해주시고, 추천의 글까지 써주신 유해룡 교수님, 횃불트리니티 신학교 이강학 교수님, 윤종모 주교님, 이만홍 교수님, 연세대 권수영 학장님, 감신대 홍영택 교수님께 깊은 감사를 드립니다.

남편을 일찍 여의고, 어린 두 아들을 홀로 키우시며 숱한 역경 속에서도 인생의 숭고함과 신앙의 고귀함을 몸소 삶을 통해 가르쳐주신 어머니에게 사랑과 존경을 담아 감사의 인사를 전합니다. 무엇보다도, 여러모로 부족한 사람과 인생의 어려운 시기를 지혜롭게 잘 견뎌준 아내와 두 딸에게 사랑을 전합니다. "와이프, 사랑해! 재윤아, 재인아! 아빠의 자랑스러운 딸이 돼주어 고마워! 사랑해!"

2019년 봄의 길목

숭실대 교정에서

The third millennium has puzzlingly launched with mixed feelings of expectation and concern, since no human being has yet walked this pilgrimage. As the academic and public enterprises both seem to seek for a new paradigm appropriate for the new era, Christian spirituality has played a significant role in providing a new platform for discussing the mixed feelings of the human species about the last two decades. The famous term in socio-religious disciplines, "NRBS or SBNR" has become a predominant concept for characterizing the new generation, and its main features have been discovered beyond geographical boundaries. So has Korean society and Christianity. Even though the desire for spirituality has been intensifying, religious institutions and churches seem to be have failed to respond in proper ways. It is a delightful observation, however, that some Christians look for spiritual practices and join in spiritual direction programs that appreciate the valuable wisdom and profound insights of Christian spiritual heritages. Would it be possible for Korean Christianity and churches to quench the spiritual thirst? This book has sprouted out of the humble desire to respond to that crucial question.

Christian spirituality as an academic discipline facilitates the hermeneutical approaches to appropriating human experiences about the Trinity. One primary purpose of the discipline is to foster and cultivate spiritual experiences so that a soul's relationship with God would be rejuvenated or transformed in the situations that life gives. Especially, this book takes cultural contexts into serious consideration, as the academic conversation about human experiences, including the spiritual sphere, are formed, shaped, or formulated by mutually interacting with cultural components. My academic and ministerial disciplines have firmly convinced me that academic comprehension and research on Christian spirituality should be based on the conviction that the presence of God is incarnated within cultures. All that we know about a culture helps us discover the presence and activity of God in life situations. This book compiles academic articles published in America and Korea, with which I have engaged for three years after returning in Korea, and extensively for the 15 academic years I spent in America. As is easily recognizable, most research has taken Korean or Korean-American contexts seriously into consideration based on the cultural implications of Christian spirituality. Its theoretical or practical implication could, however, be implemented in universal ways, I believe.

Part I contains academic works on spiritual direction and practices. Chapter One attempts to prove the way in which the psychological characteristics and spiritual dynamics of "Centering prayer," a modern spiritual practice of apophatic tradition, could lead to transformation and growth of young adults' spirituality. Chapter Two analyzes the original text of Ignatius' *Spiritual Exercises*, demonstrating that a primary goal of spiritual practices is to make a sacred choice facilitating contemplative imagination. In Chapter Three, I endeavor to analyze ecofeminist Rosemary Reuther's theological frame for delineating the formation of spiritual direction. Chapter Four explores the ways in which an Asian (Korean) male identity could affect ministry in providing spiritual direction, and in which cultural components should be acknowledged in self-awareness.

Part II focuses primarily on spiritual discernment as the core of spiritual formation and practices. Chapter Five redefines the traditional notion of discernment and its internal dynamics in the writings of Jonathan Edwards, and suggests a holistic sense of discernment by borrowing from the neuroscientific information that has recently reshaped the academic understanding of the human mind. Chapter Six diagnoses the sermons of Gregory of Nyssa and draws out the centrality of desire in spiritual discernment. It proposes the necessity to purify desire as a prerequisite for an authentic process and outcomes of spiritual discernment in modern Christian spirituality. Chapter Seven attempts to introduce the communal discernment of Ignatian tradition as pastoral leadership formation for Korean Christian churches as utilizing leadership theories unfolds.

Part III consists of research on spiritual formation that attempts to respond to pastoral questions and academic challenges in a given context. Chapter Eight makes the primary assumption that ontological knowledge should be pursued in college education for genuine growth and transformation of human nature. It describes three sacred encounters that should be promoted for a spirituality-oriented higher educational curriculum. Chapter Nine defines self-identity and life vocation as primary goals for college students, and it delineates the reasons and the methods by which spiritual practices and the examination of conscience could shape the spiritual formation of college students. Chapter Ten names compassion as the core value of the spirituality of Thomas Merton, who has been very influential in the 20th Century beyond religious boundaries. It further tries to rediscover the spirituality of compassion as an alternative strategy for the Christian nonviolence movement in the hostile atmosphere of modern society. Chapter Eleven investigates the initiatives of Divine Grace sanctifying both nature and human nature. It offers a theological threshold for the concept of divine presence and divine milieu, which will be foundational for spiritual experiences and formation.

A few words could not fully express my deepest gratitude and appreciation toward the souls shaping my life. My family and I have owed much to the many saints who encouraged, supported, and even sustained us in visible or invisible ways. First of all, I would like to thank Prof. Elizabeth Liebert of the SFTS/GTU who invited me into the academic landscape of Christian Spirituality as my academic advisor and stood firmly besides me as a spiritual midwife when I underwent a dark night of the soul. Prof. Lewis Rambo showed me the good example of theological scholars who achieved a great balance between professional sensitivity and humble character. Prof. Andrew Dreitcer and Prof. Frank Rogers of the CST were the spiritual healers who helped cure me from hardships and were also the academic midwives who help resettle and hatch my academic research topic in the life-giving nest of Claremont.

I would like to show my admiration and appreciation to my mother, who raised two little boys in harsh circumstances after the loss of our father. She has demonstrated throughout her whole life that life is beautiful and noble, and that the Christian faith is sublime and dignified, which is the spiritual and sustainable resource for me. Most of all, my love and gratitude go to my wife, Byeonghee, and our two daughters, Clair and Jane, who have walked faithfully with me even in life-challenging situations.

Spring of 2019

Soongsil Campus

C . O . N . T . E . N . T . S

I. Spiritual Practice & Direction

2 Centrality of Imagination in *Election* within *Spiritual Exercises* • 55

III. Spiritual Formation for Next Generation

Christian Spirituality in Context

I.
Spiritual Practice
& Direction

1

From "Disconnected" to "Centered":

The Implication of Centering Prayer
for the Korean Young Adults

I. Introduction

In a modern society where most young Koreans are college-educated and have a background in secular psychology, an emerging generation has been taught a heightened personal reflexivity and the value of self-awareness. They furthermore are not motivated by the Church which currently uses dogmatic teaching methods and catechisms that are accelerating the decline in the younger population getting connected with Church life.[1] Knowledge-oriented education in Church such as Bible study, however, does not satisfy the new generation's core feature: a longing for and reliance upon personal experience.

Most assuredly, Christian spiritual practice can play a threshold role in transforming and renewing the emerging Korean generation's

---

[1] Sungbin Lim, "A Christian Cultural Perspective on the N-Generation," *Church and Theology* 54 (2003), 57. The author does not decisively differentiate Generation X from Generation N by stressing that their features are discovered as mixture in Korean society.

spiritual life and religiosity.[2] Based on Liebert's definition of spiritual practice as "the intentional and repeated bringing of one's lived spirituality" into every dimension of life,[3] genuine spiritual practice will not only enhance and cultivate a person's felt experiences and understanding of God, but also revitalize and transform his or her spirituality. I propose in this paper that Centering Prayer is the appropriate form of spiritual practice for the emerging generation in Korea. Moreover, contemplative tradition and mystical spirituality embedded in genuine spiritual practice have the potential to renew spirituality by connecting mystical experience with everyday life. I will concentrate on the transformation of the spirituality of the Korean emerging generation by introducing young people to Centering Prayer and the Christian contemplative tradition.

The following study will accomplish these tasks first by defining Generation X (Gen X) as most prominent description for emerging Young Adult in socio-religious frame, and then analyzing their characteristics in Korean society comparing them with the American Generation X. Next, the fourteenth century English spiritual text, the *"Cloud of Unknowing"* will be investigated along with an explanation given of how to appropriate this practice's rich spiritual heritage into the Korean emerging generation's spiritual formation. Lastly, I will of-

---

2 "Religiosity" refers in this paper to comprehensive religious life, such as attending worship service, Bible study, fellowship, commitment to social service, and the relationship with God.

3 Elizabeth Liebert, "The Role of Practice in the Study of Christian Spirituality," in *Minding the Spirit*, eds. Elizabeth Dreyer and Mark Burrows (Baltimore and London: The Johns Hopkins University Press, 2005), 86.

fer Centering Prayer because of its *apophatic* nature as an effective formative spiritual practice for emerging young adults in the Korean context. In the conclusion of this study, therefore, I will show that the contemplative tradition in Christian, *apophatic* spirituality not only offers a critical guide to lead the new generation into a transformation of their spirituality, but affirms that Centering Prayer is the appropriate contemplation for the spirituality of Korean young adults.

II. Korean Young Adults

1. The "*unnamed*" name

In general, Gen X is categorized as a group of people who were born from the early 1960s to the late 1970s in America. They grew up in an unprecedented time in history and passed through the tunnel of uncertainty: the break down of the institution of marriage, the rise of single parenting and the enjoyment of various TV shows as its aftermath, the advent of AIDS, and the boom of computers and internet.[4] They launched to distinguish uniqueness of their culture from any other previous generation in twenty-years-olds creating the pop-culture. Contrary to the baby-boomer generation's positive participation in social issues, they pursued a self-centered life style and were much more interested in cultivating themselves with rich resources such as money and a good education system.[5] Confronted by various values and rela-

---

4 Jason William Beyer, "Young Adult Catholics: A Contemporary Look at A Potentially Mystical Faith" (M.A. diss., Graduate Theological Union, 2003), 1.

5 Tom Beaudoin, *Virtual Faith: the Irreverent Spiritual Quest of Generation X* (San Francisco:

tivism, they were engrossed with pop-songs which symbolized their resistance towards the existing norms.[6] Because of these complicated features, this generation has been labeled as the Generation X which names the 'unnamed,' who have unstable identity. Why Generation X then? It is believed that the socio-religious term embodies the most prominent characteristics of the emerging young adults in postmodern society.[7]

2. Generation X in Korea[8]

Korean society has experienced many transitions during the last century: the Japanese Occupation until 1945; the Korean War in 1950; economics-oriented modernization by military dictatorships during the 1960s and 1970s; political democratization in the 1980s; and postmodernism in the 1990s.

Considering the cultural, political, and social circumstances, it is unreasonable to adopt strictly the term Gen X in Korean society, mainly since Korean society almost simultaneously went through the pre-

---

Jossey-Bass, 1998), 28.

6 Ibid., 4-5.

7 Postmodern is defined here as "the relativity of values, the dispersal and decentralization of the subject, the limits of reason, the fragmentation of the world, the breakdown of dogmatic virtues and encyclopedic narratives." Gary Eberle, *the Geography of Nowhere,* (Kansas City: Sheed & Ward, 1994), 21, quoted originally from Tzvetan Todorov, "Postmodernism, A Primer," Review of Steven Connor's "Postmodernist Culture: an Introduction to Theories of the Contemporary," *The New Republic* (May 21, 1990 issue), 32.

8 Agreeing with Beaudion's idea (Tom Beaudoin, *Virtual Faith*, 28), it will be more reasonable to categorize this group of people not by their ages, but by cultural feature, based on the conviction that its features must be regarded as cultural, rather than as age group. Nevertheless, the age relevantly ranges from 40 to 25 in Korea.

modern and modern eras. For instance, while Gen X used to be considered the sons and daughters of the baby boom generation in America, the Korean baby boomer generation—from post-Korean War (1953) to pre-economic-oriented modernization (1963) is located just before the emergence of the Korean Gen X.[9] Generally, Gen Xers in Korea can be identified as those who were reared during the economic boom in the early 1970s through the early 1980s and were able to enjoy its abundance and surplus. Social and political participation became a significant determiner to differentiate this generation from the "386 generation."[10] Similar to Gen X of America, however, upon graduating from college, they became the most devastated victims of the national economic bankruptcy due to the International Monetary Fund crisis in 1997.[11] In socio-religious sense, these young adults have been experienced the unprecedented booming of the protestant churches and its cultural influence in 90s, and abrupt antipathy against the churches during the last decades in Korean society. Even if the young adults have been aware that the church should be changed for emerging young generation, they seems to be suspicious of church's capability to renew or nurture their spiritual life of emerging young adults.

Professor Jang articulates well in his article, the unique character-

---

9 Real Culture, ed., *The Theory of New Generation: Chaos and Order*, (Seoul: Lab of Real Culture, 1999), 7.

10 This terminology indicates specifically in Korean society the group of people who were the age of thirties (30s), attended college during the 1980s, the political turbulence era, and born in the 1960s, the poverty and baby booming era.

11 According to Jason William Beyer, American Gen X tasted sour frustration through the economic depression when they entered job market. Beyer, *Young Adult Catholics*, 2.

istics of Korean Generation X.[12] First, they pursue emotional individualism contrary to the individualism rooted in modern rationalism. It is their own feelings which become the focus of the world. Second, they resist authorities or totalitarianism of institutions which tend to deny the uniqueness of each individual. Third, the new generation seeks to be a consumer rather than a manufacturer. Lastly, their identity has been extremely expanded by cyber space which is the virtual locus to accomplish their virtual desires and virtual dreams.

After investigating Gen X identities, I conclude with three characteristics: directionless, nameless and centerless. The place they stand is in the mist of uncertainty and complication. Nothing clearly identifies them with any specific values because they tend to reject the predominating frame of reference. So, they seem to be embarrassed by the fact that they do have **directionless**. Even if cyberspace would be an alternative, their desires still remain unsatisfied. Nevertheless they do not allow themselves to be named in any specific ways and therefore remain **nameless**. The feeling only remains as the subject to identify themselves. Lastly, the postmodern world represented by fragmentation and alienation decentralizes values and truth. It emphasizes subjectivism rather than eliminates any center of the world, leaving Gen X **centerless**. Thus, the generation seems to wander looking for utopia which, however, ironically means 'no place.'[13]

---

12 Jongchul, Jang, "The Values of New Generation and its Task for Christian Education," *Theology and World* 34 (1997), 213-235.

13 Gary Eberle, *the Geography of Nowhere*, (Kansas City: Sheed & Ward, 1994), 143. In an interview, a Gen X was asked why he kept exploring the internet, and what he obtained from it. The answer was striking enough to be still memorized; "it's just fun. That's it. I don't intend to go specific place to get anything from it [directionless]. I'm not gotta ana-

3. Spirituality of Korean Young Adults

Boaudion summarized the spirituality of Gen X by five characteristics.[14] Firstly, they say **no to religion**, and yes to spirituality. What they deny is not about religiosity as a whole, but about religion as an institution. For instance, Gen X Christians want to have an intimate relationship with Jesus, through a personal encounter, but not as a symbolized image of the institution through dogmatic teachings.[15] Secondly, rather than communal, it is **personal** experience by which they evaluate their personal feeling, as the subject in the world. Thirdly, they pursue **mystical** experience of the divine through pop music, because "there is a constant yearning (in the message of music), both implicit and explicit, for the almost mystical encounter of the human and divine."[16] This tendency affects their fourth feature of **overcoming the dualistic view** between the body and the soul.[17] They seem to pursue embodying the soul through their bodily experience so that it fantasizes the virtual divine in the experience of human and the divine, mediated by the human nature. Lastly, it is their **ambiguity of faith identity** that is the most distinguishing character of Gen X that differentiates it from any other generations. Equality and anonymity of cyberspace tremendously con-

---

lyze it [nameless]. Just let it entertain me since it makes me aware of nothing [centerless]."

14 Even if Beaudion's socio-religious descriptions of GenX could not universally be acceptable, this research regards its relevancy and legitimacy in Postmodern generation of Korean context. Sungbin Lim employed Beaudion's description to explain the sociological features of Korean N-generation. Sungbin Lim, "A Theological Analysis on the Culture of N-Generation," *Korean Presbyterian Journal of Theology* 18 (2002): 367- 370.

15 Beaudion, *Virtual Faith*, 64-65.

16 Ibid., 74.

17 Ibid., 79.

tribute to their unlimited accessibility to information so that it causes them to see any kind of religion as equal. Moreover they make use of anonymity to satisfy their various personas and purse accomplishment of their unfulfilled dreams in the real world.

As a consequence, Korean young adults found themselves standing on the edge of "orthodoxy and heterodoxy, the sacred and the profane, and blasphemy and sanctity."[18] While they seem to enjoy their freedom on the edge of ambiguous areas with anonymous multiplicity of selves, the Gen Xers eventually find a fragmented, divided, and distorted self. In other words, their instabilities become the ground to discover themselves as directionless, nameless and centerless. In the end, these give impetus to asking a fundamental question of themselves which portrays their profound ambiguity as Beaudion notes: "'Will You Be There for Me?' They ask this of them selves, bodies, parents, friends, partners, society, religions, leaders, nation and even God."[19] Because their key questions are launched by querying everything including even their 'selves' on the ground of their fidelity, the final question reflects an undeniable assent of infidelity in regard to their relationship with God, of being isolated from every directions, of being dried up in their reliable resources, and of stretching their hands out looking for help. That is **disconnectedness**. It is noteworthy to look at Elizabeth Johnson's definition of postmodern spirituality. In summarizing it, she writes:

> In a word, postmodern spiritual experience prizes not isolation but essen-

---

18 Ibid., 122-138.

19 Ibid., 140.

tial connectedness; not body-mind dualism but the holistic, embodied person; not patriarchy but inclusive feminism; not militarism but expenditure for the enhancement of life; not tribal nationalism but global justice.[20]

It is manifestly demonstrated that it is **disconnectedness** that is the core feature of the emerging Korean generation's spirituality. They are disconnected from all kinds of relationship, from God, and even from themselves. Considering spirituality as "a lived faith experience of the relationship between the human spirit and the Spirit of God" following the Schneiders' definition,[21] a lack of experience of God in spiritual life as well as in faith community has played a critical role in removing Korean emerging young adults' spirituality from their religiosity. Its correlation with the ambiguity of faith identity triggers their isolation and disconnection from everything. They are unidentified from the whole community, even from churches.

4. Limitation of Church Education and Necessity of Spiritual Practice

From my investigation, the church's education is called into question since, despite clearly noticing the new spiritual characteristics of the Korean emerging generation, Korean scholars are still clinging to

---

20 Elizabeth A. Johnson, *The Search for the Living God* (Toronto: University of St. Michael's College, John M. Kelly Lecture of 1994, printed edition), 7, quoted in Beyer, *Young Adult Catholics*, 19.

21 Sandra Schneiders, "The Study of Christian Spirituality: Contours and Dynamics of a Discipline," *Minding The Spirit*, eds. Elizabeth A. Dreyer and Mark S. Burrows (Baltimore and London: Johns Hopkins University Press, 2005), 5-6.

the absoluteness of Bible teachings.[22] While the emerging Korean generation is looking forward to a personal experience of God, the church yet talks of knowledge of God; while young people are anxious to go through a mystical dimension of faith life, the church keep teaching the visibility of an invisible God; while new generations share the authentic meaning of holistic salvation through spirituality, the church harshly demands devotion and commitment without rewards; while they are looking for heaven in the here and now, the church stubbornly insists that it is located above.[23]

Under these circumstances, it is not a coincidence that Liebert's assertion on knowledge is applicable here. Her article, "The Role in Practice in the Study of Christian Spirituality" notes a difference between *epistemological* knowledge — I know something that I did not know, and *ontological* — my knowing existentially changes me.[24] Using the educational theory that "the relationship of the knower to the known becomes the basis for the relationship of the actor to the world,"[25] she verifies the necessity of spiritual practice that epistemo-

---

22 Mi-Ja Sa, "The Theological Education Fostering the Truthful Life," *Church and Theology* 51 (2002), 65-73; Jong-chul Chang, "The Values of New Generation and its Implication of Christian Education," *Theology and World* 34 (1997), 224-234.

23 This study recognizes that the academic or pedagogical endeavor to integrate the scientific knowledge of our ages with spiritual experiences of young generation in academic field and Christian higher education overcoming the dualistic worldview. Moon Son, "The Public Search of Religious Education in Christian Higher Education," *Theological Forum* 78 (2014), 323-353.

24 Elizabeth Liebert, "The Role of Practice in the Study of Christian Spirituality" in *Minding The Spirit*, eds. Elizabeth Dreyer and Mark Burrows (Baltimore and London: The Johns Hopkins University Press, 2005), 79-99.

25 Ibid., 88.

logical knowledge which excludes ontological or existential knowledge would prevent one from fully grasping the essence of spirituality. It is the ontological knowing that achieves one's holistic knowing.

Now, it is clearer why the spirituality of the new Korean generation is denoted as *disconnectedness*. An absence of the ontological knowledge through spiritual practice leads them into fragmented epistemological knowing, and then it gives rise to be disconnected the known from the knower, God. Hence, it is evident that spiritual practice plays a significant role in facilitating an experience of ontological knowledge of God. Liebert's insight on spiritual practice is drawn from the history of contemplative tradition.

III. Wisdom of the Contemplative Tradition

I will hereafter suggest Centering Prayer as a formative spiritual practice for transforming the Korean emerging young adults' spirituality from disconnectedness to centeredness. Since Centering Prayer is rooted in apophatic contemplation, it is essential to investigate the contemplative tradition.

1. *Apophatic*[26] and *Cataphatic*

Most western Christian theology has tendency to be "affirmative" or "*cataphatic*," in that it is based, most fundamentally, upon the belief

---

26 The word comes from Greek verb meaning "to say no; to deny." James A. Wiseman, *Spirituality and Mysticism; A Global View* (Maryknoll, NY: Orbis Books, 2006), 93.

that God has revealed himself and uses creatures as vehicles for his self-disclosure. Although no creature is God, every creature yet bears witness to its Creator. It is a sacramental view of the universe that is the most developed form of the *cataphatic* tradition, which means a vision that the whole world is seen as a communicating symbol of the divine. This supports the legitimate of liturgy, religious art, and theological images or ideas. On the other hand, ancient Judeo-Christian roots prohibited making graven images because they had a strong tendency towards idolatrous image making.[27] God cannot be reduced to any of our notions, words, or physical images because He is always 'other,' transcendent.

This became the bedrock of negative theology or *apophatic* tradition which emerges from the recognition that God is always beyond our words, our ideas, even our experience of the divine.[28] Pseudo-Dionysius first systematized the theology of apophasis in Christianity. He outlined a method of prayer (spiritual practice) in his book *Mystical Theology* that "denies any properties traditionally associated with God-goodness and wisdom since our human conceptions of them inevitably fall short of the supreme reality they are trying to signify."[29] He ended up articulating that when we let all mental concepts of God go away, we enter a 'darkness of unknowing.' According to him, in the intellectual darkness we can be mystically united to the unknowable

---

27 Harvey D. Egan, "Christian Apophatic and Kataphatic Mysticisms," *Theological Studies* 39 (1978), 400-402.

28 Edward Howells, "Apophatic Spirituality," in *The New Westminster Dictionary of Christian Spirituality*, ed. Philip Sheldrake (Louisville, KY: Westminster John Knox Press, 2005), 117.

29 William Johnston, *The Mysticism of The Cloud of Unknowing: a Modern Interpretation* (New York: Desclee Company, 1967), 33.

God.[30] Here we find the historical roots of the *Cloud of Unknowing*, since the author himself drew consciously on the *apophatic* tradition while translating the book of Dionysius into English.[31]

2. *The Cloud of Unknowing*[32]

There are two significances of *The Cloud of Unknowing* in the historical sense; first, it succeeded to the contemplation tradition ranged representatively from St. Gregory of Nyssa[33] to Pseudo-Dionysius. Second, the author[34] also formulated the *apophatic* tradition into a specific practice form such as monastic life remarkably pursuing a single-minded mysticism of love. The writer of *The Cloud* believes God to

---

30 Edward Howells, "*Apophatic* Spirituality," 118.

31 Julia Gatta, *Three Spiritual Directors: For Our Time* (Cambridge, MA: Cowley Publications, 1986), 94.

32 It is not necessary to treat a whole horizon of the spiritual tradition in this chapter. But, William Johnston's book *the Mysticism of the Cloud of Unknowing* is recommended for in-depth information and commentary. In Korean academic sphere, Soo-Young Kown delineates well the spirituality of *Cloud of Unknowing* in "Spirituality Oriented Christian (Pastoral) Counseling: An Integrative Encounter between Western Spirituality and Eastern Orthodox Spirituality," *Theological Forum* 72 (2013), 7-36.

33 This fourth-century Cappadocian Father was the first Christian writer to develop a full theology of *apophasis*. Using the biblical image of Moses meeting God in the 'cloud,' he established his primary metaphor for divine nature, "luminous darkness-Moses 'saw' God in the darkness," James A. Wiseman, *Spirituality and Mysticism: A Global View*, 94, "This is the seeing that consists in not seeing, because that which is sought transcends all knowledge being separated on all sides by incomprehensibility as by kind of darkness' (*Light of Moses* 2.163) in Howells, "*Apophatic* Spirituality," 118.

34 The authorship of the *Cloud of Unknowing* is still controversial in an academic sense. But according to Dom David Knowles' suggestion, the author was committed in a Dominican tradition since the *Cloud* was embedded with Thomist influence regarding a thoroughgoing view of grace. Oliver Davies, *God Within; The Mystical Tradition of Northern Europe* (NY & NJ: Paulist Press, 1998), 163.

be accessible to our *capacity to love* rather than our *capacity to know*. For the author of *The Cloud*, the key to this life is the intense desire for God (**chap. 1**) and therefore, it is possible for everyone (**chap. 27**) only to go through experiencing God in the deep center of our being.

Let us pay more attention to the paradoxical meaning of the 'cloud,' which offers a decisive clue for knowledge of God. The dominant characteristic of the 'cloud' can be presented in twos: it prevents us from either perceiving God 'in the clear light of rational understanding' or from 'experiencing his loving sweetness.' The following is the first passage dealing with the 'cloud;'

> For when you first begin to undertake it, all that you find is a darkness, a sort of cloud of unknowing; you cannot tell what it is, except that you experience in your will a simple reaching out to God. This darkness and cloud is always between you and your God, no matter what you do, and it prevents you from seeing him clearly by the light of understanding in your reason, and from experiencing him in sweetness of love in your affection.[35]

That is, the 'cloud' is the locus of our desire for God and our upward striving towards him, but it is also 'dispersed or lessened by the sharp dart of longing love' (**ch. 12**). We can tell that the meaning of the cloud or darkness is very paradoxical; when we abandon reason or comprehend God, we can obtain the presence of God under silence

---

35 James Walsh ed., *the Cloud of Unknowing*, Classics of Western Spirituality (Mahwah, NJ: Paulist Press, 1981), 120-121.

which leads us into a different kind of knowledge of God. Thus, the author is able to state that it is 'through mind of love' that we can reach out in the highest act of contemplation, which leads us into the presence of God, or the so-called "blind beholding."[36] As a consequence, we can validate the presumption from *The Cloud*'s perspective that our knowledge of God can be obtained by a unique manner of 'knowing' which is based not upon intellect but upon a perceptive love.[37]

3. Appropriation of the *Apophatic* Wisdoms

Several critical insights and wisdoms from *The Cloud of Unknowing* have the potential of transformation from disconnectedness to centeredness. First of all, the spiritual practice directs us to on authentic notion of **knowledge** of God. When we experience the love of God, we can identify who God is, obliterating an ambiguous faith identity. So, the new notion can become a watershed for the Korean Gen X to acknowledge God ontologically and to shape their holistic knowing of God. Secondly, the spiritual practice validates their **personal** experience and relationship with God by the encounter of transcendence within the existential dimension. Third, the spiritual practice arouses **mystical** experience, the presence of God. Encounter with a Being beyond words and reasoning can invite them to stay in the divine indwelling, where they overcome a dualistic worldview and embody the divine. Last, this investigation on spiritual practice helps the generation appreciate the Christian tradition, so that they could have a chance

---

36 Oliver Davies, *God Within: The Mystical Tradition of Northern Europe* (N.Y. & NJ: Paulist Press, 1998), 169.

37 Ibid., 170.

to appreciate again the value of **religion** as an institution as well as spirituality. Now, let us turn to the main question, "Can the spiritual practice of *Cloud*'s method be a formative spiritual practice for Korean Gen X's spirituality?

IV. The Journey to Union

The spiritual practice described in *The Cloud of Unknowing* would not be an appropriate contemporary spiritual practice since the ancient practice still holds an inclination of disconnectedness.[38] Specifically, since it clings strictly to a dualistic worldview of body and soul, it does not offer appropriate insight to the relationship between soul and self which has newly been cultivated by psychology. Notably, new insight from psychology on human nature generates a bigger division between the two eras of fourteenth century England and twenty-first-century Korea. I believe that a relevant spiritual practice for contemporary society must be equipped with a psychological understanding of the human being. It is Centering Prayer that relevantly harnesses psychological insight for a spirituality of centeredness.

---

38 Philip Sheldrake articulated persuasively four reasons *The Cloud of Unknowing* could not be directly adopted in the contemporary spiritual practice form: first, the tone of the Cloud is too individualistic; second, it presupposed contemplation as limited as to an elite experience; third, the worldview of body and soul is too dualistic; lastly the spiritual journey was exclusively directed to ascent away from the material world. Sheldrake, *Spirituality and History* (Maryknoll, N.Y.: Orbis Books, 1998), 186-188.

1. Centering Prayer

Centering Prayer first originated from an endeavor of a group of people, including Fr. Thomas Keating, to discover a specific spiritual practice for contemporary people, who were fascinated with the meditation practices of eastern religions, and who had left the Church in the 1970s. Accompanying the onset of Centering Prayer, Fr. Keating seriously took into consideration how to put the Christian contemplative tradition into a form accessible to active people.[39] Obtaining theological methodology from apophatic contemplation, especially from Pseudo-Dionysius, and practical method from *The Cloud of Unknowing*, Keating elaborately devised the elements of the Centering Prayer form with four guidelines.

1) Choose a scared word as the symbol of your intention to consent to God's presence and action within.
2) Sitting comfortably and with eyes closed, settle briefly and silently introduce the sacred word as the symbol of your consent to God's presence and action within.
3) When you become aware of thoughts, return ever-so-gently to the sacred word.
4) At the end of the prayer period, remain in silence with eyes closed for a couple of minutes.[40]

In practicing the Centering Prayer, Keating highlights two important points; first, God is totally present to us all the time: God is closer

---

39 Thomas Keating, *Intimacy with God: An Introduction to Centering Prayer* (New York: The Crossroad Publishing Company, 2005), 15.

40 Ibid., 64.

than thinking, breathing, choosing, or consciousness itself.[41] Second, it is emphasized therefore on 'to be totally open to God.' Namely, since God is present, the purpose of the prayer is to move beyond ourselves into God. We turn ourselves over completely to God and consent to God's presence at the deepest level of our being—the divine indwelling. So, it is *intention* that we have to facilitate, rather than *attention*. Contrary to concentrative meditation with a *mantra* or awareness method, Centering Prayer encourages us to bypass focused attention and to work directly with intention itself.[42] It is subsequently expected to bring about 'letting it go and giving away,' because it represents an intention to die to self, which for Keating is the crucial bedrock for the journey to union with God.

2. From Disconnected to Centered

One of the far-reaching contributions of Centering Prayer is that it expands the horizon of relations between Christian contemplation and human nature by adopting psychological elements and offers insightful analysis on *the self*.[43] Resonating with Augustine, Keating asserts not only that the consequences of original sin are illusion, concupiscence, and weakness of will,[44] but at the same time, he also states that

---

41 Thomas Keating, "Practicing Centering Prayer" in *The Diversity of Centering Prayer* (New York: The Continuum Publishing Company, 1999), 16.

42 Cynthia Bourgeault, *Centering Prayer and Inner Awakening* (Cambridge, Mass.: Cowley Publications, 2004), 20-21.

43 Bourgeault makes the statement that Keating's contributions is "his interlinking of the 'dark night' or 'cloud of unknowing' of the traditional *apophatic* path with the psychological process." Bourgeault, *Centering Prayer and Inner Awakening*, 95-96.

44 Keating, *Intimacy with God*, 73.

original sin manifests as a *false self*, in psychological terms. God is so close that in some sense he is 'our true self.' However, original sin has removed us from our *true self* without the experience of union with God. Thus, "we as '*the false self*' do not know where true happiness is to be found."[45] Only in excavating the true self does there appear a threshold of experience of divine indwelling and union with God.

Practicing Centering Prayer according to Keating ushers one into divine indwelling with the following four aspects: 1) Divine Consciousness, 2) Inner Healing, 3) Purification of the False Self, and 4) Unitive Selfhood. First, the more intentionally the silence of the prayer becomes established, the closer one is to **divine consciousness** or awareness which ordinary awareness detects as a vacuum. This new perception triggers a growing sense of connectedness with the ultimate ground of being. Finding oneself in God and acquiring the perspective of God, one is aware of interconnection within God and the world. Knowing that, therefore, nothing can possibly fall out of God, one express it as St. Paul, "whether I live or die, I am the Lord's" (Roman 14:8).

Second, centering prayer inevitably brings about **inner healing**, the, so called, "Divine Therapy."[46] When an authentic spiritual practice, the moment of deep spiritual rest in the presence and action of God takes place, the unconsciousness, which used to be immersed under the surface of consciousness, begins to unload the emotional junk of a lifetime. This includes repressed memories, pain, accumulated hurts, and

---

45 Thomas Keating, *Open Mind, Open Heart: the contemplative dimension of the Gospel* (New York : Continuum, 2000), 128.

46 Thomas Keating, *Intimacy with God*, 72.

feelings, which remain unresolved in the unconscious level while the false self invests oneself with illusions. At this point, centering prayer does not encourage acknowledging the thoughts that emerge from the unconsciousness, but lets it go.

Third, as these wounds are gradually surfaced and released in prayer, the false self weakens and the true self gradually emerges. This is **the purification of the false self**. For Keating, this is the inevitable process of transforming union, since the true self emerges with divine indwelling, while the false self undergoes purification. Thus, one could undergo negative emotions such as anger, sorrow and bitterness, which is correspondent with the second aspect of the cloud: it prevents us from either perceiving God 'in the clear light of rational understanding' or from 'experiencing his loving sweetness. After all, this status prompts spiritual freedom from the consequence of original and personal sin and from illusion and weakens of will. What remains for Keating is a state of divine union.

Finally, as a sequence of above, it is **unitive selfhood** that is a critical contribution for Keating. He asserts that transforming union with God proceeding to self-transcendence could not be perceived with our *cataphatic* awareness. It rather impedes us to enter into the deeper level of the mystical experience. Namely, *cataphatic* consciousness, owing to its self-reflective tendency, can not usher one into take an illuminative level among the three step of Christian spiritual development model — purgation, illumination, and union. On the other hand, even though *apophatic* awareness surrenders the self, paradoxically the self does not diminish, but discover the true self in Trinitarian Relationship.[47] It is *apophatic* consciousness that experience of union with God through Christ, and by Holy Spirit brings about. Just as *apophatic* darkness is neither just dark of soul nor emptiness, "*Apophatic* self"[48] is not nothingness, but "a kind of intuitive hologram knowingness which is the core motion of unitive consciousness and the foundation of unitive selfhood."[49] That is, in the center of one's nothingness one meets the infinitely real. Hereafter, union with God in loving relationship is "knowing in being unknown."[50]

3. Centering Prayer for Korean Emerging Young Adults[51]

A Korean young adult group in church ministry[52] has been invited

---

47 Ibid., 148. Keating sees Centering Prayer as Trinitarian in origin since the divine indwelling, mentioned by Jesus in biblical narrative, means that God's own life is being communicated to us. Therefore, he considers the focus of the Prayer from Christology. The union is accomplished through Christ, through existential relationship with Him.

48 Bougeult coins the term in her book. Bourgeault, *Centering Prayer and Inner Awakening*, 51.

49 Ibid., 51.

50 Thomas Keating explains that Meister Eckhart calls contemplation 'unknowing knowing of God," Thomas Keating, "Practicing Centering Prayer" in *The Diversity of Centering Prayer*, ed. Gustave Reininger (New York: Coninuum, 1999), 17.

51 This research recognizes that the qualitative research method within Practical Theological frame would also be relevant for demonstrating the way in which the spiritual practice would critically function. This research however employs the "self-implication" method in Christian Spirtualty as academic discipline, which Sandra Scheniders elaborates in her article, "Approaches to the Study of Christian Spirituality," *The Blackwell Companion to Christian Spirituality*, ed. Arthur Holder (Malden: Blackwell Publishing, 2005), 29-30. The academic method asserts that christian spirituality as academic discipline should use the experiences of the researcher as legitimate since "the analogue experience of the researcher is virtually necessary for understanding."

52 This young adult group mostly consists of ten members ranging from students, salary men, to office workers of Korean or Korean American living in Northern California, US.

to practice the Centering Prayer for the three months. They were asked to follow the direction strictly that the prayer must be practiced at least once a day for twenty minutes and to participate in the group session once a week. The experience transformation and self-transcendence by Centering Prayer is significant. Eun-Jin, a thirty-five year old female interior designer, had once felt dismissed from all dimension of life, family, friends, church, self and God after a divorce—**disconnectedness**. She began to attend our church last year while she struggled with traumatic memories from a three-year-old divorce. Whereas she has abundant knowledge of the bible and God, her critical complaining about the dogmatic teaching and passive attitude in church did not cease.

After beginning it for first one month, she readily shared her experiences of personal centering prayer during the group session. Whenever she was doing Centering Prayer, she acknowledged at first that she naturally but unwillingly revisited the memories. So in order to escape it, she intended to bring her sacred word up in the moment. But ironically, she had enough courage to sustain that moment and suddenly discovered the presence of God (**divine consciousness**) in the traumatic incident, which she never noticed before. Next, realizing her anger had suppressed her true self, she encountered God touching and healing her painful memories and emotions (**inner healing**). Immediately she confessed her wrongdoings and selfishness (**the purification of false self**). In the following group session, she shared her story with burst of joy that she took a further step in her relationship with God: she kept feeling loved by God indwelling in her deepest self. The more she practiced the centering prayer, the clearer knowledge of God and the bible story readily became evident: God is love and she is beloved. Its aftermath affected all of her relationships significantly: life, family, church and community. She attempted not only to connect with her parent and friends, but also to commit herself to the homeless ministry of church (**unitive selfhood**). She became connected in every area of life, by being **centered in** the *apophatic* self, where the knower, the knowing, and that which is known are all one as well as where love and knowledge are infused together.

V. Conclusion

In this chapter I investigated Centering Prayer as an effective spiritual practice for prompting transformation in Korean emerging young adults' spirituality, bringing them from disconnectedness into centeredness. The contemplative tradition (*apophatic*) of Christian spirituality, embedded in *The Cloud of Unknowing*, first was examined as an appropriate bridge to enable Korean young adults to integrate ontological knowledge of God with epistemological knowledge through mystical experiences of union with God. This practice made overcoming this target group's spiritual disconnectedness possible by connecting knowledge of God with experience of and encounter with God. Next, I explored Centering Prayer's contributions in interlinking *apophatic* contemplation with psychology principles as well as its relevance to Korean emerging young adults' spirituality. Centering Prayer's ability to connect self with God, to promote the healing process in unconsciousness, and to expand the notion of union with God into a holistic and integrative understanding of selfhood was evident. This spiritual practice's capacity to transform and transcend Korean emerging young adults' disconnectedness to centeredness was illustrated and demonstrated.

In any attempt to transplant Centering Prayer in Korea, it will be critical to help Koreans be aware of history of contemplation tradition in Christianity since the early church period. There is dominating prejudice that contemplation with silence might have originated from Buddhist meditation. I believe, however, Centering Prayer, supported by psychological benefits, will contribute to Korean emerging generation not only in integrating spirituality with religiosity, but also in all dimensions of life. Moreover, it will convincingly be conducive to nurturing the maturity of Korean Christianity enough to create a mutual reciprocal milieu in the multi-religious society. Hopefully this chapter would become a launching locus to take Centering Prayer into serious consideration as a formative spiritual practice in Korean Christianity.

Bibliography

Beaudoin, Thomas M. Virtual Faith: The Irreverent Spiritual Quest of Generation X. San Francisco: Jossey-Bass, 1998.

Beyer, Jason William. "Young Adult Catholics: A Contemporary Look at a Potentially Mystical Faith." M.A. diss. Graduate Theological Union, 2003.

Bourgeault, Cynthia. Centering Prayer and Inner Awakening. Cambridge, MA: Cowley Publications, 2004.

Davies, Oliver. God Within: the Mystical Tradition of Northern Europe. N.Y. & NJ: Paulist Press, 1998.

Dreyer, Elizabeth A. and Mark S. Burrows, eds. Minding the Spirit: The Study of Christian Spirituality. Baltimore and London: Johns Hopkins University Press, 2005.

Eberle, Gary. The Geography of Nowhere: Fining One's Self in the Postmodern World. Kansas City: Sheed & Ward, 1994.

Egan, Harvey D. "Christian Apophatic and Kataphatic Mysticisms." Theological Studies 39 (1978): 399-426.

Gatta Julia. Three Spiritual Directors: For Our Time. Cambridge: Cowlegy Publications, 1986.

Howells, Edward. "Apophatic Spirituality." in the New Westminster Dictionary of Christian Spirituality, ed. Philip Sheldrake, Louisville, Kentucky: Westminster John Knox Press, 2005.

James Walsh., ed. The Cloud of Unknowing. Classics of Western Spirituality. Mahwah, NJ: Paulist Press, 1981.

Jang, Jong-Chul. "The Values of New Generation and its Implication of Christian Education." Theology and World 34 (1997): 213-235.

Johnston, William. The Mysticism of the Cloud of Unknowing: A Modern Interpretation. New York: Descless Company, 1967.

Keating, Thomas. Open Mind, Open Heart: The Contemplative Dimension of the Gospel. New York: Continuum, 2000.

_____. "Practicing Centering Prayer." The Diversity of Centering Prayer, ed. Gustave Reininger, New York: Continuum, 1999.

_____. Intimacy with God. New York: The Crossroad Publishing Company, 1994.

Kwon, Soo-Young. "Spirituality Oriented Christian (Pastoral) Counseling: An Integrative Encounter between Western Spirituality and Eastern Orthodox Spirituality." Theological Forum 72 (2013): 7-36

Liebert, Elizabeth. "The Role of Practice in the Study of Christian Spirituality." In Minding the Spirit: The Study of Christian Spirituality., eds. Elizabeth Dreyer and Mark Burrows, 79-99. Baltimore and London: The Johns Hopkins University Press, 2005.

Lim, SungBin. "Theology for Church: A Christian Cultural Perspective on the N-Generation." Church and theology 54 (2003): 57-63.

_____. "A Theological Analysis on the Culture of "N-Generation." Korean Presbyterian Journal of Theology 18 (2002): 355-372.

Real Culture, ed. The Theory of New Generation: Chaos and Order. Seoul: The Lab of Real Culture, 1999.

Reininger, Gustave, ed. The Diversity of Centering Prayer. New York: Continuum, 1999.

Sa, Mi-Ja. "Theology for Church: Theological Education Fostering a Truthful Life." Church and theology 51 (2002): 65-73.

Schneiders, Sandra. "Approaches to the Study of Christian Spirituality." In The Blackwell Companion to Christian Spirituality. edited by Arthur Holder, 15-33. Madlen: Blackwell Publishing, 2005.

_____. "The Study of Christian Spirituality: Contours and Dynamics of a Discipline." In Minding the Spirit: The Study of Christian Spirituality, eds. Elizabeth Dreyer and Mark S. Burrows, 5-24. Baltimore: The Johns Hopkins University Press, 2005.

Sheldrake, Philip. Spirituality and History. Maryknoll, N.Y.: Orbis Books, 1998.

Son, Moon. "The Public Search of Religious Education in Christian Higher Education." Theological Forum 78 (2014): 323-353.

Wiseman, James A. Spirituality and Mysticism: a Global View. Maryknoll, N.Y.: Orbis Books, 2006.

2

Centrality of Imagination in *Election* within *Spiritual Exercises*

I. Introduction

Most scholars noticeably recognize these two words, imagination and decision-making, as basics elements in the *Spiritual Exercises* of Ignatius of Loyola. Scholars agree that Ignatius and his *Exercises* established the foundation for systematically describing *Election* (*Electio* in Latin, and *Eleccion* in Spanish, 'choice' or 'decision*) as the ultimate goal of spiritual practices.[1] In addition, it is noticeable that facilitating imagination is the other most groundbreaking feature of Ignatius' *Spiritual Exercises*. I argue in this regard that imagination is a universal phenomenon of human nature, and anyone who existentially or ontologically perceives imagination as one of human faculties may benefit from its use in their spiritual practice. Despite their vital role in the *Spiritual Exercises* of Ignatius, imagination and election together have rarely been dealt with together in the literature. As a creative

---

1 Javier Melloni, S.J. *The Exercises of St. Ignatius Loyola in the Western Tradition* (Leominster: Gracewing, 2000), 49-53.

endeavor, this research will examine the role of imagination as formatively inevitable and essential for authentic *Election*.

This research engages deeply with analyzing and interpreting the text of *Spiritual Exercise* of Ignatius of Loyola. First it will explore Election as the ultimate purpose of Ignatius's *Spiritual Exercises*, investigating briefly the *First* and *Second Week* where election is presented. Then, I will explore imagination or imaginative contemplation comprehensively in Ignatius' *Autobiography* and the *Exercises*. And lastly, the intimate association between imagination and election will be explored by considering the essential elements of indifference and desires in my argument. Consequently, I will show that imagination is the formative instrument for Election; in other words, Election is the end result of the *Spiritual Exercises*, and imagination is the means to the end. These two interrelated aspects of the *Spiritual Exercise* mutually transform end into means, and means into end. This procedure will implicitly demonstrate the way in which the spiritual practices equipped with imaginative contemplation and election would play crucial role in establishing spiritual formation and in fostering the spiritual enhancement in Christian community.

II. Ignatian *Election* in *Spiritual Exercise*

1. Election in the *Principle and Foundation*

Election is an absolutely unique concept as it appears in the tradition of Christian discipleship inherited specifically from Ignatius of Loyola and his spiritual legacy, the *Spiritual Exercises*. I will first acknowledge his perspective on human beings and then figure out the reason he composed the book, noting that Election is the aim of the exercises. Ignatius firmly believed that each human being is created for a purpose, which is, 'to praise, reverence and serve God our Lord and by so doing to save his or her soul' [*Spiritual Exercises* (hereafter SE), 22]. Remarkably, Ignatius carefully defined the well-being of the human soul, and he held that human life is totally dependent upon the person's realization that God is their origin[2]: God and its ultimate purpose (praise Him). Therefore, this fundamental understanding leads Ignatius to confirm that human self-realization and good order are rooted in consistency between that ultimate purpose and the choices which men and women make in particular circumstances.[3]

All choices that human beings make need to be consciously related to that ultimate purpose. Ignatius also seems to pay attention to the fact that all human decision is vulnerable to external elements and contradictory factors contained in every human context. Even interior factors of human life, the so called motions in the Ignatian context, such as feeling, thinking, willing and desires, are conceivably swayed by disordered or distorted patterns. This helps us understand the purpose behind Ignatius' *Spiritual Exercises*: the overcoming of self and the

2 Dyckman, Garvin and Liebert borrow the Jungian term individuation to represent the totality of one's person becoming an *imago Dei* in light of who God calls one to become. Whole articulation indicates the possible resemblance between election and individuation and furthermore the fact that the active imagination is taken into account for accomplishing their purpose in both. See more details in Katherine Dyckman, Mary Garvin, and Elizabeth Liebert, *The Spiritual Exercises Reclaimed: Uncovering Liberating Possibilities for Women* (New York: Paulist Press, 2001), 124.

3 David Lonsdale, "Ignatian Election," in *The New Westminster Dictionary of Christian Spirituality*, ed. by Philip Sheldrake (Louisville, KY: Westminster John Knox Press, 2005), 269.

ordering of life on the basis of a decision made in freedom from any ill-ordered attachment' [SE, 21]. For Ignatius, any decision or choice must be in accord with the ultimate purpose of each human being.[4] The *Spiritual Exercises* were hence explicitly composed to discover each human being's lifelong vocation and to help each person make choices or decisions based on that vocation. The comprehensive methods employed in the *Spiritual Exercises* are consciously directed at those who attend a retreat and are guided by a director. After all, a person on retreat recognizes that the authentic election, which entails seeking, finding and following God's will is intimately connected to discovering one's lifelong vocation and making large and small choices through the process described in the *Exercises*.

2. Election in the *First Week*

Not only is it important to acknowledge that election is the primary goal of the *Spiritual Exercises*, but it also is significant to notice that election occupies a certain part in the exercises of the Second Week. It is be worthwhile briefly to articulate the ways in which an exercitant is directed by *Spiritual Exercises* before encountering election. In the First Week, a time when most retreatants experience themselves as alienated or desolate by seeing the misery of the world around them, they also discover themselves as sinful. The experience of sinfulness is mainly encountered in this week of the retreat, and each retreatant may go through alienation from God, the self and the world. The medita-

---

4 Michael Ivens, S.J. *Understanding the Spiritual Exercises* (Trowbridge: Cromwell Press, 1998), 128, 130; Dyckman, Garvin, and Liebert, *The Spiritual Exercises Reclaimed* (2001), 282.

tion on sinfulness, meanwhile, deliberately brings about a new awareness of responsibility for alienation: the person making the retreat has sinned against the light. The more his or her inner awareness of being alienated and desolate grows, the more vital and growing is their desire to be a disciple and to follow Jesus. This experience thus leaves a person at the threshold of the Second Week of the Spiritual Exercises.[5]

3. Election in the Second Week

The retreatant who has had a deep First Week experience now in the Second Week enters the contemplation of the life of Christ with enthusiasm and gratitude. Contemplation of Jesus concentrates on Jesus' life journey and his kindness and sympathy. This experiences turns out to be an invitation to help retreatants recognize what discipleship means and furthermore what their real choice might be. As Dyckman et al. put it, it is not about whether to give up cigarettes or not, but about whether to let one's life be ruled by the Lord and His Plan.[6] On the way to election, Ignatius's deliberation designed in *Spiritual Exercises* indicates that any exercitant should take at least two preliminary dimensions. First, a person is presupposed to practice regularly the Examen prayer to notice the way in which God is at work in his or her life and how to respond to it. The prayer helps the retreatant acknowledge the grace of the *Exercises* in all dimension of daily life [SE, 24-26]. If, in addition, an exercitant follows the exercises faithfully, they will

---

5 William Barry, "The Experience of the First and Second Weeks of the Spiritual Exercises," in *Notes on the Spiritual Exercises of St. Ignatius of Loyola*, ed. by David L. Fleming S.J. (St. Louis, MO: Review for Religious, 1983), 95-100.

6 Ibid., 101.

equip him/her with the ability to discern good and bad spirits through reading the inner motions (will, intellect, affection, etc.).

It is legitimate to say, Election weaves throughout the Second Week and forms its climax.[7] Specifically, through the exercises on the Call of the King, the Two Standards, the Three Classes of People, and the Three Kinds of Humility, Ignatius intends to nurture in retreatants the ability to recognize and choose God's will when it is made known. Ivens confirms this in his commentary that the process of election starts precisely with identifying the crucial questions in the Call of the King: who is this Jesus and what is it like to follow him? [SE, 91-101]. In answering these questions, the retreatants discover their new self-image as the knight for the heavenly kingdom; they are no longer the shamed knight of the First Week. The new self-image spurs their desire to be more intimate with Christ, the Lord. Meditating on the Two Standards [SE, 136-148] on the fourth day of the Second Week challenges the retreatant to make a clear choice between Jesus and the Prince of Darkness.[8] The Two Standards, promoting the dispositions the retreatant needs in order to be able to hear Christ's call, help prepare them for the radical conversion of outlook and desire that constitutes the true life in Christ.[9]

The meditation on the Three Classes of Persons [149-157] sheds light upon the grace to choose what is more for the glory of the Trinity rather than being attached to money and possession. The meditation trains the exercitant to attain a disposition of indifference and detach-

---

7 Dyckman, Garvin, and Liebert, *The Spiritual Exercises Reclaimed* (2001), 280.

8 Ivens, *Understanding the Spiritual Exercises* (1998), 103.

9 Ibid., 105.

ment which is in accord with the Principle and Foundation. Indifference is what the meditation on the Three Classes of People is all about. The meditation focuses the seekers to ask themselves about their level of generosity. And it also causes them to increasingly long to serve Jesus Christ. This desire alone is the cause of their accepting anything or of their relinquishing anything [155]. Next, when asked to meditate on the Three Kinds of Humility, retreatants are concerned about their relationship with the person of Christ. Their relationship to money is confronted by the Three Classes of People. Ignatius urges retreatants to seek a new disposition of soul and a new relationship to Christ. Since the *Exercises* are a major step in the life-process of maturing in Christ, Ignatius clearly advocates the view that the paradoxical way of the third kind of humility embodies a radical choice to give one's life entirely to Jesus, no matter what the consequences might be. Thus, humility is conceived as nothing other than the love of God. While all three preliminary steps tune one's disposition with God, election is introduced with continuing contemplations on Christ's life.

4. Election and its Three Times

The location of election in the *Spiritual Exercises* is not accidental. Ignatius' deliberate elaboration of the process of moving toward election creates the exercise context in which the retreatant becomes more intimately acquainted with the personal life of Jesus as they become more accustomed with the workings of their spirit. Under the strong conviction that the *Exercises* are designed to help persons find God's will in making personal life decisions [169], Ignatius requires that the prerequisite state of the soul is indifference [170].[10]

Then, he indicates three different Times (situations) when a correct and good choice related to one's life may be made in the context of faith. The First Time is when God so moves the soul that there can be no mistaking God's call. God's will is being revealed clearly, in a way that cannot be doubted. What marks this Time is the certainty it yields. The Second Time asks the exercitant to acknowledge what consolation and desolation are and to attain clarity through discerning the movements of spirits. The comparison between consolation and desolation helps the retreatant understand how motions (thoughts, feelings, and imaginings) influence the affectivity of a person.[11] This is the place where the Rules of Discernment [313-327] become a comprehensively and elaborately instrument for election.

5. The Third Time and its Two Methods

The Third Time is one of tranquility, which implies an absence of any spiritual movements which could of themselves determine choice, and second, a freedom from all negative feelings that might obstruct rational deliberation.[12] In case an election is not made in the First or the Second Time, Ignatius suggests two methods of discovering what God wants from a person in the Third Time. In the first method, which he calls the method of Third Time, reason weighs the advantages and disadvantages of, for example, a particular marriage [181]. The rea-

---

10 Ignatius considers matters about which a choice may be made [170-174]. These matters are called unchangeable choices, for example, priesthood and marriage.

11 Ivens, op. cit., 137.

12 Ivens, op. cit., 138.

soning process is taken into consideration for the process of confirmation of election.

It is critical, however, to notice two things: indifference and the
desire for grace [179]. Retreatants should first hold themselves in freedom like a balance at equilibrium, since without that freedom the reasoning process is thought of as simply tallying the advantages and disadvantages. Requesting the grace that is desired also plays an essential
role in accomplishing the authentic rational process [180]. Harnessed
readily by freedom and a desire for grace, the reasoning process approaches its confirmation of election. We have difficulty recognizing
the clear outlines of confirmation of election when we see the text
itself due to its ambiguity and lack of articulation. Despite its vague
expression, the significance of confirming election at the sixth point
should not be underestimated in Ignatius' method for election.[13] After
all, how do people know whether God accepts and confirms their decision? Not from what they have gone through in their reasoning process
but from the humble realization that all decisions are tentative. They
need to examine the beginning, middle and end of the process.

The second method for good election begins with Ignatius's con-

---

13 Borrowing from Toner, Liebert and her colleagues elucidate five features of Ignatius's
   confirmation. First, seeking confirmation is, in Ignatius's mind, essential. Second, actually receiving it depends upon the weightiness of the matter for discernment the faith
   perspective underlying election holds that God would give some disconfirmation. Third,
   confirmation might consist in spiritual consolations such as courage to proceed fourth,
   seeking confirmation entails waiting, actively reviewing the process and outcome, a final
   aspect comes after the completed election: appropriate authorities confirm the decision
   (288-289). This is originally from Jules Toner, *Discerning God's Will: Ignatius of Loyola's
   Teaching on Christian Decision Making* (St. Louis, MO: Institute of Jesuit Sources, 1991),
   201-232.

fession that the matter in question should descend from above, from the love of God [184], and this plays a part in renewing indifference. Afterward, Ignatius suggests the techniques of role playing: imagining ourselves giving advice [185], imagining we are on our deathbed [186], or imaging ourselves on the judgment day [187]. Ignatius skillfully convinces the retreatant of how powerful imagination is to offer a way for making election through these exercises. The election relies heavily on the way in which the exercitant imagines the situation. After all, the retreatant has a striking opportunity to take new or fresh perspectives on the subject matter so as to enable a tentative decision and bringing it to God for confirmation. That is, imagining scenes from the Bible gradually readies the retreatant to perceive their new identity as the self in Christ. And then, the process invites the retreatant toward choosing an identity in Christ, which entails that all choice is made in Christ. Here is the crucial locus for developing my argument on the relationship between imagination and election. The formative role of the imagination in the election process emerges at this stage. Next, I will address a crucial connection between imagination and Ignatius' life experiences and the *Spiritual Exercises*.

III. Imaginative Contemplation in Ignatius' Works

1. The Centrality of Imagination in Lived Experiences

The most salient feature of the *Spiritual Exercises* besides election is readily recognizable as Ignatius' emphasis on the imagination. What Ignatius constantly requires of the retreatant is, above all, an exercise of imagination. Ignatius believes strongly that achieving the conversion and freedom which are the main goals of the *Spiritual Exercises* requires that the imagination be fully engaged.[14] He specifically notes its significance in this statement, I am "to see with the eyes of the imagination the road from Nazareth to Bethlehem; considering its length, breadth,..."[112]. For him, the appeal to the imagination is the inevitable path to the ultimate end of the spiritual exercises.

What is imagination as a human capacity? In what ways have humans employed imagination in their lived spiritual experiences? In the modern scientific era, imagination in the epistemological landscape has been dismissed except in the cognitive sphere. However, recent cognitive research has acknowledged the intimate connection between intellect and imagination. Any cognitive activity is able to accomplish its function through the imagination in such a way that it complements conceptual and intellectual approaches to truth.[15] That is, imagination clearly provides a decisive way to overcome the dualistic view derived from acquiring knowledge and reading a text.[16] But it also plays a bridge role in enabling the mundane to express the sacred.[17] Imagination enables one to see a double vision of reality which makes it ex-

---

14 Brendan Byrne, 'To See with the Eyes of the Imagination': Scripture in the Exercises and Recent Interpretation. *The Way Supplement* 72 (Autumn 1991): 6.

15 Dyckma, Garvin, and Liebert, op. cit., 122.

16 Antonio T. De Nicolas, *Powers of Imagining: Ignatius de Loyola*, foreword by Patrick Heelan, S.J. (Albany, NY: State University of New York Press, 1986), 32.

17 Chaedong Han, "The Horizontal and the Vertical: Imagination in the Contemporary Homiletic Debates," *Theology and Praxis* 34(Feb. 2013), 121-165. Moses Kim, "The Importance of Ligature of Relationship and the Use of the Semiotic Methods in Crisis Counseling," *Theology and Praxis* 41(Sep. 2014), 336-337.

plicitly possible for humans to perceive that what is revealed in Jesus is that human are in the place where God is present.

Consequently, humans can dwell in two dimensions at once, composed of their ordinary events and of God's presence in these events, without contradiction.[18] It is thus legitimate to say that the imagination is an indispensible medium for the experience of God. It is intrinsic to human nature; it is a natural instrument of religious and spiritual experiences. Why is it so? This is so, as Fischer rightly observes, because imagination leads from earth to heaven in human desire to God; at the same time, it leads from heaven to earth in God's desire, working through the willing cooperation of human beings, for salvation of the world.[19] Consequently, imagination is the human capacity to experience the divine mystery.

2. Imagination and Ignatius's *Autobiography*

Ignatius of Loyola is considered one of the most important contributors to our understanding of the role of the imagination in experiencing the divine mystery. It is well known that while recovering from his wounds, Ignatius repeatedly read the only two books in his house, *Vita Christi* by Ludolph of Saxony (1314-1378) and the *Flos Sanctorum* by James of Vorgine. There is a consensus that Ignatius first became conscious of spiritual matters through this reading. Imagining the life

---

18 Kathleen Fischer, "The Imagination in Spirituality," *The Way Supplement* 66 (Autumn, 1989): 98.

19 Paul G. Crowley, "Between earth and heaven: Ignatian Imagination and the Aesthetics of Liberation," in *Through a Glass Darkly: Essays in the Religious Imagination*, ed. by John C. Hawley (New York, NY: Fordham University Press, 1996), 63.

of Jesus and the saints progressively fostered his spiritual senses and his desire to follow Jesus and imitate the saints. What if I should do what St. Francis did, and found good, always proposing to himself what was difficult and burdensome? [7]. Even before his injury and convalescence, Ignatius was given to imagining himself as a knightly hero winning the favor of a great lady. He would spend hours in such daydreams. However, the Gospel stories and the lives of the saints fired Ignatius's imagination so that he gradually noticed how God's spirit helped him to receive the lasting joy of being with Christ. It is valid to assume that engagement with the Gospel stories and the lives of the saints through the kernel of imaginative contemplation helps shape authentic images of God, the self and the world.[20] Most of all, Ignatius found that the image of the humble Christ was his principal image of God and helped him understand his own inability to gain total purity through his own efforts.

Ignatius's *Autobiography* presents many accounts of encountering divine images, visions, and seeing with the interior eyes, such as the images of the Madonna with the child Jesus [10], seeing the humanity of Christ in Manresa [29], and Christ's appearance to him [41, 44].[21]

---

20 Even though the specific methods are introduced in the Second Week of Spiritual Exercises, it is helpful to consider briefly the characteristics of imaginative contemplation. Contemplation employing imagination is supported by will, memory and intellect as opposed to meditation. Imaginative contemplation asks us not only to recall but actually to recreate the events prompted by the reading of the Scripture and the action of the Holy Spirit, both by situating oneself imaginatively within it and by desiring interior knowledge of it. Meditation employs reasoning, supported by memory and imagination, contemplation employs imagination, supported by memory and reasoning. Dyckma, Garvin, and Liebert, op. cit., 118.

21 Clarifying the notion of *Autobiography*, Boyle calls into question whether Loyola's *Acts* is

It is interesting that Ignatius firmly believes that the divine images are apprehended through the imaginative facility. The *Autobiography* maintains that it does not matter in the end whether God created the good image in the soul or if he imprinted it on the soul. The imagination is thought of as the word of God.[22] The *Autobiography* furthermore indicates that these sights become the main sources for Ignatius' discerning whether the divine images come originally from God, even if he sometimes receives very great consolation by the images for a considerable time.

For Ignatius, these experiences resulted in at least two consequences: First, his interior vision seems to play a striking role in incurring Ignatius's desire to imitate Jesus and his way of life. Second these experiences prompt him to realize that imaginative contemplation disposes him for the divine mystery with spiritual affection.[23] His experiences with imaginative contemplation of divine visions heavily influenced Ignatius in his composition of the *Spiritual Exercises* since the book

---

real autobiography. She is suspicious of assumptions that it is completely factual because the account of Ignatius's life was likely to go through at least five steps at the hands of *da Carmera*: audition, memorization, notation, composition, and transcription. She maintains that the text was invented by imitating Ignatius's story rather than by copying what he said word by word. *Da Camara* listened to Ignatius, and repeated what he heard. Marjorie O'Rourke Boyle, *Loyola's Acts: The Rhetoric of the Self* (Berkeley, CA: University of California Press, 1997), 1-21.

22 Ibid., 40.

23 In Ignatian Spirituality, the term Affection can be characterized as particular motions that arise from sensations, reflections about sensations, and choices about following them (affectivity, intellect, will). Thus, it is more inclusive than feelings, because affection includes reflections on feelings and the choices with respect to them. Therefore it can be used interchangeably with tendency, inclination, propensity, and attachment. Ivens, op. cit., 2.

confirms the practice of imaginative contemplation of Christ in the Gospel mysteries and many of the methods of praying which he later taught in the exercises.

3. Imagination in the *Spiritual Exercises*

1) The First Week

In the Principle and Foundation of the First Week the retreatant is reminded that the purpose of *Spiritual Exercises* is to bring about a transformation in human nature in such a manner that a person is able to make decisions in conformity with the will of God (Election). Entering into the first week with the 'Examen' prayer,[24] the first exercise focuses on the composition for meditation about the three sins: the sins of Angels [50]; the sins of Adam and Eve [51]; and the sins of those is gone to hell [52]. In the next composition, the imaginative meditation on Christ suspended on the cross takes place in Colloquy [53]. These processes intend to direct the retreatant to see in imagination and to consider my soul as imprisoned in this corruptible body and my wholeself as an exile in this valley among brute animals [47]. What Ignatius initially proposes through this meditation is to consider the soul's imprisonment in the corruptible body.

However, the inner knowledge of my sins and an abhorrence for

---

24 The purpose of the Examen Prayer, one of the unique prayers derived from Ignatian Spirituality, is to prepare retreatants for the meditations of the First Week by opening their eyes to know the sins of their past life. Official Directory of 1599, in M. Palmer, *On Giving the Spiritual Exercises: The Early Jesuit Manuscript Directories and the Official Directory of 1599* (St. Louis: Institute of Jesuit Sources, 1996), 313.

them [63] does not aim to cause guilt about the contaminated human nature but instead aims to make the exercitant become fully aware of human inability to make a good decision in conformity with the will and desire of God. Furthermore, the ultimate endeavor is to recreate the image of God as loving and merciful. In the imaginative contemplation, the Trinity revealed in the cross is imagined as blessing us, presenting itself to us, laboring for us, and energizing us for our salvation.[25] Through the image of a vulnerable person, God is present as constant love. This exercise in imagination brings up gratitude as the proper human response, and the retreatant is led into realization of the Grace of the First Week which is to see oneself as a loved sinner.

Now I discuss the Additional Directives [73], which direct the imaginative contemplation to a sinner in chains [74 & 85]. This series of exercises pertains to penance, which leads to self-denial and to being in accord with God's desire. Presumably, the experience of the interior and exterior penances prompt the imagination about the passion and pain of Christ on the Cross in such a way that it enhances the exercitant's inner awakening to the reality that the loved sinner is also a responsible companion to Christ. This new awareness is considered as the potential locus for making a life decision.

2) The Second Week

The imaginative contemplation is introduced more fully to the retreatant in the Second Week. Ignatius urges the retreatant to seek inti-

---

25 John J. English, *Spiritual Freedom: from an Experience of the Ignatian Exercises to the Art of Spiritual Guidance* (Chicago: Loyola University Press, 1995), 253.

mate knowledge of our Lord, who has become man for me, that I may love him more and follow him more closely [104]. In the imaginative contemplation of the Incarnation and the Nativity, seekers are invited to imagine what is behind the text. The imagination enables people to go beyond the gospel text, recreating the events both by situating oneself imaginatively within it and by desiring interior knowledge of it.[26] By seeking to be intimately present in the events, people arrive at a new understanding of themselves.

In the composition of the place of the Nativity, for instance, Ignatius triggers free imagination by saying,

> Here it will be to see in imagination the road from Nazareth to Bethlehem. Consider its length and breadth, whether it is level or winds through valleys and hills. Similarly, look at the place or cave of the Nativity: How big is it, or small? How long or high? And how is it furnished? [112].

Even though Ignatius had visited the Holy Land, he does not tell us how the terrain looks in reality. Each person is free to imagine what the terrain and place might look like. In the imaginative contemplation proper, he again advises us to look at the people, to listen to what they are saying, and to consider what they are doing. He also adds a new character to the scene, a maidservant, and suggests that I will make myself a poor, little, and unworthy slave, gazing at them, contemplating them, and serving them in their needs, just as if I were there [114]. Such suggestions open the individual's imagination to see themselves

---

26 Dyckma, Garvin, and Liebert, op. cit., 119.

in the biblical scene in ways in which Ignatius expects that God will ultimately reveal the desire to know Jesus more intimately.

Another place featuring the imagination is the fifth contemplation of the first day, when the five senses are harnessed to the subject matter of the first and second contemplations. I note here the how *Directory* clarifies the use of the five senses:

> It [the 5th exercise] consists in using our imagination to see the persons, to hear their words or any other sounds, to touch or kiss places or persons. The sense of smell is applied by our Father Ignatius to smelling the soul's fragrance from God's gifts, and the sense of taste to tasting its sweetness; both of these betoken a kind of presence of the reality or person we are meditating, joined with a relish and heartfelt love for them.[27]

The above passage clearly indicates that the aim of this mode of prayer is to render the events of salvation 'present' in our minds and to obtain the direct experience of love and divine consolation which is the utmost purpose of the whole Spiritual Exercises.[28]

Ivens correctly spells out the primary process of the Second Week: election and growth in the true life taught by Christ.[29] Both are un-

---

27 Palmer, M. Official Directory of 1599, *On Giving the Spiritual Exercises: The Early Jesuit Manuscript Directories and the Official Directory of 1599* (St. Louis: Institute of Jesuit Sources, 1996), 321 (no.154).

28 Ernest Ferlita C, S.J., "The Road to BethlehemIs it Level or Winding?: The Use of the Imagination in the Spiritual Exercises," in *Studies in the Spirituality of Jesuits* 29/5 (November 1997): 17. This is quoted from Hugo Rahner, *Ignatius the Theologian* (New York: Herder & Herder, 1968), 194.

29 Ivens, op. cit., 74.

questionably intertwined in the second week since the former points to how the imaginative contemplation of Christ's life gives us examples of various states of life, and the latter shows how we begin to explore and inquire in what state or way of life doe the Divine Majesty wish us to serve him?[135]. Ignatius seems to be convinced that imagination offers the possibility of discovering what our true feelings are by imagining a certain situation and seeing ourselves in that situation.[30]

Ignatius therefore proposes imaginative contemplation On the Three Classes of Persons, moving toward Making a Good Election [149-157]. The retreatant imagines a considerable amount of money, but not purely or properly for the love of God. Despite all the desire of all three classes of people to get rid of their attachment to money, they proceed in three different ways. As we put ourselves in each person's place, Ignatius asks us directly to imagine how we feel about each situation. The desired hope is clearly to discover in oneself feelings similar to the person of the third class, which is someone who desires to get rid of all attachments.

Our discussion now is returning to the second method of the Third Time in the Election, where imagination plays a significant role. Equipped well by the previous exercises, facilitating the imaginative contemplation culminates in the election process. Herein Ignatius advises us to imagine three situations: first, giving advice to others in the same situation from an objective perspective; second, considering the situation from the perspective of your deathbed; third, imagining yourself on judgment day [184-188]. While engaging with these imaginary

---

30 Ferlita, op. cit., 18.

situations, retreatants are asked to make a decision for themselves in each situation. Similar to the way in which the retreatant discovers feelings through this exercise, they are advised to make the same decision in the process of election. Significantly Ignatius offers imaginative contemplation for discerning one's affective knowing and decision making (election). My contention that Ignatius's ultimate purpose in the *Spiritual Exercises* is chiefly initiated and progressively actualized by imaginative contemplation is affirmed in this part of the election process. Let us examine the intimate relationship between election and imagination within the horizon of the *Spiritual Exercises*.

IV. Imagination, the most Formative Dynamics for Election

1. Indifference as the Preliminary Stage

Among several prayer forms and practices presented in *Spiritual Exercises*, nothing can be more substantial than indifference. For Ignatius, indifference is the eventual prerequisite for imagination and election. Its significance appears when the Annotation describes indifference as a balance at equilibrium, without leaning to one side or the other [15].[31] Then, Ignatius explicitly describes in the Principle and Foundation sections what indifference looks like: on our part we

---

31 This research clearly acknowledges that the retreatant is not directly approaching *Annotation*, but the director is. Thus, it must be noted that through the introduction to the Election [169] the retreatant learns about indifference, and thus the advice concerning indifference from director must be complementary.

ought not to seek health rather than sickness, wealth rather than poverty, honor rather than dishonor, or a long life rather than a short life [23]. The embedded core ideas we discover here are reduced to two principles: First, indifference comes only from an awareness of God's love and a consciousness of God's goodness, found in all things or creatures. Second, indifference implies that we are so consumed by love for Christ (which is actually Christ's love for us) that we are free from all desires.[32]

Ignatius continues, We ought to desire and choose only that which is more conducive to the end for which we are created [23]. In the end, indifference is valuable not for its own sake but for allowing us to choose what is more conducive to some end. Our aim in choosing is to conform ourselves freely and entirely to what God chooses. For us, indifference is a crucial element in our freedom, the freedom that we leave open to God's loving intimations.

Dismissing indifference in the further practice of the imagination is highly unlikely to produce the pure and uncontaminated images possible from imaginatively contemplating the biblical accounts, since the imagining process would be preoccupied with attachments that range from desire elicited by physical objects to memories of the past. Without doubt, a lack of indifference distracts retreatants not only from authentic imaginative contemplation but also from achieving a new interior knowledge of God, self, and the world. This will result in a resistance to allowing our authentic desires to conform our choice to what God chooses.

––––––––––––––––––

32 English, *Spiritual Freedom* (1995), 36-37.

2. Imagination as Impetus to Desires and Election

From the very beginning, Ignatius urges the exercitant to ask God our Lord for what I want and desire [45], because the positive anthropology of Ignatius enables him to see desires as being implanted in us in virtue of our unique creation.[33] Therefore reading and following these innate desires is a part of realizing our integrity, which involves the Holy Spirit working through these desires. The Holy Spirit accommodates our desires to conform to God's desire. Being equipped with the real desires, the personal relationship of a retreatant with Jesus Christ is now established in a foundational fashion. Barry supports this view by saying that true relationship is based on authentic desires. Unless we engage our desires, developing a relationship with Jesus or God is not constructive.[34]

Because of this cultivation and enhancing of the intimate relationship with Jesus, Ignatius asks people to take advantage of the power of the imagination. The *Spiritual Exercises* claim, Imagine yourself before Christ on the cross and ask yourself what you want to do for Christ; imagine yourself before Christ the King and see if you do not desire to respond to his call; imagine yourself with Christ in the Garden and see if you don't desire to experience sorrow with Christ? Through it Ignatius encourages retreatants to see if it fits you and make it your own. The imaginative contemplation takes place in a subjective way, so that each individual has his or her own style or method of imagining

---

33 In comparison with the contemporary Protestant understanding of human nature, Ignatius' anthropology was firmly in accord with the Catholic traditional perspective on human cooperation with divine grace.

34 William A. Barry S.J. *Letting God Come Close* (2001), 28 & 40.

the biblical account. This exercise prompts us to discover how essential our desires are in the process of making a choice. In other words, the authenticity of desires is vindicated by the way in which one makes a choice. A desire that comes from God is a decision that is made in conformity with God's desires. This desire is a crucial element, then, in making an authentic election. Consequently, desires are elicited by imaginative contemplation and election is informed by desires.

3. Imagination and Election in Ignatius

We have acknowledged that the *Spiritual Exercises* is an instrument designed for the purpose of discovering God's wills [1]. All details of the practices aim at determining the will of God. Everything, all the meditations, all the contemplations, all the rules are at the service of the Election, of the making of a vital decision. Ignatius says as much in his Introduction to Election, when he points out how the imaginative contemplation of Christ's life gives us examples of various states of life and how, while continuing our (imaginative) contemplations of his life, we begin simultaneously to explore and inquire: in which state or way of life does the divine majesty wish us to serve him? [135]

Election becomes embodied in many of the imaginative contemplation practices as part of process of asking the retreatant to choose a way of life. The four meditations in the Second Week, Call of the King, the Two Standards, the Three Classes of People, and the Three Kinds of Humility, shape and nurture the seeker's disposition to be in conformity with God's. As the retreatant contemplates imaginatively each subject matter step by step, imagination at first opens his or her inner eyes to challenge the retreatant's present life, and it also leads to a recognition that the retreatant falls short of imitating Jesus' life. Next, the imagination ignites the retreatant's dispositional change by firing his or her desires (Spirit-given desires) to follow and imitate the life of Jesus. In addition, imagination inflames the desire to form one's mind and soul to attain a disposition of indifference. Through this process, the retreatant is implicitly directed to the election exercises of seeking and finding and responding to God's here-and-now word. This implies that imagination plays a formative role in preparing the human disposition to make an authentic election in accord with Principle and Foundation. It is apparent that without dispositional transformation by imagination, the way to election is fruitless.

Meditating on the biblical text is another good way to prompt imaginative contemplation. Imagining the biblical stories allows the historical events to be 'present and actual' and also allows the retreatant to encounter Jesus in personal and existential ways. The encounter shapes the interior knowledge of Jesus and leads them to confess, I do know who Jesus is. This interior knowledge also improves the use of the five senses in meditation, and the retreatant becomes noticeably aware that the knowledge residing within the retreatant's mind and soul becomes the primary resource for making an election.

It is in the second method of the third time of election where my argument concerning the formative role of the imagination in actualizing election culminates. The three imaginative situations direct the exercitant to contemplate them imaginatively and with the purpose of looking at the election process from three different perspectives: a third-person perspective; a perspective from the deathbed; and a judgment day perspective. Ivens identifies two reasons why an exercitant might not be able to make an election: (1) He or she is not at the moment faced by any sufficiently substantial issue; (2) even though the situation might contain matter for election, the exercitant has no readiness of will to deal with it.[35] In either case, the fruit of the imagination is to bring about renewal and transformation of the retreatant's perspective through looking at the decision from an objective viewpoint or the critical life situation. Imagination enables one to make a tentative election that confirms the will of God.

The configuration of the relationship between imagination and election now becomes more obvious. My examination of this topic has demonstrated several features of the dynamic relation between imagination and election in the Ignatian writings. First, indifference or spiritual freedom is critical for imaginative contemplation. Second, imaginative contemplation makes situations directed by the *Spiritual Exercises* to be present to the retreatant. Third, these experiences ask the retreatant to strengthen his or her desire to make a choice. Fourth, the most noticeable contribution to imagination to election lies in shaping one's disposition to seek, find and respond to God's will.

Consequently, according to Ignatius election without imagination is infeasible and unauthentic. It is like corporality without a skeleton to support the concrete shape. Election equipped with imagination or imaginative contemplation, however, guarantees tangible outcomes from the attempt to seek and find the will of God.[36] On the other hand,

---

35 Ivens, op. cit., 144.

36 Seeking the will of God asks the retreatants for the discipline of spiritual discernment and for spiritual guidance by spiritual director. Han-Sang Cho and Jong-Hyeok Sim, "A Comparative Study of Spiritual Discernment between Ignatius of Loyola and Jonathan Ed-

imagination without election is like a daydream or illusion. Imagination elicited or motivated by election produces authentic images of God, the self, and the world and enables a person to realize the will of God. The greater the interdependent and reciprocal mutuality between imagination and election, the more vitality is reflected in each constitutive aspect in the Ignatian context. As emphasized above, election is the end of the *Spiritual Exercises*; imagination is formative and an essential means to the ends.

V. Conclusion

One of the contributions of this research would be the first endeavor to elucidate the intrinsic relationship between imagination and election within the context of Spiritual Exercise. It has explored election as the goal of the Ignatius' *Spiritual Exercises* and examined its dynamic and development in the First and Second Weeks. It discovered through this investigation the significance of imagination, which includes meditation and contemplation. I also determined that authentic election inevitably entails imaginative contemplation.

An analysis of imagination has been presented for two of Ignatius's works. Ignatius's encounter with the divine images and visions portrayed in his *Autobiography* is likely to be imaginative. These ex-

---

wards," *Theology and Praxis* 46(Sep. 2015), 335-359. Kyungeun Kim, "Spiritual Direction: from the Integrating Perspective of Everyday Life and Spirituality," *Theology and Praxis* 44(May, 2015), 279-301. Kyungeun Kim, "The Positive Role of Spiritual Direction for Social Reconciliation," *Theology and Praxis* 43(Feb. 2015), 267-292.

periences very much influenced Ignatius's ideas that he developed in the *Spiritual Exercises*. Exploring the critical role of imagination in the First and Second Week demonstrates that Ignatius suggests that the deliberate use of imagination is the most essential human faculty not only for experiencing God, but also for enhancing and fostering our desires and indifference for finding and seeking the will of God, which is the process known as election.

In the last part of this chapter I attempted to demonstrate the vital dynamic and interdependent relationship between these constitutive components: indifference, desire, imagination and election. This examination reveals that imagination is the formative and essential means for election, which is the goal of the *Spiritual Exercises*. Two future tasks remain: analysis of the correlation between imagination and affectivity, and analysis of the role of discernment in the dynamic relation between imagination and election.

Bibliography

Barry, William S.J. *Letting God Come Close: an Approach to the Ignatian Spiritual Exercises*. Chicago: Jesuit Way, 2001.

Boyle, Marjorie O'Rourke. *Loyola's Acts: The Rhetoric of the Self*. Berkeley, CA: University of California Press, 1997.

Byrne, Brendan. 'To See with the Eyes of the Imagination': Scripture in the Exercises and Recent Interpretation. *The Way Supplement* 72 (Autumn 1991): 3-19.

Cho, Han-Sang and Jong-Hyeok Sim. "A Comparative Study of Spiritual Discernment between Ignatius of Loyola and Jonathan Edwards." *Theology and Praxis* 46(Sep. 2015), 335-359.

Crowley, Paul G, S.J. Between Earth and Heaven: Ignatian Imagination and the Aesthetics of Liberation, in *Through a Glass Darkly: Essays in the Religious Imagination*. Edited by John C. Hawley. New York, N.Y.: Fordham University Press, 1996.

De Nicolas, Antonio T. *Powers of Imagining: Ignatius de Loyola*. Foreword by Patrick Heelan, S.J. Albany, NY: State University of New York Press, 1986.

Dyckman, Katherine, Mary Garvin and Elizabeth Liebert. *The Spiritual Exercises Reclaimed: Uncovering Liberating Possibilities for Women*. Mahwah, N.J.: Paulist Press, 2001.

English, John J., S.J. *Spiritual Freedom: From an Exercise of the Ignatian Exercises to the Art of Spiritual Guidance*. 2nd edition. Chicago, IL: Loyola Press, 1995.

Ferlita, Ernest C, S.J. The Road to BethlehemIs It Level or Winding?: The Use of the Imagination in the Spiritual Exercise. *Studies in the Spirituality of Jesuits* 29 (November 1997): 1-23.

Fischer, Kathleen. The Imagination in Spirituality. *The Way Supplement* 66 (Autumn, 1989): 96-105.

Fleming, David L, S.J. *Notes on the Spiritual Exercises of St. Ignatius of Loyola*. St. Louis, MO: Review for Religious, 1983.

Gallagher, Michael Paul. Imagination and Faith. *The Way* 24 (April 1984): 115-123.

Han, Chaedong. "The Horizontal and the Vertical: Imagination in the Contemporary Homiletic Debates." *Theology and Praxis* 34(Feb. 2013), 121-165.

Ignatius of Loyola. *Spiritual Exercises and Selected Works*, ed. George E. Ganss. New York: Paulist Press, 1991.

Ivens, Michael S.J. *Understanding the Spiritual Exercise: Text and Commentary; a Handbook for Retreat Directors*. Leominster: Gracewing, 1998.

Kim, Kyungeun. "Spiritual Direction: from the Integrating Perspective of Everyday Life and Spirituality." *Theology and Praxis* 44(May, 2015), 279-301.

_____."The Positive Role of Spiritual Direction for Social Reconciliation." *Theology and Praxis* 43(Feb. 2015), 267-292.

Kim, Moses. "The Importance of Ligature of Relationship and the Use of the Semiotic Methods in Crisis Counseling." *Theology and Praxis* 41(Sep. 2014), 325-351.

Kinerk, Edward E S.J. Eliciting Great Desires: Their Place in the Spirituality of the Society of Jesus. *Studies in the Spirituality of Jesuits* 16 (November, 1984): 1-29.

Liebert, Elizabeth. *The Way of Discernment: Spiritual Practices for Decision Making*. Louisville, Kentucky: Westminster John Knox Press, 2008.

Melloni, Javier S.J. *The Exercise of St. Ignatius Loyola in the Western Tradition*. Leominster: Gracewing, 2000.

O'Donoghue N. D. The Mystical Imagination, in *Religious Imagination*. Edited by James, P. Mackey. Edinburgh: Edinburgh University Press, 1986, 186-206.

Official Directory of 1599. in Palmer, M. *On Giving the Spiritual Exercises: The Early Jesuit Manuscript Directories and the Official Directory of 1599*. St. Louis: Institute of Jesuit Sources, 1996.

Palmer, M. Official Directory of 1599. *On Giving the Spiritual Exercises: The Early Jesuit Manuscript Directories and the Official Directory of 1599*. St. Louis: Institute of Jesuit Sources, 1996.

Ribadeneira, Pedro de. *The Life of B. Father Ignatius of Loyola* 1616. London: The Scolar Press, 1976.

Sheldrake, Philip. Imagination and Prayer. *The Way* 24 (April 1984): 92-102.

Tellechea Idgoras, Jos Ignacio. *Ignatius of Loyola: The Pilgrim Saint*. Chicago: Loyola University Press, 1994.

3

Feministic Theological Approach to Spiritual Direction:

Centered on Rosemary R. Ruether

I. Introduction

Spiritual direction is one of the most important spiritual practices employed in Christian ministry, and it plays a significant role in cultivating the spiritual formation of Christians.[1] It is defined as a spiritual conversation between two persons, a director and a directee, in which the directee gives expression to her experience of faith and discerns the movement of Spirit in her life.[2] Through spiritual companionship, the directee may attain an increasing sense of spiritual openness and responsiveness to God's presence in her life.[3] Not does only the prac-

---

1 William A. Barry & William J. Connolly, *the Practice of Spiritual Direction* (New York: Harper-Collins Publishers, 1986), 3-12; Bang-Sik Oh, "A Study of Thomas Merton's Spiritual Direction," *Theology and Praxis* 52 (Dec., 2016), 393.

2 Susan S. Philips, *Candlelight: Illuminating the Art of Spiritual Direction* (New York: Morehouse Publishing, 2008), 3-10; Kang-Hack Lee, "Lee Sejong's Spiritual Direction and Its Application to the Ministry of the Korean Church," *Theology and Praxis* 49 (June 2016), 220-221.

3 Mary Rose Bumpus, *Supervision of Spiritual Directors: The Assistance of an Absent Other*, eds.

tice assist the directee to enhance her sense of the leadings of the Holy Spirit, but it also cultivates the genuine sense of the self at a deep level of spiritual awareness in the directee's relationship with God.

As a spiritual director, my experiences with female directees have implicitly but critically led me to be aware that the traditional theological frameworks, including male-oriented symbols and patriarchic concepts within the Christian Church, have significantly hindered female directees from being connected deeply with the holy and from cultivating their genuine selves in their relationship with God.[4] Moreover, the values embedded within the biblical world have supported the view of females as inferior to males, which has created a barrier that keeps many Christian women from deepening their relationship with God. For this reason, women's spiritual experiences and voices have easily been marginalized and dismissed in the Christian faith context.

Some Christian scholars and spiritual practitioners have explored the resources of feminist approaches to assist directees in seeking a deeper relationship with the divine feminine through spiritual direction.[5] Fischer thoroughly explains why spiritual direction with female

---

Mary Rose Bumpus & Rebecca Bradburn Langer (New York: Morehouse Publishing, 2005), 3-5.

4 It is ministerial and professional endeavor to integrate Christian spirituality and everyday life. Kyungeun Kim, "Spiritual Direction: from the Integrating Perspective of Everyday Life and Spirituality," *Theology and Praxis* 44 (June 2015), 280-282; Joohyung Lee, "Social and Cultural Self-Awareness in Spiritual Direction: Reflection of an Asian Male Director," *Presence: International Journal of Spiritual Direction* 21(Dec. 2015), 40-46.

5 Even if the practical context would be different, the feminist approaches to pastoral counseling would somewhat be applicable to this research's interest. Hee-Sung Chung, "A Reconstruction of Developmental Theories from the Perspective of Feminist Pastoral Counseling," *Theology and Praxis* 48 (Feb. 2016), 195-219; Hee-Sung Chung, "An Exploration of Womanist Pastoral Theology in the Korean Context," *Theology and Praxis* 29 (Nov. 2011),

directees should be undertaken using a feminist approach, maintaining that women need someone who will hear their stories on their own terms and help them find their own horizons.[6] Vest proposes the concept of Godde as an essential tool for feminist spiritual direction, helpful in overcoming the predominantly male images and belief systems in Christianity that can be disruptive of the prayer life and spiritual experience of feminists.[7] Ruffing also notes it is significant to pay attention to the experiences and needs of women and its theological sensitivities in that the female spiritual directors are majority in the society of the spiritual director.[8] Little work has been done, however, on developing theological themes for the construction of a feminist theological frame of reference for spiritual direction. This study is based on the awareness that a feminist theological approach could enhance the core nature and features of spiritual direction. The primary goal of feminist theology—constructing a new Christian theological structure based on relations of equality and mutuality—should also be a critical foundation for spiritual direction. This study will demonstrate that the feminist theological framework can be a formative tool for the authentic practice of spiritual direction.

This study affirms that a basic tenet of spiritual direction is that the

---

157-179.

6 Kathleen Fischer, *Women at the Well: Feminist Perspectives on Spiritual Direction,* (New York: Paulist Press, 1988), 7.

7 Norvene Vest, "In the Image of Godde: Feminist Spiritual Direction," in *Tending the Holy: Spiritual Direction across Traditions,* ed. Norvene Vest, (Harrisburg, PA: Morehouse Pub., 2003), 186.

8 Janet K. Ruffing, *Spiritual Direction: Beyond the Beginnings,* (New York: Paulist Press, 2000), 3.

director should not forcefully impose any particular theological agenda upon the directee's spiritual journey.[9] In order to avoid this possibility, this research will endeavor to construct a theological framework that takes into account this basic nature of spiritual direction. Thus, this inquiry is built upon the rudimentary assumption that the feminist theological framework is formative of spiritual direction at a deep level. Meanwhile, it is important to acknowledge that spiritual direction sometimes requires the director to play the role of a guide to ensure that the directee is open to learning of the feminist theological approach as a renewing or transformative perspective in the individual dimension of spiritual direction.

This study starts with the primary assumption that reorienting or reestablishing the right relations of equality and mutuality is necessary in the pursuit of spiritual direction. First, spiritual direction that is engaged in from a feminist theological perspective strongly affirms the female identity of the directee, so that the directee is more able to honor her own femininity in her spiritual experiences. Second, the honoring of her feminine identity could lead the female directee to undergo both liberation from oppressive systems and restoration of her female identity at the center of her spiritual journey. Third, this perspective entails deepening the directee's spiritual relationship with God, based on her genuine identity. In addition, the feminist theological framework helps prevent male directors from being blinded by hierarchical or patriarchal points of view, which end up distorting their role as spiritual director.

---

9 Ibid., 57-65.

The first section of this research will discuss the limitations of the traditional theological frameworks in relation to the concept of sexism, based upon the theological arguments of Rosemary Ruether. Why Ruether? It is undeniable fact that she is one of the most influential and "quoted" feminist theologians in the academic fields as well as activists in the Christian contemporary society.[10] Her theological terms and frames will help articulate why the prevalence of male language in Christianity can be a barrier in the context of spiritual direction with Christian women. Second, it will explore deconstructed and reconstructed concepts in feminist theological understanding of topics ranging from the images of God, Christ, and human nature to salvation; these concepts are essential for reformulating the feminist paradigm in spiritual direction. Next, the most appropriate components of feminist theological understanding will be employed in establishing a feminist approach to spiritual direction, so that certain critical features of feminist approaches to spiritual direction will be addressed as constitutive components.

II. Beyond Sexism in Spiritual Direction

Julie Han, a thirty-year-old Korean American woman, has felt discomfort and unease about attending worship service, since she recognized that the new senior pastor of her church strongly emphasizes

---

10 Whitney A. Bauman, Dirk von der Horst, & Emily Leah Silverman, "Introduction: Divining Prophetic Voices," in *Voices of Feminist Liberation: Writings in Celebration of Rosemary Radford Ruether*, (New York: Routledge, 2014), 1-3.

obedience to God as a necessary response to divine grace. The pastor has often described ways in which obedience should be embodied and practiced in congregants' relationships with the ministers in church and within marital relationships in families. Besides forceful requests for larger offerings as a desirable way to express obedience to God, the senior pastor has forced the laypeople to submit to and obey God's commands and the pastor's teachings. Most of all, on her spiritual journey Julie has realized that obedience is not necessarily the best choice in her relationship with pastors or with her husband. Rather, her past experiences in the church have led her to understand that over-emphasizing obedience distorts the pastor-layperson relationship, as well as her marital relationship. She has agonized over this struggle in her spiritual direction sessions, questioning whether she should stay or leave the church where she has attended and built relationships over the last decade.

Jee-Yeon, who is a Korean female minister, was educated in seminary to follow her divine call to be a minister. Training in CPE and pastoral counseling has also helped her to discern her life vocation in the ministry. Since she is aware of the necessity to be ordained as a pastor for a more effective engagement in the ministerial context, she has felt frustrated that her denomination does not allow the ordination of women. She acknowledges that the ordination door has not yet been opened to females, but she feels frustrated or angry by the disrespectful and indiscreet attitude of the denomination office: any further consideration of her being ordained could not be made within that circle. Denominational representatives have told her that if she wants to be ordained, she will have to transfer her membership to a different denomination.

Most contemporary women in Christian churches are not convinced that God has had a different theological and relational agenda or salvation plan for men and women from the beginning of Christian history. Current Christian spiritual practices and traditions have fallen into crisis because the contradiction between traditional theological interpretation and individual experience is growing. The perceptions and experiences of today's Christians lead to questions: Have the experiences of inferiority and discrimination within female circles been consistently observed throughout the history of Christianity? Or, has the inferior status of women systematically developed in the Christian community based upon contextualized historical circumstances? Rosemary Ruether, the prominent feminist theologian, answered the question well by drawing on the countercultural movement discovered in early Christianity. Under the influence of Jesus' movement within the prophetic tradition, the writers of the New Testament recognized that Jesus' new vision enabled the new community to envision social transformation in regards to racism, slavery, and sexism. Ruether considers the baptismal formula in the Pauline letter to the Galatians as representative of an egalitarian view of the world, through which a new equality between all social groups could be established in Christian community.[11] This is vivid evidence that the early Christian community worked to treat females as equal members of the community, even in religious and social relations.

---

11 Rosemary Ruether, *Sexism and God-talk: Toward a Feminist Theology,* (Boston: Beacon Press, 1983), 33.

Then, if the inferiority of females was not established as the inherent social order of the early Christian community, when and why did it become embedded in the structure of the religious community? Ruether points to the canonization process as a critical pivotal procedure through which the concept of women's social inferiority came into the religious institution.[12] As the early church community realized the necessity of having a canon, the authorities in control set the criteria for determining or selecting the most authoritative sources among all the possibilities, turning down heretical or less authenticated scripture. This procedure led to the dominant (earlier) perspectives permeating the interpretation of the sources so that some branches of the community were marginalized and suppressed.[13] The dominant authority or controlling value system adopted a hierarchic and patriarchic worldview as the normative rule, and the social idea of the inferiority of women pervaded the canon of Scripture.[14] The first council of Nicaea, called by the emperor Constantine of the Roman Empire, is recognized as the initial place where the original faith of the primitive Christian community was censored and codified according to the controlling authority and where the inferiority of females was initially systematized, dismissing the egalitarian views of Jesus' original message.[15]

---

12 Rosemary Ruether, *Goddesses and the Divine Feminine,* (Berkeley, CA: University of California Press, 2005), 121-132.

13 Ruether, *Sexism and God-talk,* 14.

14 The females in Korean church also claim the canonization as main obstacle hampering their identity and experiences to be contextually authenticated. Young Sil Choi, "Korean Feminist Theology and the Bible," *Korean Journal of Christian Studies* 90 (2013), 319-342.

15 Rosemary Ruether, *Women and Redemption: A Theological History,* (Minneapolis, MN: Fortress Press, 2012), 37-41.

Ruether clarifies that restoring the egalitarian framework that had originated in and overcome female inferiority in the Christian community is the primary goal of feminist theology. She maintains that the critical principle of feminist theology is the "promotion of the full humanity of women" and that the full humanity of women should be reflected upon the divine and in authentic relation to the divine, and in the authentic nature of things, and in the message of an authentic redeemer, and in a community of redemption.[16] She identified the essence of the distortion and oppression experienced within Christian churches as sexism, writing that the "naming of males as norms of authentic humanity has caused women to be scapegoated for sin and marginalized in both original and redeemed humanity."[17] Feminists set the primary goal that women's identity, experiences, and full humanity should be included in the definition of inclusive humanity as well as of the divine-human relationship.[18]

Serene Jones also argues that feminist theology is not just interested in women's flourishing and in liberating women from their multilayered experiences of oppression.[19] But she additionally implies that embracing women's lives and stories and their hope in the theological enterprise can function as constitutive in nourishing and renewing Christian experiences and faith as a whole. This has since become a

---

16 Ruether, *Sexism and God-talk*, 18-19.

17 Ibid, 19.

18 Ae-Young Kim, "A Study of Rosemary R. Ruether's Ecofeminist Theology," *Korean Journal of Christian Studies* 44 (2006), 114-115.

19 Serene Jones, *Feminist Theory and Christian Theology: Cartographies of Grace*, (Minneapolis: Fortress Press, 2000), 13-15.

core feature of feminist theology—it ranges from liberating, prophetic, and inclusive to communal, self-critical, and truth-seeking. Feminist theology can play more than a complementary role; it can play an essential role in reshaping and reconstructing all sections of the theological enterprise and, furthermore, in building up a healthy and authentic community embracing the next generation of Christians.

As a tactic of deconstruction, how should feminist theology facilitate its insights and wisdom in creating alternative ways? Ruether suggests a *midrashic* reading of the scripture as the most relevant method for drawing upon women's experiences within the Christian community. This is because midrashic interpretation sheds light upon redrawing and rediscovering the symbols, metaphors, language, and images that have been denied or rejected in the Christian tradition. On the other hand, as a way to de/reconstruct the Christian theological enterprise, Jones is convinced that the doctrines are still effective in playing a normative role since they provide the basic outline of the theological drama within which the Christian story unfolds. As theological drama, the doctrines could construct an imagistic and conceptual terrain within which people of faith locate and interpret their lives and the world around them. This chapter will attempt to explore feminist theological frameworks centering on the writings of Ruether and other feminist theologians, thus laying a foundation for understanding women's lived experiences and for developing an interpretive framework within spiritual direction.

III. Feminist Theological Themes

1. Renaming God/ess

Julie Han has identified that her struggle with the pastor's exclusive emphasis on obedience is grounded in his hierarchic and patriarchic understanding based on his theological formation. The male-oriented worldview is built upon the vertical, dynamic, hierarchic orderings of God-male-female and God-pastor-laypersons. This traditional theological frame has even distanced her from her sense of belonging with her faith community and from her connection with God. Her identity as a female has not been appreciated in the church, so she has felt marginalized and isolated.

Norvene Vest argues strongly that introducing the concept of the Goddess or female God is necessary for female directees so that they may embrace constructively their female identity as well as appropriate it for their spiritual lives in their lived experiences. It is evident that the predominance of male images and language has critically prevented many female directees not only from being intimately connected with the male God, but also from cultivating intrinsic self-identification with God.[20] So, for Vest it is essential for female directees and for Christians in general to reshape the working image of Goddess for overcoming the oppressive aspects of the prevalence of male images of God.

Exploring the historical prevalence of the female divine in the

---

20 Norvene Vest, op. cit., 187.

Ancient Near East, Ruether pays attention to the fact that the female divine was replaced by male monotheism when nomadic herding societies were established.[21] This shift in social structure gave rise to strengthened masculine functions and entailed focusing on the image of God as the Sky-Father.[22] Male monotheism reinforced the social hierarchy—patriarchal rule—through its religious system, which caused a weakening of the feminine in the divine image so as to solidify the dualistic or subordinated orderings: the masculine god ruled over the feminine, and the latter was more dependent on the former. The reverse of the divine image between the two genders became the critical basis of male monotheism and of distortion in images of God and social relations: female was subordinated to male. This historical distortion permeated the Christian community so that hierarchic and patriarchic frameworks affected the shape of the value system and worldview. In the end, female inferiority in the divine image and in social relations was solidified and accelerated in Christendom under canonization and other Constantinian initiatives.[23]

Ruether suggests four theological concepts as alternative ways to illuminate God/ess beyond its patriarchic image. First, the prophetic tradition in Christian scripture demonstrates that God was identified as justice-loving by protesting on behalf of the rural peasantry against the hierarchical, urban, and landowning society in the Old Testament. Jesus in the New Testament was also portrayed as a redeemer of those

---

21 Ruether, *Gaia and God: An Ecofeminist Theology of Earth Healing*, (San Francisco: HarperCollins, 1992), 15-30.

22 Ruether, *Sexism and God-talk*, 53.

23 Ruether, *Gaia and God*, 143-170.

who were marginalized, deprived, and oppressed, such as slaves, women, and gentiles. Here, salvation is defined as deliverance from social oppression and as restoration of an egalitarian society. Despite the absence of explicit description, it is evident that the prophetic consciousness shed light on women as oppressed and deprived. And this liberates God from the patriarchic image.

Divine sovereignty is identified as the second God-language necessary for overcoming the patriarchic image. Ruether explains that divine sovereignty was claimed in order to liberate people from the bondage of human kings and kinships (in the Old Testament). The divine sovereignty also seeks liberation from "human dominance-dependence relationships based on kinship ties or master-servant relationship"[24] and replacement with a new community of brother and sisters in the New Testament. Since this community was characterized by mutual equality without any class, race, or gender divisions, God-language can employ neutral or non-patriarchic images. The proscription of idolatry is named as the third biblical tradition significant in this context. Ruether points out that Christian artistic and verbal representations specify a particular image of God, exemplifying an authoritative father or old wise man image, as a consequence dismissing all other images including the feminine God. Ruether therefore asserts that in order for the theological representation to be inclusiveness in language, which includes the images and experiences of both genders, naming the God/ ess with both female and male metaphors is essential.[25]

---

24 Ruether, *Sexism and God-talk*, 64.

25 Ibid., 66-67.

Last, Ruether highlights the biblical examples of naming the God/ess as female and male through metaphors such as the parable of the mustard seed. The scripture illustrates the equality between female and male, and the images were not drawn from the dominant social groups but from marginalized Galilean peasants.[26] In addition, the parables portray the divine action in non-parental terms. This analysis supports that metaphor treating females and males as equals already existed in the biblical sources, and they can become the bedrock for renaming or characterizing God in more valid ways. Now I will discuss the ways in which renaming God/ess could affect the concept of female nature.

2. Female nature

Feminist theologians consider the historically and culturally constructed inferiority of the feminine nature to the masculine to be a prominent problem within patriarchal civilization and Western Christianity. Rosemary Ruether elucidates how the theoretical problem in this patriarchal anthropology is its uncritical and naive endeavor to "link woman only with the sin-prone part of the self," thus denying female *redeemability* in a theological construction.[27] This theological misconception of Western theologians has thus regarded the woman as an 'inferior mix,' assuming that she is incapable of holding the image of God as does the man, who is seen as representing the rational and spiritual part of the self.

Questioning the essentialist perspective on women's nature, Se-

---

26 Ibid., 68.

27 Ibid., 94.

rene Jones agrees that the theological concept of feminine inferiority has been characterized as a fundamental and indispensable property of female persons. Hence, feminine nature is confined by expressions with negative connotations such as passivity, instability, emotionality, innate, native, and inborn. Both Ruether and Jones point out that a dualistic worldview, a prevalent condition in Western Christianity, has intensified the theological anthropology of feminine inferiority as following the form of culture/nature, reason/intuition, public/private, subject/object, civilized/primitive, etc.[28]

Despite their consensus on identifying dualism as a main problem, Ruether uniquely and relevantly conceives of three marginalized traditions as offering an egalitarian view.[29] First, the eschatological feminism of early Christianity, found also in the theology of the Shakers and the Quakers, viewed the church as anticipating the final redemption of humanity and restoration to its original equality. Second, liberal feminism, which arose during the eighteenth-century Enlightenment, argued for the equal rights of all human beings regardless of gender. Its focus was on transforming the social, political, and economic institutions of this world. Third, the many forms of romantic feminism see masculinity and femininity as equal yet complementary dimensions of the human personality. Ruether argues that we need to find a 'creative synthesis' between liberalism and romanticism. As one way to develop a synthesis, she questions the use of the term *androgyny*, which refers to possession of both male and female characteristics.

---

28 Serene Jones, op. cit., 28.

29 Ruether, *Sexism and God-talk*, 99-109.

Ruether states that the primary question in feminist theological anthropology is how the theological dualism of the *imago dei*/fallen Adam connects with sexual duality, or humanity as male and female.[30] As noted earlier, she first prohibits the use of the term *androgyny*, since it indicates that males and females possess both a 'masculine' and a 'feminine' side to their psychic capacity. As a preliminary step, she calls for integrating the rational and relational capacities in both genders. She argues that that we should not be confused by the concept of *androgyny*, which affirms the commonality of the essential human nature of both men and women. Within Ruether's frame, the differences between male and female are therefore centered on the issues of gender, not those of biological or physiological origin. She asserts, thus, that to restore redeemed humanity, reconnected with the *imago dei*, the recovery of psychic potentials that have been repressed by cultural stereotypes require integration with social engagement, which draws on an egalitarian understanding of human nature. The primary goal of feminist theological anthropology can be established by the recovery of holistic psychic capacities and egalitarian access to social roles, which can overturn the church's patriarchal structures.

On the other hands, Jones begins with a different question drawn from the 'nature and nurture' debates. She devises "strategic essentialism" as a theoretical tactic through which the endeavor to integrate essentialism and constructivism takes a compromising stance. Then, the following questions come up: "How is strategic essentialism implicated in Christian theology?" "What kind of remapping can take

---

30 Ruether, *Sexism and God-talk*, 94.

place in the academic enterprise?" Reconsidering women's nature leads Jones to propose theological mapping in a reverse way, so that sanctification must precede the justification. That is, women's journey to redemption should start with calling upon women to become the subject in their relationship with God.[31] In the Western theological concept, women were only "guilty and saved by association (men)."[32] Before being called into the divine court for justification, women need to be identified as agents responding to God's love, which empowers them to move 'in body' toward perfection. This creates a new space for women to reorient themselves and to start a new beginning of faithful living in relation with God, resisting falsely gendered versions of the self. How might justification function then? Jones claims that justification implies forgiving the sins of constructions that bind us, so that the liberating or emancipatory work of the Holy Spirit may open the door for women. By justification, women may be released from restrictive conceptions of gender, and this may bring about new life.[33]

3. Female Christ

In a spiritual direction session, Jee-Yeon shared the stunning information that the forbidding of women's ordination in her Korean Protestant denomination is based on the fact that Jesus was male; thus, any female could not fully represent Christ in the priesthood or ministry. This hierarchic or patriarchic assumption that the man is the nor-

31 Rosemary R. Ruether, *Introducing Redemption in Christian Feminism,* (Sheffield, England: Sheffield Academic Press, 1998), 16-19.

32 Serene Jones, op. cit., 61.

33 Ibid., 65-66.

mative human being and the woman is defective physically, morally, and mentally has been deeply embedded in the theological concept of ordination. For Jee-Yeon, the Jesus portrayed by the denominational authority does not validate her spiritual experiences and conviction. It is highly problematic that Jee-Yeon's personal spiritual experience and her spiritual vocation on the basis of her relationship with God have been dismissed by the institutionalized concepts and dogma.

Ruether's delineation of the history of patriarchy in Christianity questions whether the church policy against women's ordination would be validated in the light of contemporary Christological understanding. In the Hebraic history and spiritual tradition, the idea of the Messiah was associated with the coming reign of God, the eschatological hope of regaining the Davidic kingdom. Jesus' way of proclaiming the kingdom of God, however, was different from the hope of a Davidic messiah. His message and life instead presented the kingdom of God as radicalized in the prophetic lineage so that the coming reign of God would be among the poor, the oppressed, and other marginalized groups. "Jesus' vision of the Kingdom is neither nationalistic nor other-worldly."[34] Jesus' reinterpretation of the messianic symbol shifted from a king to a servant so that he reversed the social reference of divine redemptive activity, identifying redemption with the lowest persons in society rather than the highest.

The other reformulation of Jesus' messianic symbol, according to Ruether, is found in his emphasis on the 'present' reign of God. Jesus' concept of Spirit facilitated the presence of divine prophecy,

---

34 Ruether, *Sexism and God-talk*, 120.

rather than canonizing past prophecy. Jesus attempted to verify that the kingdom of God will be present here and now, and the presence of Spirit will prove it. This liberated religious experiences from the "fossilization of past traditions"[35] and enabled people to access the divine presence in its "present" form. This representation of Jesus about the messianic vision or idea of Christ plays a critical role in emancipating people's spiritual experiences from institutionalized bondage, as well as in prompting the sense of God's prophetic and redemptive activity in the present time.

Then, in what ways can women discover a legitimate concept of Christology, one that validates female identity and experience? Ruether argues convincingly that it should start with Jesus' new prophetic vision that the kingdom of God is incompatible with the current social or religious hierarchy and patriarchy.[36] Women could function as spiritual guides who are led by the radical calling of the Spirit into a new reality in which marginalized and oppressed people are invited to become initiates in the coming reign of God. The social relations in God's kingdom are overturned since in God's new order the lowly, marginalized, and oppressed are considered as the subjects.

Ruether further reminds us of the ways in which the synoptic Gospels portray women in relationship with Jesus.[37] Even though females were considered as lowly in the historical context, the female disciples played an important role in witnessing Jesus' new vision of social relations. Socially lower-class women are represented as uncovering the

---

35 Ibid., 121.

36 Ibid., 135.

37 Ruether, *Women and Redemption: A Theological History*, 14-20.

intrinsic features of the messianic vision. For instance, Mary is portrayed as the first figure to encounter Jesus resurrected and the first witness of what turned out to be the foundation of the first Christian church. This means that even though the social order of the existing society could treat females as lowly and marginalized, the hierarchic and patriarchic social ordering could not prevent females from becoming genuine disciples and participating authentically in God's kingdom here and now. Rather, the female disciples were disclosed as main characters who recognized and were the first to join in the kingdom of God proclaimed by Jesus.

As a liberator, Jesus proclaims that he "renounced the system of domination and seeks to embody in his person the new humanity of service and mutual empowerment."[38] The *messiahship* of Jesus is verified by his embodying the new reality of God's kingdom, by his liberating the oppressed from systematic social oppression, and by his rescuing the marginalized from social dismissal and disregard. "As the representative of liberated humanity and the liberating Word of God, Jesus manifests the kenosis of patriarchy, the announcement of the new humanity through a lifestyle that discards hierarchical caste privilege and speaks on behalf of the lowly."[39] This enables us to say that the maleness of Jesus is not significant theologically. Instead, it tells Christian women that to become a disciple of Jesus or a minister is to become a witness against the religious or social idolatrous system of patriarchal privilege. It is thus a reasonable claim that the church

---

38 Ruether, *Sexism and God-talk*, 137.

39 Ibid.

policy against women's ordination is not even Christological, since the institutional policy explicitly limits the messiahship of Jesus within the hierarchical and patriarchal privilege so that it disregards seriously the liberating and redemptive activity of God in women's ordination and spiritual experiences.

Carter Heyward offers the insightful perspectives that the stance of institutionalized religion against women's ordination is external evidence of moralism in Christianity. Moralism is the conviction that "we and we alone know what's right and, moreover, that we have a moral, or ethical, duty to make others see things our way irrespective of how actual human, divine, and other life may be affected."[40] Moralists are secure in the assumption that there is only one right perspective and that those who have it are right. Heyward is conscious that moralism could be embodied as authoritarian power relations, which elicits oppression and distortion in relationship since the morally superior side that sees only one right perspective tends to rule over the inferior side.

Given this, Heyward maintains, Jesus' way to overcome or overturn moralism and its oppression and distortion is to go through the passion led by Spirit. This was the inevitable journey of Jesus as he followed the spontaneous leading of the Spirit out of the divine desire to establish mutual right relationships. This is the reason Heyward states, that Jesus' passion comes out of "the fullness of his embodied life, the depth and power of his embodied spirit, the openness of his body to risk and struggle in the spirit of God."[41] That is, the God that

---

40 Carter Heyward, *Saving Jesus from Those Who Are Right: Rethinking What It Means to Be Christian* (Minneapolis: Fortress Press, 1999), 119.

41 Carter Heyward, *Saving Jesus from Those Who Are Right*, 122.

Jesus loved passionately was and is a Spirit that compelled Jesus, as it compels us all, to live in such a way that our lives are themselves protests against structures of injustice and exploitation in our religious institutions and in the larger society.[42] Jesus' passion is the fruit of the mutual relations among God, Jesus, and Spirit, and it challenges the moralism embedded in religious authoritarian relations of power.

Heyward's theological reconstruction extends into the concepts of atonement and incarnation, which have misled us into relations steeped in authoritarian, moralistic, and violent dynamics in the traditional theological framework. She points out that this central doctrine of Christianity has historically been constructed with a male-centered frame. It was built upon the assumption that bodies are inferior to spirit, so our bodies need to be liberated by our spirit. The traditional treatments of incarnation and atonement have functioned primarily to separate us from God, Jesus, and one another. She states that this is not the way Jesus bore his passion, in which the Spirit drew him into an intimate relation with God and the messianic vision. The incarnation is the Christological articulation of divine desire and the idea that "as our Sacred, Sensual Power, deeply infusing our flesh, root of our embodied yearning to reach out to one another, God was indeed in Jesus as God is in us."[43] The atonement as the other side of divine desire, moreover, represents the way in which the incarnated God is redeeming or liberating us through our mutual relations.

Heyward spells out that God's salvific invitation asks human be-

---

42 Ibid., 136.

43 Ibid., 126.

ings to take part in mutual relations with God and Jesus. God's call to participate in incarnation and in atonement is therefore considered as an act of solidarity and as the mutual embodiment of right relationship among God, Jesus, and humans. Not only is it a spiritual event, but also a "political, social, ecological, and pastoral movement of liberation from larger and smaller forces that are cruel, violent, apathetic or ignorant of what humans and other creatures need in order to live and thrive."[44] Jesus is standing in the central locus of the divine desire to establish mutual right relations between Creator and creatures, Liberator and the oppressed.

IV. Feminist Theological Strategies for Spiritual Direction

There are several significant insights or benefits of the feminist theological approach relevant to spiritual direction in the Christian context. The first is the liberation theme. The feminist theological frame contributes to liberating our image of God from humanly generated images that have elicited distortion or misrepresentation of the divine nature. God's image and the nature of God associated with that image have been misrepresented by the male-dominant language used by Christian religious institutions. Feminist theological insights assist us in restoring the original form of the divine image or of nature by demystifying a false conceptualization and by overcoming a dualistic worldview. It is helpful to learn that God does not want to be confined

---

44 Ibid., 122.

to manipulated images generated historically or culturally in hierarchic or patriarchic contexts. In addition, liberation from hierarchic and patriarchic images of God entails the liberation of human beings from subordinated or obedient relationships with God, family, and society. A new self-representation or self-image of Christian women could emancipate them from oppression or marginalization in subordinated or obedience-reinforced relations. They are not secondary or sin-elicited beings, but ones in whom the divine image is equally represented. Authoritative and oppressive images of God are no longer permissible or viable; the God who is longing to have an intimate relationship with humans and to accompany humans is more relevant and legitimate.

Next, the feminist theological frame leads us to realize two significant features of the Holy Spirit: spontaneity and simultaneity.[45] Noticing the spontaneous and simultaneous leadings of the Spirit is a critical tool for overcoming the fossilization of religious institutions and for living out the renewing power of the presence of God in given situations.[46] This demands that we not be stuck with social systems that bring about oppression or subordination. But it also strongly asks us to participate in the liberating work of the Holy Spirit taking place spontaneously and simultaneously every moment and everywhere.[47] Fol-

---

45 Janet Ruffing, op. cit., 65-66.

46 Elizabeth Liebert, "Supervision as Widening the Horizons," in *Supervision of Spiritual Directors: Engaging in Holy Mystery*, eds. Mary R. Bumpus and Rebecca B. Langer (New York: Morehouse Publishing, 2005), 133-134.

47 The spiritual directees were guided with spiritual reading of the Scripture and the historical writings especially written by the female saints and theologians. The spiritual practices played implicitly significant role in facilitating female experiences and identity, and enhancing the dynamic in prayer so as to reshape spiritual formation.

lowing the Spirit implies discerning the movement of the divine will and desire 'here and now,' so it requires that we cherish each moment and each place. A lively response to the spontaneous and simultaneous movement of the Holy Spirit is required of the spiritual pilgrim. This might give rise to a new spiritual awareness that the leadings of the Spirit invite female directees to embody their spiritual wisdom and insights in various aspects of lived experiences, engaging actively with community, society, and the world, since they are not subordinated, insufficient, or deformed beings but a divine being bearing the image of God.

Finally, feminist theological insights can equip the spiritual director with the essential theological concept of mutual interrelation and reciprocity.[48] One of the primary characteristics of the divine nature as reformulated by feminist theology is the concept that God is seeking mutual interrelation and reciprocity in the relations with the human. God calls human beings not as servants or subordinates, but as companions, active partners on the divine journey in human history. Here, human beings are not the objects of the divine milieu; they are called as co-creators or co-agents in the world. Salvation is redefined as the right mutual relations between God and human beings and others. These concepts can guide spiritual direction, determining where its essence should be grounded. The profound insights from feminist theology will formulate the core characteristic of Christian spiritual direction: mutually respectful and right relations with God and other beings

---

48 Cf) Janet, Ruffing, *Spiritual Direction*, 135-154.

and the environment.[49] This enables us to state that one of the primary goals of spiritual direction is to bear witness that the soul should initially establish, seek for, enhance, or restore right mutual relationships among God, the self, and the world. It further leads us to embrace the egalitarian vision as our Christian vocation, since this is the original form of the right mutual relations that God wills.

The use of these feminist theological approaches as formative strategies in spiritual direction is illustrated by the following example. Since being introduced to the historical construction of the patriarchic image of God, Julie Han, the Korean-American Christian minister whose situation was discussed above, has been convinced of the theological irrelevancy of obedience as necessary for spiritual formation. She has decided that maintaining her membership in the church will not nurture her spiritual life and will even worsen her inner sense of oppression and marginalization in the church. In several subsequent spiritual direction sessions, she has named the sense of agony and frustration that she experiences due to the emphasis on obedience, and she has begun, for the sake of her spiritual life and for healthy marital relations in her family life, to make the tentative decision to leave the church. Even though this will be a hard decision, she and her family members have become convinced that engaging in a spiritual journey to seek the right mutual relations with God, themselves, and others will bear fruit in other aspects of their lives.

Jee-Yeon has taken advantage of spiritual direction as a discerning process for her ordination process and her current association with a

---

49 Elizabeth Liebert, op. cit., 130-135.

particular denomination. She was initially angry and frustrated by the fact that her religious denomination, the Korean Presbyterian Church Abroad (KPCA), has not opened and does not plan to open ordination to women. She has noticed, however, that her desire to be ordained as a Christian minister has not been extinguished by the lack of support by the religious institution, since she has discovered it is related to one of her life vocations. She mentioned in one of the direction sessions that this frustration has rather awakened her social consciousness of the need for the oppressive structure that has stemmed from patriarchic society to be changed or transformed as an authentic way to incarnate the message of Jesus Christ and to embody right mutual relations in her context. Her inner compassion toward the denomination and the church authorities has surprisingly become a new motivation that guides her actions for change. She has recently been engaged in communal solidarity with other female ministers to campaign for the ordination of women in her denomination.

V. Conclusion

This study has endeavored to demonstrate that feminist theological approaches can be a formative strategy for spiritual direction in the Christian context. The chapter began with the problematic discrimination against women that has been systematically constructed and is currently experienced by Christian women. The prevalence of male language in the traditional hierarchic and patriarchic theological structures was identified as a critical impediment for female directees to affirm not only their self-identities, but also their spiritual experiences within the Christian frame. Feminist theological themes, ranging from divine images and Christology to human nature, shed light upon deconstructing and reconstructing the theological frameworks within Christian theology. So, this study attempted to demonstrate the ways in which the traditional Christian theological approaches reconstructed with feminist approaches could play a significant role in cultivating the spiritual experiences of female directees and enhancing their spiritual identity. The feminist theological approaches contain formative and constitutive components for renewing or authenticating spiritual direction for female directees.

In the next stage of this research, the theological and practical implications of the feminist theological approaches for male spiritual directors who are working with female directees will be relevant. The study will focus more on the ways in which the feminist theological frame could cultivate the self-representation of male spiritual directors and enhance their awareness of the cause and effects of patriarchic frameworks in direction sessions as well as religious institutions.

Bibliography

Aquino, Maria Pilar, Daisy Machado, and Jeanette Rodríguez. *A Reader in Latina Feminist Theology*. Austin: University of Texas Press, 2002.

Barry, William A. and William J. Connolly. *The Practice of Spiritual Direction*. New York: HarperCollins Publishers, 1986.

Bauman, Whitney A., Dirk von der Horst, and Emily Leah Silverman. Introduction: Divining Prophetic Voices, in *Voices of Feminist Liberation: Writings in Celebration of Rosemary Radford Ruether*. New York: Routledge, 2014.

Bumpus, Mary Rose. Supervision of Spiritual Directors: The Assistance of an Absent Other. In *Supervision of Spiritual Direction: Engaging in Holy Mystery*. Edited by Mary Rose Bumpus & Rebecca Bradburn Langer. New York: Morehouse Publishing, 2005.

Choi, Young Sil Choi. "Korean Feminist Theology and the Bible." *Korean Journal of Christian Studies* 90 (2013), 319-342.

Chung, Hee-Sung. "A Re-construction of Developmental Theories from the Perspective of Feminist Pastoral Counseling." *Theology and Praxis* 48 (March 2016), 195-219.

_____. "An Exploration of Womanist Pastoral Theology in the Korean Context." *Theology and Praxis* 29 (Nov. 2011), 157-179.

Fischer, Kathleen. *Women at the Well: Feminist Perspectives on Spiritual Direction*. New York: Paulist Press, 1988.

Heyward, Carter. *Saving Jesus from Those Who Are Right: Rethinking What It Means to Be Christian*. Minneapolis: Fortress Press, 1999.

Jones, Serene. *Feminist Theory and Christian Theology: Cartographies of Grace*. Minneapolis: Fortress Press, 2000.

Kim, Ae-Young. "A Study of Rosemary R. Ruether's Ecofeminist Theology." *Korean Journal of Christian Studies* 44 (2006), 111-139.

Kim, Kyungeun. "Spiritual Direction: from the Integrating Perspective of Everyday Life and Spirituality." *Theology and Praxis* 44 (June 2015), 279-301.

Lee, Kang-Hack. "Lee Sejong's Spiritual Direction and Its Application to the Ministry of the Korean Church." *Theology and Praxis* 49 (June 2016), 219-244.

Lee, Joohyung. "Social and Cultural Self-Awareness in Spiritual Direction:

Reflection of an Asian Male Director." *Presence: International Journal of Spiritual Direction* 21(Dec. 2015), 40-46.

Liebert, Elizabeth. *Supervision as Widening the Horizons, in Supervision of Spiritual Directors: Engaging in Holy Mystery*. Edited by Mary R. Bumpus & Rebecca B Langer. New York: Morehouse Publishing, 2005, 125-146.

Mitchem, Stephanie. *Introducing Womanist Theology*. Maryknoll, NY: Orbis Books, 2002.

Norvene Vest. In the Image of Godde: Feminist Spiritual Direction, In *Tending the Holy: Spiritual Direction Across Traditions*. Edited by Norvene Vest, 186-203. Harrisburg, PA: Morehouse Pub., 2003.

Oh, Bang-Sik. "A Study of Thomas Merton's Spiritual Direction." *Theology and Praxis* 52 (Dec. 2016), 393-420.

Philips, Susan S. *Candlelight: Illuminating the Art of Spiritual Direction*. New York: Morehouse Publishing, 2008.

Ruether, Rosemary R. *Sexism and God-talk: Toward a Feminist Theology*. Boston: Beacon Press, 1983.

_____. *Gaia and God: An Ecofeminist Theology of Earth Healing*. San Francisco: HarperCollins, 1992.

_____. *Women and Redemption: A Theological History*. Minneapolis, MN: Fortress Press, 2012.

_____. *Introducing Redemption in Christian Feminism*. Sheffield: Sheffield Academic Press, 1998.

_____. *Goddesses and the Divine Feminine: A Western Religious History*. Berkeley: University of California Press, 2005.

Ruffing, Janet K. *Spiritual Direction: Beyond the Beginnings*. New York: Paulist Press, 2000.

4

Social and Cultural Self-Awareness in Spiritual Direction:

Reflections of an Asian (Korean) Male Director

I. Social Awareness as a Spiritual Director

Engaging in spiritual direction implies the participation in the indwelling work of the Holy Spirit. My training in the Diploma of Arts in Spiritual Direction program of San Francisco Theological Seminary led me to realize that to be effective, the spiritual director should be grounded in profound self-awareness or self-perception in the social context, since participation in the full presence of the Holy Spirit requires the director to be fully aware of the holistic aspects of his or her "self." This is instrumental when taking part in the present or real-time work of the Holy Spirit on behalf of both the directee and the director. In that sense, Kelly Arora's guidelines about the social identity of a director provide an intriguing tool for reflecting upon myself, especially my social status, values about systems, worldviews, assumptions, etc.[1]

---

1 Kelly Arora, "Not-Knowing in Spiritual Direction: Reflections on Social Identity," *Presence* 17, no. 2 (June 2011): 19–26. Arora's guidelines, captured by the acronym SHARES, categorize

These are constitutive elements of who I am, and these affect how I function in spiritual direction. Acknowledging my social identity and assumptions is crucial for my directees, since spiritual companionship is constructed with them and so my social identity implicitly or explicitly affects their spiritual journeys. By reflecting on my social identity here, I expect to enhance my awareness of my potential to judge or disengage from certain people who seek companionship as directees on their spiritual journey.

Following the SHARES acronym described by Arora, I will begin with my Sexual orientation and gender identity. I am heterosexual, married to a Korean woman, and live with my two biological daughters, who are twelve and ten years old. As a male director, having a female directee would be challenging for me due to the gender difference, especially in the Asian cultural context where the gender roles are rigid and strict. Conversations with my wife and the raising of two daughters have better prepared me, however, to understand the key features of the psychological and spiritual journeys of female directees. Most of all, I find that practical wisdom from fellow spiritual directors offers guidance on prominent themes in direction with females. For instance, Janet Ruffing presents four key themes to help male directors bring about the flourishing of female directees.[2] In addition,

---

the social identity of spiritual directors into six dimensions: Sexual Orientation and Gender, Health, Age and Generational Influences, Religious and Spiritual Beliefs and Practices, Ethnicity, National Origin, and Racial Identity, and Socioeconomic Status. Arora created the SHARES model by modifying the ADDRESSING framework for therapists developed by psychologist Pamela A. Hays.

2 Janet Ruffing, "Spiritual Direction with Women: Reclaiming and Reinterpreting Key Themes from the Spiritual Tradition," *Presence* 12, no. 3 (September 2006): 36–46. Ruffing elabo-

my longterm friendships with several LGBT individuals and couples is another spiritual asset in that knowing their life stories and issues not only helps compensate for my lack of any firsthand experience of homosexuality or transexuality but also enables me to understand deeply those who are in conflict over or troubled by sexual orientation issues. For instance, one of my lesbian friends has shared with me over the last decade about her marriage, adoption of two infants, and raising of her children in American society. Engaging with her life story has enhanced my knowledge of the existential concerns and still-ambivalent atmosphere in contemporary society about sexual orientation and the civil rights of LGBT people, which has helped me cultivate a compassionate presence in spiritual direction.

The other embedded factor in relation to sexual orientation stems from my religious community. My religious denomination and community (the Korean Presbyterian Church) has expressed negative views on sexual orientations other than heterosexuality. Despite this, my close fellowship with LGBT friends helps me advocate for the spiritual journey of a gay/lesbian directee in my ministry of spiritual direction. I have been aware of the potential for my sexual orientation to lead me to disengage from homosexual people who have experienced violence due to their sexual orientation. Another potential case might be doing direction with those coming from broken families. For

rates four key themes from the spiritual traditions, taking into account their potentially negative effects on women in order to clear the way for appreciating their positive contribution to women's spiritual growth: silence vs. silencing/voicelessness; enclosure, sanctuary, withdrawal vs. confinement and incarceration; ego-lessness, self-naughting, self-denial vs. self-possession; and desire vs. restraint of desire or extinguishing of desire.

instance, divorce could be a challenging issue for me to face since my religious community tends to pose legalistic stance on moral values grounded in biblical literalism. My training in Clinical Pastoral Education and my engaging in Christian counseling in pastoral ministry over the last decade, however, have prepared me to respond to the woundedness or brokenness identified in spiritual direction sessions beyond the religious rigidity. I recognize that spiritual direction and pastoral counseling require different approaches. My training as a professional counselor has assisted me in deepening my compassionate presence when encountering brokenness without trying to analyze or evaluate the directee's inner journey.

Next, I will deal with Health issues in direction. While physical health has not been a concern of mine, my experience with psychological depression has engaged me actively with people in similar situations. I have been able to feel compassionately connected with directees going through depression or depressive affective disorder. In addition, my compassionate presence with those who are suffering from physical illness and with their family members has been deeply grounded in two life-changing experiences. I lost my father to lung cancer when I was young, and my wife has had surgery on her spine and still suffers from chronic back pain. Empathy and compassionate presence is embodied within my soul in spiritual direction with regard to directees' health issues and concerns.

My Age and generational status are also socially influenced. As a person in my late 30s, I have been aware of this age as a time for developing life skills and preparing for the later part of my life. And I feel a strong sense of responsibility for my family and for raising my two daughters, which is one of my current primary goals. In a generational sense, I grew up in a political transition from a military dictatorship to a democratic movement. My country's poverty issues were partially overcome and its overall economy was boosted when I was young. The new generation in Korean and Korean American society is emerging in the postmodern or multicultural context. My ministerial experience with this transitional generation assists me in embracing the experiences and the historical context of directees ranging from the younger to the older generations. As I grow into middle age, I might be better able to comprehend older or senior directees' experiences. It would be challenging for me to engage with seniors who underwent the Korean War and the Cold War; their social and political perceptions seem to be polarized among Korean people. Honoring the sacrifices of the older generation and the hidden wholeness within their suffering, however, could be embodied in the same way I honor my parents who sacrificed their whole lives for me and my younger brother.

I am identified as a Christian minister and director trained under formal Christian educational systems (Religious and Spiritual Beliefs and Practices). The discernment process for religious vocation is one of my main fields in the direction context, so I have helped several young adult Christians discern their life vocation based upon their spiritual journey. Nevertheless, I recognize other religions and am willing and open to having constructive dialogue with other religious professionals. My most challenging direction session was held with a Christian pastor who relied heavily on a rigid dogmatic belief system, and this clearly indicates the high potential for me to disengage from people from a similar background to that pastor.

And fifth, I am Ethnically Korean, having grown up in Korea and identifying myself as a Korean who is grounded in Korean cultural values and assumptions. In my academic journey, I have also realized that Neo-Confucianism has deeply shaped and formulated most of the conscious or unconscious aspects of my life at the individual and collective levels. This social background has tremendously assisted me in my spiritual direction role with Korean people. There is, however, the other side of the coin as well; the challenge of having a director from a different cultural or ethnic background is immense. I notice that as a director I have tended to put too much energy into collecting a lot of background information from non-Korean directees since I was preoccupied by the assumption that I lacked cultural data about non-Koreans. While my direction will be more focused on the Korean Christian context, the multiethnic or multicultural experiences in the direction context might lead me to disengage with a directee from a different cultural or racial background.

In terms of Socioeconomic status, I was raised in a middle-class family in one of the suburbs of Seoul, and this prevented me from experiencing economic hardships or poverty issues for a long time. Experiencing the recent bankruptcy of my family's business, however, has led me to become interested in social and economic justice issues and to extend my compassionate eyes to see those who are experiencing the harsh reality of economic pressure due to financial shortages and poverty. My current socioeconomic status asks me to be accountable for clear consciousness in direction sessions since systematic corruption or structural problems inherently embedded in capitalism have intensified economic polarization, income inequality, and discrimination as well as social conflict. My economic status has equipped me with the socioeconomic lens to understand the way in which economic and financial conditions in a society could affect the directee's individual life and inner dynamics. This sheds light upon the director's role in comprehending the interrelatedness or interdependence of social justice and personal morality in various aspects ranging from the intrapersonal to the interpersonal and social levels. It invites me to engage implicitly and explicitly with the pastoral endeavor to embody the core values of Christian truth regarding spiritual solidarity and liberation through the ministry of spiritual direction. Meanwhile, I have been awakening to the realization that I was not trained properly in ways to enhance my financial independence. So, making an effort to support my family financially is also crucial in order for me to sustain a stable spiritual direction ministry.

I have reflected upon my social identity that is potentially present or embedded in the spiritual direction process, and my self-awareness will help to prevent me from judging or disengaging from a directee. Thus, it is reasonable to ask the question, how can these multiple aspects of myself be facilitated in spiritual direction in a constructive and productive way? Pamela Cooper-White gives a useful insight on this topic.[3] The multiplicity perceived within us (the self) should not be fragmented or partially broken, but it can be utilized to cultivate a sense of empathy with the otherness within ourselves. Basing her work on a psychoanalytic framework, Cooper-White states that there are several

_____

3 Pamela, Cooper-White, "The 'Other' Within: Multiple Selves Making a World of Difference," _Reflective Practice: Formation and Supervision in Ministry_ 29 (2009): 23–37.

inner parts within the psyche that are variable and that ebb and flow. With greater awareness of these inner parts, we can "better predict our autonomic responses in the face of unconsciously perceived threats and learn to soothe, manage, and override our animal reactivity."[4] The multiplicity of the human psyche is constructed by its nature from the inherently dynamic instincts of aggression and fear, out of which one responds to an outer stimulus such as violence, attack, etc, Both the aggressive and vulnerable parts within the self coexist. She argues persuasively that the most appropriate way to treat the multiple aspects of human nature, including its aggression and vulnerability, is not embodied by pretending to transcend our bodily needs but by embracing our complexity and befriending each part. That is, rather than evading the strangeness within ourselves, through befriending and knowing more about the strangeness we can be aware of our own aggression and its origins as well as speculate about how to renew it as part of ourself. Furthermore, Cooper-White maintains that once we are aware of our inner multiplicity, we can serve others in an appropriate way. In the spiritual direction context, empathy or compassion toward a directee could more effectively be facilitated through coming to know, accept, and even embrace our multiple selves.[5]

---

4 Ibid., 27.

5 Ibid., 25.

II. Culture as Constitutive Component of Spiritual Direction

I am a Korean. I believe that my call to be a spiritual director of Koreans and Korean Americans has grown and manifested in my spiritual journey little by little. My vocational journey as a spiritual director has been discerned or examined within the whole dimension of my life over the last several years, especially as reflected in my academic interests and my spiritual practices. Standing on the threshold of this significant ministry in my spiritual journey, my reflections on spiritual direction have consistently reminded me of my identity as "a Korean." Since committing to inner work and spiritual practices, never have I been ignorant of my identity as a Korean. "Being a Korean" is the overarching concept of my identity that enables me to interpret or understand the entirety of my experience and my life ranging from my family background and social relationships to church life and mysterious experiences related to the divinity. "Being a Korean" implies a comprehensive experience beyond the fact of national identity, including the founding of Korea and the history of the forefathers, the multireligious and syncretistic culture, neo-Confucianism, the agricultural economy, Japanese occupation and the Korean War, the modern economy and political dictatorships, the division between North Korea and the political democracy of South Korea, the Korean wave in Asian countries, etc.

As the above list implies, encountering a Korean in spiritual direction is an encounter with the past, present, and future of Korea. Encountering a Korean Christian, therefore, leads to listening to a story that a soul has undergone in the context of the holistic history of Korea. Therefore, it should be assumed that the Korean directee's experiences of a transcendent being or deity have been influenced and sometimes significantly shaped by the cultural characteristics and historical events of his or her context. The directee's cultural background and experiences are the constructive factors of their spiritual experiences.

My self-reflective articulation of my identity has uncovered the reason I keep seeking the cultural component in spiritual direction. The significance of cultural aspects as constitutive components of spiritual direction is affirmed in an article by Susan Rakoczy.[6] Her article challenges me to meet and embrace diversity; spiritual directors are not exempt from this reality and experiences. She maintains that what makes spiritual direction sacred is that it is the encounter not only between two souls, but also between two different cultures. All beings have a "home" culture that gives us values that will have an effect on forming our life and our ministry as spiritual directors, since we meet the directee in an interpersonal relationship in which two cultural worldviews interact. Once we recognize that a different cultural framework has been encountered within the directee's worldview, how should we as a director respond to the difference?

My reading of the literature brings me again to the concept of the "stranger" within oneself. In contrast to Cooper-White's reliance on empathy, Rakoczy elicits the necessity of *interpathy* in spiritual direc-

---

6 Susan Rakoczy, "Responding to Difference: Challenges for Contemporary Spiritual Directors," *Reflective Practice: Formation and Supervision in Ministry* 29 (2009): 91–104.

tion in a culturally different context. Grounded in the biblical terms "kenosis" and "self-emptying," interpathy is described as "crossing over into another's frame and experiences and returning different— enriched, disturbed, humbled."[7] The utilization of interpathy raises several questions and prerequisites to ponder: Will the directee feel a sense of accompaniment with me? If I have been aware of empathy, sympathy, or interpathy in a session, what are they teaching me about myself or God? Which part of the other's worldview, image of God, and image of self and community has not been shared? Rakoczy notes that interpathy is always partial and incomplete since I am always my- self. If the crossing over into another's culture is incarnated with hu- mility and authenticity, the desired fruits of spiritual direction can be borne even in the context of cultural differences. I am convinced that her articulation of three modes of ecumenical direction experiences can be applied to spiritual direction in three different ways by employing interpathy in culturally different contexts. First, interpathy can bring about "wisdom sharing," in which the directee's worldview or value system is secured or accepted by the director. This might cultivate the director's comprehension of the other's life and stimulate the sharing of wisdom and learning from each other. Second, interpathy can lead to "paradigm shifting," in which a director enters as completely as possible into the world of the seeker and thinks and feels within the di- rectee's life. This shifting is a way to participate in the seeker's native language and cultural framework and to perceive or speak from within. But, due to its always being partial and incomplete, the director is still

7 Ibid., 97.

grounded in his/her own culture. The third way is termed "beyond cultural difference," which rarely happens. The director and the directee might not perceive any cultural differences and are not limited by their own cultural references, but they transcend their existential difference and feel connected and encountered deeply with each other. This might be the fruit to savor the most in spiritual direction.

The crucial role of culture in spiritual direction has been vividly manifested in sessions I have held with Korean immigrants or Korean American people. These experiences lead me to agree with Sophia Park's explanation of three perceived rhythms.[8] At first, some Korean directees hold firmly to the cultural heritage and value systems of their home country. This is mostly observed in first-generation Korean immigrants. While holding tightly to the historical roots of their cultural legacy tends to be presented as cultural or racial pride, it is likely to be a fundamental reason they are isolated from mainstream society in the United States. I have observed that a few directees have shared with me some concerns about conflicts or implicit problems in the parent-children relationship. The parents in the family, mostly first generation, show a strong tendency to treat or raise their children, who are second generation, as they themselves were treated in the homeland, where Confucian rigidity and the patriarchal structure were dominant in family relationships. But the children have trouble with their parents' authoritative relationship and one-way communication style because they have been educated in or become accustomed to the American culture

---

8 Jung Eun Sophia Park, "Cross-Cultural Spiritual Direction: Dancing with a Stranger," *Presence* 16, no. 1 (January 2010): 46–52.

and its style of relationship formation. The conflict between two generations of immigrant families is well illustrated in the book *American Born Chinese*.[9] This story of a Chinese-American adolescent portrays his agony and difficulty understanding his parents, since his Americanized worldview and intercultural perspective, derived from his school education and personal relationships with other Americans, hindered his comprehension of his parents' cultural attitudes and expectations at home.

I have also encountered a second group of people who have undergone assimilation with American culture and society so that they do not appreciate their Korean racial and cultural roots. Their spiritual and racial journeys that have led them to disregard their cultural roots have various origins. It would not be correct to assume that their resentment or despair toward their homeland is the sole reason they have distanced themselves from their origins; several other situations could also cause the disconnection or separation. Spiritual direction with people in this group has a strong tendency to review the biblical account of the Israelite discovery of Canaan as an exploration of a new land, a blessed place for them to live. It is reasonable for them to rely on this story since their existential or spiritual journey draws them to adjust wholeheartedly to this new land rather than to regret being separated from the homeland.

The third group of people, identified as "between two different cultures," is the most challenging and need to be treated in a more sophisticated or deliberate way since they are usually found to be lack-

---

9 Gene Luen Yang, *American Born Chinese* (New York: First Second Books, 2007).

ing self-confidence due to their ambiguous identification. Because they don't belong to any one culture, their inner conflicts are mostly associated with their sense of belonging or of having deserted their origins (family or homeland). Thus, theological and cultural themes should be taken into careful consideration in direction since whenever a director leans toward any concept or belief that is deeply rooted within the directee's culture of origin, the directee might resist.

In addition, my academic exploration of Neo-Confucianism as the constitutive ideology in the East Asian Christian context demonstrates that Korean Christians have implicitly and culturally been affected by the Confucian worldview and its cultural formation. Even though they identify as Christian, their ways of decision-making, developing relationships with others, and engaging socially are still influenced by core concepts of Neo-Confucianism, such as the concept of a holistic, interconnected world with simultaneity between opposite logics. These kinds of cultural components make spiritual direction with Korean Christians unique and distinctive from any other Christian spiritual direction context.

III. Concluding Remarks: Hidden Wholeness

In what way can I describe the effects of spiritual direction on my life? It is a sacred calling to bear witness and live out the hidden wholeness, the mysterious but graciously gifted life.[10] My life jour-

---

10 The concept of a hidden wholeness originated with Thomas Merton. It is employed in

ney with spiritual direction has led me to discover the threefold divine blessing hidden in my life. Why should I call it a divine blessing? Accompaniment in spiritual direction leads me continuously into sacred exploration of the divine milieu. I discovered the first aspect of the divine blessing in the inner journey to myself. Without exaggeration, every time I have encountered a spiritual director or a directee, it has caused me to see myself, an inner space, innermost place within my soul and spirit. I am on a spiritual journey to unveil and cultivate my true self, which is covered by unessential elements derived from a fragmented life. This contemplation-oriented ministry has allowed me to reflect upon my current location so as to help me be centered in the sacred presence.

Second, the ministry of spiritual direction greatly assists me to see the divine presence and to hear the voice of the Holy Spirit within the spiritual journey of the seeker or the directee. Being aware of the holy presence within someone else's spiritual life is a very humbling and privileged experience. Listening to another's spiritual story has taught my inner attention to perceive the movements and works of the Holy Spirit, and furthermore it has trained me to hear more carefully or sensitively the stories unfolded by souls whom I might have previously disregarded or dismissed. I would say that all dialogue and conversation with all people can be considered as a sacred moment in which to notice the trace of the Holy Spirit within one's life.

Lastly, the threefold blessing of spiritual direction is fully accom-

---

Parker Palmer's book *A Hidden Wholeness: The Journey Toward an Undivided Life* (San Francisco: Jossey-Bass, 2004).

plished when my spiritual perception is thoroughly embodied in the social or communal dimension. Engaging with and encountering seekers' stories of the divine has enhanced my sense of compassion on the communal or social level so that it asks me to embody my spiritual awareness in community, society, and country in terms of justice issues.[11] I am firmly convinced that without engagement with social or communal justice, the spiritual journey through spiritual direction is somewhat hypothetical and does not bear genuine fruits. Engaging in spiritual direction can proceed into a theological endeavor to articulate the human nature and divine presence in a newly appropriate way. I believe that my ministerial vocation of spiritual direction embodies these integrative and authentic features of the threefold blessing of spiritual direction: dwelling in divine milieu, hearing the sacred voice, and embodying social justice in comprehensive ministry.

---

11 Eleazer S. Fernandez, *Reimagining the Human: Theological Anthropology in Response to Systematic Evil* (St. Louis, MO: Chalice Press, 2004).

Bibliography

Arora, Kelly. "Not-Knowing in Spiritual Direction: Reflections on Social Identity." *Presence* 17, no. 2 (June 2011): 19-26.

Cooper-White, Pamela. "The 'Other' Within: Multiple Selves Making a World of Difference." *Reflective Practice: Formation and Supervision in Ministry* 29 (2009): 23-37.

Fernandez, Eleazar S. *Reimagining the Human: Theological Anthropology in Response to Systematic Evil*. St. Louis, MO: Chalice Press, 2004.

Palmer, Parker. *A Hidden Wholeness: The Journey Toward an Undivided Life*. San Francisco; Jossey-Bass, 2004.

Park, Jung Eun Sophia. "Cross-Cultural Spiritual Direction: Dancing with a Stranger." *Presence* 16, no. 1 (January 2010): 46-52.

Rakoczy, Susan. "Responding to Difference: Challenges for Contemporary Spiritual Directors." *Reflective Practice: Formation and Supervision in Ministry* 29 (2009): 91-104.

Ruffing, Janet. "Spiritual Direction with Women: Reclaiming and Reinterpreting Key Themes from the Spiritual Tradition." *Presence* 12, no. 3 (September 2006): 36-46.

Yang, Gene Luen Yang. *American Born Chinese*. New York: First Second Books, 2007.

II.
Spiritual Discernment

5

Christian Discernment
Through the Neuroscientific Lens:

Within Jonathan Edwards' *Religious Affection*

I. Introduction

Christians living in the contemporary world use spiritual discernment as an essential component of their spiritual formation and discipline. Discernment is defined as "the Christian practice of seeking God's call in the midst of the decisions that mark one's life."[1] It stands on the initial premise that the ultimate aim of one's spiritual life and journey is to seek to be tuned in to the Holy Spirit's guidance. The decisions and choices Christians make in their daily lives should consistently resonate with this guidance. This critical engagement requires a practical procedure for figuring out which given options outweigh others so that individual decisions or choices reflect one's values, life goals, or vocation. Discernment is the most important Christian spiritual practice for cultivating and transforming one's spiritual life and

---

1 Elizabeth Liebert, *The Way of Discernment: Spiritual Practices for Decision Making*, 1st ed. (Louisville, KY: Westminster John Knox Press, 2008), ix.

journey.

Our contemporary world has recently paid attention to the advanced information from neuroscience since the research data and its outcomes have provided us with new understanding and knowledge about human nature. Christian concern toward the scientific findings has initially been intensified since some neuroscientists have presented a reductionist perspective on the existence of human spirit/soul. It is undeniable that the reductionist view on human soul would threat the critical role of religiosity and spiritual experiences in human life.[2] Nevertheless, I am convinced that their findings of brain function and its mechanism is worthwhile to taking into consideration of our theological discourses since it expands and deepens the understanding of spiritual experiences.[3] This study sets its quest for the way in which neurosceintific insights would assist to cultivate our knowledge about spiritual experiences and to facilitate new frame of reference in spiritual formation. This interdisciplinary study will make experimental endeavor to prompt the constructive dialogue or theological discourse

---

2 Since the year of 2001, *Newsweek* article, "God and the Brain," the comprehensive conversations among ministerial professionals, neuroscientists and theological scholars have been spurred regarding interrelatedness between braining functions and religious experiences. Most controversial issue has clearly been uncovered in the way to answer the critical questions of whether spiritual or mysterious experiences would be resulted from neuron's connection or not. If yes, spiritual experiences would take reductionist view that all human experiences including cognition, emotion and spirituality as physical or materialistic frame. (c.f.) Kevin S. Seybold, "Introduction," in *Explorations in Neuroscience, Psychology, and Religion,* Ashgate Science and Religion Series (Aldershot, England: Ashgate Publishing, 2007), 1-2.

3 Cf) Kyung-Dong Yoo, "A Study on the Ethical Community over the Problems of the Brain Function and the Brain Consciousness," *Korean Journal of Christian Studies* 96 (2015), 36-66.

between two disciplines: Christian discernment and neuroscience.

This study stands on the preliminary conviction that Jonathan Edwards' understanding of religious affection and its centrality in Christian discernment are still relevant and appropriate, given that neuroscientific researches bring about new understanding of human cognition and mind. Rather, the neuroscientific evidences shed lights upon the significance of affection in practicing spiritual discernment. This study argues that neuroscientific insights are constructively relevant and practically applicable in understanding or embodying Jonathan Edwards' understanding of religious affection and its centrality in Christian discernment.

Constructive dialogue between two disciplines prompts the primary question of this research: how does the groundbreaking information of neuroscience would tell about human cognition, emotion, affection and their relations? In what ways could the neuroscientific knowledge be applicable to spiritual experience and practices? How could the new conceptualization of human affection be implied into the spiritual practice of Christian discernment? What are the insights of neuroscience helping to facilitate or support the centrality of affection in spiritual discernment?

My first presupposition is that affections/emotions play the central role in the practice of spiritual discernment.[4] Contemporary people,

---

4 Several contemporary scholars have also emphasized the role of the affections in the discernment process. Elizabeth Liebert states that "discernment refers to the process of attending to the movements experienced interiorly, assessing these in such a way that one becomes increasingly able to judge by one's own affective responses whether a situation or choice leads toward one's deepest self." Evan Howard emphasizes affectivity in his definition of discernment: "Discernment is the affective-rich process and act of coming to

regardless of their geographical location, live in a postmodern milieu that challenges the modernist belief that reason is the only trustworthy guide to understanding life. Most postmodern thinkers no longer alienate the emotions from the major aspects of the uniquely human nature.[5] This research sets forth the premise that understanding and treating emotion properly should be prioritized in the practice of spiritual discernment. That is, even though this project primarily focuses on the Korean Protestant context, I believe that engaging comprehensively with emotion in the process of Christian discernment is universally appropriate.[6]

Regarding the context, this study presupposes that the Korean Protestant Church already has abundant resources for cognitive discernment based on these key features: sermon-centered services, Bible study groups, discipleship training programs, and conferences.[7] How-

---

identity and knowing in a given situation, in the light of one's Christian faith tradition, that which is significantly related to God (or significantly not related to God)." Elizabeth Liebert, *Changing Life Patterns: Adult Development in Spiritual Direction* (New York: Paulist Press, 1992), 21-22; Evan B. Howard, *Affirming the Touch of God: A Psychological and Philosophical Exploration of Christian Discernment* (Lanham, MD: University Press of America, 2000), 11.

5 It may not go too far to say that the scientific examination and discourse of the modern world, which is based heavily upon Rene Descartes' methodology, tend to reject all that is immeasurable or unproved. This approach leads modern thinkers to avoid intentionally or unintentionally taking emotions into consideration.

6 The writer is also aware, however, of the difficulties experienced by those who suffer from suppressed or unresolved emotions and of the limitations of focusing on attention to emotion as a universal way for spiritual discernment.

7 These resources seem to help Korean Protestants take practical steps to use reason and analyze their experiences so that they can discern God's movement and will through the cognitive discernment process. Theological analysis in the Korean context, for instance, has produced Minjung theology, the Korean liberation theology, suggesting that a Korean cognitive discernment process has been taking place.

ever, the cultural and religious perspectives on emotion/affection have not been positive or constructive within Korean protestant church due partly to the dualistic understanding of reason and emotion and due partly to the negative views on emotions.[8] It results critically in the absence of comprehensive understanding of Christian discernment by dismissing the significant role of affection in spiritual discernment.[9]

This research begins with exploration of neuroscientific understanding on emotions which would overcome the dichotomous view of human nature as composed of reason and emotion. The scientific contribution of neuroscience to spiritual practice will be briefly presented as a way to appropriate affective aspects in spiritual practice and discernment. Ultimately, this approach has the potential to offer indispensable perspectives on affective discernment. At next, Jonathan Edwards' understanding of the religious affections, which is presented in his book *Treatise on Religious Affections* (1746), is explored as a significant element not only for cultivating the affections in spiritual practice but also for fostering the Korean Protestant discernment process. Consequently, this study will contribute to formulating an improved comprehensive method of Christian discernment in the Korean Protestant context, with emphasis on a renewed perspective on the affections.

---

8 Seongho Cho, "Against Dualistic view of Christian Spirituality in Korea," *Korean Journal of Christian Studies* 97 (2015), 189-208. This study assumes that while Korean protestant churches have promoted emotional burst-out or ecstasy mainly by employing the cry-out prayer (통성기도), they are less likely to facilitate spiritual formation to integrate reasoning with emotion, which is intrinsic experiences as spiritual resources to discern the movement of Holy Spirit.

9 This study acknowledges that the significance of affection in Christian discernment has been introduced and practiced within Korean protestant context mainly employing Spiritual Exercise of Ignatius of Loyola.

II. Neuroscientific Insights on Affection

Recent significant advances in the fields of neuroscience and neuropsychology, particularly research concerning the brain, are changing the prevailing understanding of many human processes.[10] This neurological information has been pivotal in the postmodern renewal of interest in emotions, for such research reveals significant data about the biological factors contributing to the experience of emotionality.

1. Neuroscience and Emotion

Psychologists have historically focused on intrapsychic phenomena perceived to occur only within the mind.[11] They often define emotions in psychological terms that neglect the biological context of mental processes. Neurological research has led to new insights and understanding of "affective programs"—that is, identifiable activities of the brain related to the experience of emotion.[12] Researchers used to think that all primary emotions—anger, fear, joy, and sorrow—were processed in the same brain system, but now they acknowledge that different emotions occur within diverse neurological systems. In other

---

10 Kevin S. Seybold, "Neuroscience," in *Explorations in Neuroscience, Psychology, and Religion*, Ashgate Science and Religion Series. (Aldershot, England: Ashgate Publishing, 2007), 3-10.

11 Psychoanalysis, a predominant school in psychology discipline, such as Sigmund Freud (1856-1939) has historically contributed to investigate how human unconsciousness has immensely affected the consciousness and in what ways it shapes human mind.

12 Jaak Panksepp, *Affective Neuroscience: The Foundations of Human and Animal Emotions, Series in Affective Science* (New York: Oxford University Press, 1998), 41.

words, though physiological arousal specific to such feelings as grief, fear, and anger have their individual biological markers, all emotional arousal seems to include complex biological, physiological, and neurological processes in the human body.

How are emotions connected physically to the body in any given life situation? The following description presents a pattern of mechanisms of the brain and body. A person's senses encounter stimuli in the environment, and the raw data through sensors is sent to the thalamus, the part of the brain that seems to be responsible for the first stage of collating and organizing data from sensors. The thalamus then forwards this information through two kinds of neurological systems—first, the amygdala/limbic system, and second, the neocortex/prefrontal lobe system. The amygdala/limbic system is the most primitive, which means it developed much earlier in humanity's biological history, and it includes organs referred to as the mammalian brain. The neocortex/prefrontal lobe system is related to the development of human levels of consciousness and cognitive ability.[13]

2. Emotional and Thinking Brain

At one time, the prevalent idea was that all emotional responses fall under the control of the neocortex, which manages rational or cognitive processes in the brain. Recent research, however, indicates that neurological pathways directly connect the thalamus to the amygdala and limbic system. Information perceived and sensed is transmitted

---

13 Joseph E. LeDoux, *Synaptic Self: How Our Brains Become Who We Are* (New York: Viking, 2002), 1-12.

directly to the more primitive amygdala and limbic system, bypass-ing the neocortex. More convincingly, the primitive senses, including seeing and hearing, are wired directly to the amygdala and perhaps other parts of the limbic system, which explains how certain sights and sounds trigger immediate responses. This mechanism is called the "emotional" brain, which functions without immediate input from the neocortex.[14]

The other critical function of the amygdala is to participate in the process of memory: recording, storing, and recalling events from the past. When receiving sensory information, the amygdala runs a quick check to see if the message is associated with any past events that call for a mobilization of the body or an arousal response of some type. All kinds of trauma instigate this mechanism. For example, this can be ob-served in war veterans with Post-Traumatic Stress Disorder. Many vet-erans respond strongly to the sound of an airplane flying or of electric tools from a construction site, because these stimuli prompt flashbacks of their war experience. These emotional arousals are manifestations of typical patterns of the emotional brain.[15]

The other pathway from the thalamus, proceeding forward to the neocortex, is called the "reasoning" or "thinking" brain. The neocortex is the brain's primary switchboard among sensing, interpreting, and responding to environmental events more clearly connected to psycho-social events.[16] The main role of the neocortex, therefore, is to enable

14 Joseph E. LeDoux, *The Emotional Brain: The Mysterious Underpinnings of Emotional Life* (New York: Simon & Schuster, 1996), 179-224.

15 LeDoux, *Synaptic Self*, 290-294.

16 Ibid., 35-36, 88, 210-211.

people to think through their encounters with the environment, make decisions, and tie behavior to needs and desires that go beyond physical survival.

When it comes to the relationship with emotionality, the thinking brain by itself is unable to generate emotions. It is dependent on the subcortical structure of the brain "below" the neocortex, which is more primitive,[17] having developed earlier in humanity's biological history, to generate the physiological arousal of feeling. When perceiving messages from the thalamus and discovering something in the environment that calls for a specific response, the neocortex interprets an external event, sends a warning message to the amygdala, and makes a decision as to whether any form of response would be appropriate to the situation.[18]

Even in the decision-making process, the neocortex is significantly influenced by felt response. It cues the neocortex to organize the storage of memories; these later become the basis for interpretation of an environment or situation and determine appropriate triggers to an emotional response. This is not to imply that the neocortex is subordinate to the emotional brain. On the contrary, when the neocortex

---

17 Evolutionary neuroscientists presuppose that the location of each brain part gives support to the idea that the human brain has evolved according to the needs of human survival. Thus, the brain parts essential to survival have been layered in the lower area first, and the surface area such as the cortex managing complex activities developed later. The order of development is as follows: spinal cord, medulla, cerebellum, hypothalamus, thalamus, neocortex, amygdala, hippocampus, and cerebral cortex. The word, "primitive" indicates the parts from the spinal cord to the thalamus. Kevin S. Seybold, *Explorations in Neuroscience, Psychology, and Religion, Ashgate Science and Religion Series* (Aldershot, England: Ashgate Publishing, 2007), 12-16.

18 LeDoux, *Synaptic Self*, 104-5, 210-11.

perceives a dangerous signal, it commands the amygdala to send an instantaneous message throughout the body's neurological system to make the person ready to take appropriate action. Consequently, until a person physiologically responds to an external event, the neocortex and amygdala relate with each other reciprocally.[19]

Given that the neuroscientific research findings demonstrate that the thinking process in the human brain is followed by the physiological arousal of emotion, what is the theoretical implication for understanding the human mind? In what ways does the scientific information affect the understanding of the human mind? How do these neuroscientific insights shed light upon the intrinsic dynamics or relations in the cognitive and affective functions of the human mind?

3. Emotions and Feelings

1) Emotions

Neurologist and neuroscientist Antonio Damasio applies the new scientific findings to illustrate the subtle relations among emotion, feeling, reasoning, and mind. He acknowledges the theoretical procedures and core arguments proposed by the aforementioned scholars Jaak Panksepp and Joseph LeDoux.[20] Damasio puts forward, however, a slightly different but critical claim that the emotions should be differentiated from feelings. For him, emotions are manifested in public or visible areas, while feelings are always hidden or unseen, such as

---

19 Ibid., 28-31.

20 Antonio R. Damasio, *Looking for Spinoza: Joy, Sorrow, and the Feeling Brain*, 1st ed. (Orlando, FL: Harcourt, 2003), 60, 63.

mental images. Emotions play out in the theater of the body while feelings play out in the theater of the mind; emotions are unfolded in the physiological realm, whereas feelings involve cognitive perception of a bodily state. Emotions and a host of related reactions are part of the basic mechanism of life regulation, so they become the foundation for feelings.

Damasio asserts that human emotions should precede feelings since feelings presuppose an emotional state. One of the pieces of theoretical evidence for his claim is drawn from the evolutionary processes of the living body, including humans; he constructs a hierarchical structure of automated homeostatic regulation from simple to complex.[21] The concept of homeostasis is crucial for him since it suggests that all living organisms are inherently given the ability to solve problems threatening their lives without the involvement of reason. Based upon homeostatic regulation, emotions are triggered and executed through an engagement with a lower level of body mechanism ranging from immune responses, basic reflexes, pain and pleasure, to drives and motivations.

Then, how are emotions distinguishable from simple reflexes, which are found in simpler creatures such as snails? Damasio argues that emotions are not reflexes; it is more complex than this. Although the simpler living organisms produce a reflex as a reaction to a threatening stimulus, emotions come with a multiplicity of components, and the components have to be coordinated. On the basis of chemical homeostatic processes in the human body, emotions proper are activated

---

21 Ibid., 31-34.

when the presence of certain stimuli in the environment is detected. As the normal brain detects an emotionally competent stimulus (an ECS), the object or event triggers the emotion. The responses are automatic. The emotions are automatic responses but have not been programed with a certain fixed mechanism; instead, they are tentative and able to change in response to various life experiences. The ultimate goal of this response is to place the organism in circumstances favorable to its survival and well-being.[22]

Then, in what manner are emotions triggered or executed within the brain structure? Damasio identifies the amygdala and the ventromedial prefrontal cortex as emotion-triggering sites, which are responsive to both "natural stimuli, the electrochemical patterns that support the images in our minds, and to very unnatural stimuli such as an electric current applied to the brain."[23] But the sites cannot take the place of emotions; rather, the sites elicit other parts of the brain to subsequent activity, such as the basal forebrain, hypothalamus, or nuclei of the brainstem. With the participation of complex behaviors and the concerted responses at these sites, emotions are executed.[24] For instance, fear, an emotional state, is initially detected by an emotionally competent stimulus in sensory association or cerebral cortices, and it is immediately triggered inductively in the amygdala. Then the concerted participation of the basal forebrain or hypothalamus executes the transition so that the emotional state of fear unfolds. Eventually, the process of emotions faces a dual track: either it takes the path of the flow-

---

22 Ibid., 53.

23 Ibid., 59.

24 Ibid. See Figure 2.4.

ing of mental contents that bring along the triggers for the emotional responses, or it takes the path of the executed responses themselves, those that constitute emotions, which eventually lead to feelings. If taking the latter track, it leads to the stage of the assembling of feelings, entering into the mental realm. The former track, which involves staying in the emotional state, is meaningful in relation to homeostasis since all living organisms endeavor to preserve themselves without conscious knowledge of this undertaking and without engaging in a cognitive procedure.

2) Feelings

Damasio primarily pays attention to redefining feelings by arguing that they are the mental representation of parts of the body or of the whole body operating in a certain way. For him, feeling is the perception of a certain state of the body along with the perception of a certain mode of thinking or of thoughts with certain themes. Thus, the essential content of feelings is the mapping of a particular body state; the substate of feeling is the set of neural patterns that map the body state and from which a mental image of the body state can emerge. A feeling is essentially an idea of the body in certain circumstances. That is, a feeling of emotion is an idea of the body when it is perturbed by the emoting process.[25]

Damasio describes three ways in which the feeling of fear is expressed.[26] At first, the transmission of signals from the body to the

---

25 Ibid., 86-88.

26 Ibid., 90. See Figure 3.1.

brain can be affected by the triggering and execution sites in the neural or musculoskeletal system. Then, those triggering and executing sites can elicit a change in the cognitive mode with distinctive content in the amygdala realm. Lastly, direct changes are made in somatic maps that constitute the proximate neural substrate for feelings in the evaluating stage, which occurs at the cerebral level within sensory association and higher-order cerebral cortices. At this point, the mind represents not only a physiological state, but also reasoning one. That is, feeling fear is not just about horror or dread in the body or a reaction to an emotionally competent stimulus. It also contains a thought or the will to evade or escape from the threatening object or event.

The dual dynamics of feelings mean that feeling is not regarded as a passive perception to the presence of a body and a brain representation—feelings are interactive perceptions.[27] For instance, when beautiful scenery X captures a person, scenery X is perceived as an actual object at the origin X in the person's body state. Then the brain circuits endeavor to find out the means to respond approximately to the object as feelings, since the "the object at the origin" is inside the body-sensing maps represented in the brain. Hence, the object at the origin on the one hand and the object in the brain map on the other have interactively engaged within a feelings state.[28] Damasio maintains that feelings are not aroused from actual body states, but rather from the actual maps constructed in the body-sensing regions. He states that the core feature of the feelings is that they are composite representations

---

27 Ibid., 91.

28 Ibid., 92.

of the state of life in the process of being adjusted for survival in a state of optimal operation.

What are the potential advantages of the neuroscientific understanding of feelings? First, Damasio's work demonstrates that reasoning defects are not directly or primarily connected with cognitive problems, but rather with a defect in emotion and feelings.[29] Secondly, a decision made in emotion-impoverished circumstances might lead to erratic or negative results.[30] This does not mean that the emotional signal has no role in proper decision-making or reasoning. It still plays an auxiliary role, increasing the efficiency of the reasoning process and speeding it up. Third, the fact that feelings are mental events indicates that feelings help us solve complicated problems such as creativity, judgment, and decision-making, since problem-solving processes require more than simply engaging with vast amounts of knowledge.[31] But it also proves that the mental level of biological operations should be involved in order to integrate large sets of information. These findings effectively demonstrate that feelings should not be considered a separate capacity from the human mind; they have the requisite mental level to enter the operations of the mind.

Damasio's studies are making remarkable contributions firstly to overcoming the modern dualism of human beings by utilizing neuroscientific research and its new insights on the human brain and mind. At next, the differentiation of feelings from emotion is critical to reconstruct the idea of the human mind and the constitutive role of feel-

---

29 Ibid., 144.

30 Ibid., 145.

31 Ibid., 177.

ings in the reasoning process in the human mind. Thirdly, Damasio's description of feelings highlights the possibility to change the formation of the mind from a negative mental response based on previous experiences to new or positive formations. Thus, feelings can play an important role in altering the reasoning or cognitive process.

With regard to his research interests, Damasio mentions spiritual experiences as mental processes.[32] Within his frame of reference, spiritual experiences are a particular state of the organism, a delicate combination of certain body configurations and certain mental configurations. Thus, within his neuroscientific framework, we can constructively assume that spiritual experiences can cultivate a person's inner quality of life by engaging feelings and the mind in appropriate ways.

4. Implications of Neuroscience for Spiritual Practice

Neuroscientists have extensively and scientifically demonstrated the critical role of spiritual practices in shaping the human mind, consciousness, and self over the last couple of decades.[33] Among these scholars, Mario Beauregard and Denyse O'Leary are noteworthy since their research refutes the materialist approach of neuroscientists and philosophers who claim that the human mind and spirit are the by-product of electrical or chemical processes in the brain.[34] The core argument convincingly proposes that even if fMRI images of the brain

---

32 Ibid., 284.

33 Andrew Newberg and Mark Robert Waldman, *How God Changes Your Brain: Breakthrough Findings from a Leading Neuroscientist*, 1st ed. (New York: Ballantine Books, 2009), 3-20, 41-61.

34 Mario Beauregard and Denyse O'Leary, *The Spiritual Brain: A Neuroscientist's Case for the Existence of the Soul,* 1st ed. (New York: HarperOne, 2007).

of a nun who is praying contemplatively do not prove the existence of spiritual or transcendent beings, the brain does not represent the entire realm of the human mind, thoughts, and feelings.

This does not mean, however, that neuroscientific findings are only employed by those who are suspicious of the existence of the human mind and spirit. The evidence actually powerfully supports the idea that spiritual practices elicit the transformation of the human mind and spirit. Andrew Dreitcer and Michael Spezio's research, for instance, is remarkable since they employing neuroscientific research as one of the theoretical foundations for claiming that meditation is the critical vehicle in the neuroscientific study of neural and cognitive plasticity.[35] That is, neuroscientific findings verify the role of meditation or contemplation in eliciting changes in neural circuits and cognitive frames. So, negative emotions may be changed in neuron circuitries by meditation, and this cultivates a sense of relationality that stimulates and enhances the spiritual sense of compassion.[36]

In this way, neuroscience offers critical insights on the centrality of emotion in human nature as well as on the reciprocal relationship between emotion and reason. The research described above implies that all human cognitive activities include emotionality, and emotions play a vital role in initiating cognitive procedures. More specifically, feelings are not in a separate realm from the cognitive component of the human mind; rather, they are a constitutive component in triggering,

---

35 Andrew Dreitcer and Michael Spezio, "Agent-Relational Contemplative Studies of Practices in Christian Communities," in *Mind and Life Summer Research Institute 2012* (Garrison, NY: Garrison Institute, 2012).

36 Ibid., 3-4.

executing, and constructing human mentality. Now, neuroscientific insights can play a threshold role in reconnecting emotion/the affections in spiritual practices. This is a pivotal idea for overcoming the dualistic view of human nature, regarded as the most serious obstacle to the practice of discernment in the Korean Church. Actively embracing affectivity as a co-agent of human nature results in allowing emotions and feelings as well as reason to play a significant role in discerning God's will in human life.

Feelings by themselves cannot be the sole resource for spiritual discernment. Rather, acknowledging the reciprocal dynamics between reason and emotion, noticing and analyzing one's emotion, leads one into the divine milieu in which it is possible to discern the movement of the Holy Spirit. Affection is not identified as pure emotions or feelings. Rather, this term can be used interchangeably with the term "reasoning heart," where both the cognitive and emotive elements of human brain capacity are interwoven without clear distinction but are boosted by their reciprocal mutuality and interdependence. The term 'affection' reflects the human capacity to overcome the dualistic understanding of human nature.

If this dualism is lessened through the affections, with support from neuroscience's evaluation of the significance of affectivity, then Christian discernment can be exercised more effectively and holistically. What are the implications of this idea for the spiritual discernment process in the Korean context? What kinds of implications can be drawn for spiritual discernment? The endeavor to answer these questions is embodied by the work on *Treatise Concerning Religious Affections* of Jonathan Edwards, which is a historical landmark in affective discernment in the Christian spiritual tradition.

III. Jonathan Edwards and Affective Discernment

The most distinctive feature of Jonathan Edwards' work is his understanding of affection, which sheds new light on his way of discerning the movement of the Holy Spirit. It is critical to determine at this point how well Edwards' understanding of affection corresponds, implicitly or explicitly, with that of the neuroscientific view of affection. Then we will be able to appreciate how relevant Edwards' understanding of affection may be for discernment in the Korean Protestant context.

1. "Religious Affections"

When the fever of the Awakening had ended, the primary theological concern Jonathan Edwards struggled to comprehend can be encapsulated as following, "why had so many promising converts fallen away from "true religion" and returned to their old "carnal ways?"[37] He forcefully and insightfully engaged with the central question and concern, which had preoccupied him right after the Awakening: What is the nature of genuine Christian experience? How does true devotion

---

37 Jonathan Edwards, *Religious Affections, Works of Jonathan Edwards*, Vol. 2 (New Haven: Yale University Press, 1959), 93; William C. Spohn, "Finding God in All Things: Jonathan Edwards and Ignatius Loyola," in *Finding God in All Things: Essays in Honor of Michael J. Beckley S.J.*, ed. Michael J. Himes and Stephen J. Pope (New York: Crossroad Publishing, 1996), 246.

differ from false piety? How do we distinguish true religious affections from religious enthusiasm? What marks a genuine revival of religion? This gave birth to his most substantial and balanced analysis of the theological issues and pastoral problems involved in the Awakening, *Treatise Concerning Religious Affections* (1746).

Edwards had a threefold purpose in his book *Religious Affections*.[38] He sought to show that affections are an essential part of "true religion" and to offer signs for appraising them ("testing the spirits"), since he did not believe that all religious affections are genuinely from God based on his observation of the Great Awakening and the aftermath of the conversion experiences. Insisting that religious faith is more than a purely "notional" understanding of doctrine, he emphasized a love of God that kindles in believers the affections of joy, hope, trust, and peace, which is what he called "the sense of the heart." This led him to commit to the next aim, which is to test religious experiences by means of what he called the "signs" of gracious affections to be found throughout the Bible, especially in Paul's account. Edwards hoped to confound the opponents of "heart religion" who wrote that a "wild display of emotions, visionary experiences, shrieking and moaning, has no validity as signs for judging genuine religion."[39]

Edwards discusses the distinction between affections and passions in the first part of *Religious Affections*. Whereas passions are inclinations that overpower the individual, affections are active responses that

---

38 John E. Smith, "Religious Affections and 'the Sense of the Heart,'" in *Princeton Companion to Jonathan Edwards*, ed. Sang Hyun Lee (Princeton, NJ: Princeton University Press, 2005), 103.

39 Ibid.

are evoked by an idea or understanding of the nature of what affects a person. While the former includes dark, violent, and uncontrollable responses, the latter involves understanding, discipline, and desire for God.[40] The distinction arose out of Edwards' stress on the difference between a person's "merely notional understanding" of a thing, called speculation, and a person's "being in some way inclined" toward it.[41] To be "inclined," for Edwards, means a choice to accept or reject, to like or dislike. That is, unlike passion, affections are "more vigorous and sensible exercises" of inclination, which are accompanied by understanding.

In the second part of *Religious Affections*, Edwards presents the twelve negative signs, which are "signs that affections are gracious, or that they are not." Considering the weight of their relative significance and the subject, this study will focus exclusively on the eighth and twelfth signs since they are considered Edwards' distinctive contribution in the discernment tradition regarding the order of affections and the outward manifestations. (8) "Nothing can certainly be determined concerning the nature of the affections by this, that comforts and joys seems to follow awakenings and convictions of conscience, in a *certain order*,"[42] and Edwards adds that "a seeming to have this distinctness as to steps and method, is no certain sign."[43] Edwards asserts that a method and order cannot be a critical criterion in conversion experiences. His focus shifts from "the Spirit's method of producing

---

40 Edwards, *Religious Affections*, 98.

41 Ibid., 96-97.

42 Ibid., 151.

43 Ibid., 160.

them [affections]"to "the nature of the fruits of the Spirit." He had a slightly different perspective from the understanding of his contemporary Puritans. According to Howard, "saving conversion was expected to be preceded by sensible experiences of conviction, or terror, or humiliation,"[44] and nearly all people agreed with this view. The Puritans believed that it was more important for the Spirit to produce the affections than its fruits. This is the reason Edwards deliberately gave priority to the nature of the fruits of Spirit since the sovereignty of the Spirit's work should be a prerequisite for good discernment.[45] The twelfth sign reads, "Nothing can be certainly concluded . . . from this, that the outward manifestations of them [affections], and the relation persons give of them, are very affecting and pleasing to the truly godly, and such as greatly gain their charity, and win their hearts."[46] Edwards underlines the unreliability of trying to discern who is godly and who is not based upon expressed affections or outward manifestations.[47] It is necessary to be careful not to judge others only by their external affections or behaviors since this would not guarantee their true salvation.

Then, how does Edwards describe the positive signs in the third part of his book? Howard's categorization of the twelve positive signs assists in encapsulating the core features.

Edwards introduces the first four signs by language which speaks of the affections "rising from" or having their "foundation" in the sign

---

44 Howard, *Affirming the Touch of God*, 91.

45 Edwards, *Religious Affections*, 119.

46 Ibid., 127-81.

47 Ibid., 181.

mentioned (RA 197, 240, 241, 253, 254,257 and 267). The fifth through seventh signs are introduced by speaking of the affections being "attended with" certain characteristics (RA 291, 311, 340, and 395). The eighth and ninth signs supplement and enlarge the seventh. They speak of the affections as "tending to and attended with," as "begetting" or "promoting," as being "under the government of," or as "attended and followed with" (RA 344, 345, 346, and 347). The affections of the tenth sign both "are" and "extend" symmetry and proportion (RA 365 and 370). And finally, the eleventh and twelfth signs indicate consequences which flow from the affections, either as tendencies which follow changes in the affections ("higher, he more" RA 376), or as the "exercise and fruit" of the affections (RA 383).[48]

McDermott's summary also captures useful categories of the twelve positive signs, as follows: a divine supernatural source; attraction to God; seeing the beauty of holiness; a new knowing; deep-seated conviction; humility; a change of nature; a Christlike spirit; fear of God; balance; hunger for God; and Christian practice (surrender and perseverance).[49] Most distinctive is the primary interest discovered in the first sign. Here Edwards introduces "a new inward perception" or 'the new spiritual sense" that is "entirely different in its nature and kind, from anything that ever their minds were the subjects of before they were sanctified."[50] The new spiritual sense and the new dispositions will become "new principles of nature," and for this purpose the

---

48 Howard, *Affirming the Touch of God*, 121.

49 Gerald R. McDermott, *Seeing God: Twelve Reliable Signs of True Spirituality* (Downers Grove, IL: InterVarsity Press, 1995), 85-224.

50 Edwards, *Religious Affections*, 205.

affections are employed as the new foundation of the new principles of nature without compromising or intermingling with understanding and will.[51]

The fourth sign is worth paying attention to since Edwards carefully explains spiritual understanding as gracious affections. Spiritual understanding consists in "a sense of the heart, of the supreme beauty and sweetness of the holiness or moral perfection of divine things, together with all that discerning and knowledge of things of religion, that depends upon, and flows from such a sense."[52] This notion suggests that, for Edwards, affections are constitutive components of spiritual understanding, the sense of heart or the new perception of spiritual reality. This makes it clear that spiritual understanding is the epistemological foundation of Edwards' discernment.

Notably, Smith lays out the overarching contributions of Edwards' *Religious Affections* with a focus on three features.[53] First, Edwards' idea of the new sense and new nature elicits renewal of the distinctively religious dimension of life, preventing the diminishment of religion. Second, Edwards expanded the meaning of understanding into the spiritual realm by retaining and reconnecting the direct association with individual experiences, thus preventing the spiritual realm from being bound by the theoretical realm. Finally, Edwards demonstrates the way in which piety could be "subject to rational scrutiny in the form of tests aimed at revealing its genuine or spurious character."[54]

---

51 Ibid., 206.

52 Ibid., 272.

53 Smith, "Introduction," 44.

54 Ibid.

In discerning the will of God, Edwards provide a theological or spiritual method in which the rational realm and the spiritual realm are integrated or assist each other in interpreting or evaluating the present experience and context.

IV. Re-appropriating Christian Discernment

1. Edward's insights on Affective Discernment

Edwards often writes that affections are "the actings of inclination and will."[55] For Edwards, the will is identified as a complex affair: choice and judgment primarily, and overt action secondarily. "Will" is "inclination expressed in action."[56] Meanwhile, affections for Edwards are the lively inclinations that reveal the fundamental intent and direction of "the heart"—inclination expressed in the mind. Even if will and affection are neither distinctive nor identical with each other, it is in the affections that the signs of the Spirit's work and the human response are manifested. The affections take precedence over will in that affections are the lively inclinations, while the will is inclination already expressed. Therefore, the presence of God is not detected in the will but in the affections, the basic desires and dynamic habits of the heart, where the sign of conversion is discovered.[57]

Edwards' basic insight about the affections is that the affections

---

55 Smith, "Religious Affections and the 'Sense of the Heart,'" 104.

56 Allen C. Guelzo, "Freedom of the Will," in *The Princeton Companion to Jonathan Edwards*, ed. Sang Hyun Lee (Princeton, NJ: Princeton University Press, 2005), 121.

57 Ibid., 121-28.

consist in the unity of an idea and a felt response. Edwards was firmly convinced that the clear dichotomy between "emotion" and "reason," and the "heart" and the "head," prevents us from comprehending what the affections truly are. The felt response is the affection that is "raised" in us in conjunction with understanding.[58] A good example is found in the affection of the holy love of God. Love of God is not a mere "feeling" descending on us out of ignorance, but the affection that arises in the mind when we understand the ultimate being—God. For Edwards, it is impossible for anyone to have a proper understanding of divine excellence without experiencing the gracious affection that goes by the name of holy love. Neither the understanding nor the affection can stand alone; one may "know" God's true love in the sense of having a "notional understanding" gained from reading the Bible without having a "sense" of that love. However, for Edwards, the love is not genuine unless it has been affected by a proper experience and understanding of God's true nature. Genuine love for God is based upon the personal "loveliness" or beauty of God.

According to William C. Spohn,[59] Jonathan Edward understood religious affections as correlating with some specific quality of God and Christ. When God's personal beauty is disclosed in conversion, an entirely new proper object (the divine characteristics) enters the per-

---

58 Behind Edwards' whole outlook stands a thought that he learned early in his reading of John Locke's book, Essay Concerning Human Understanding. In order to explain the reciprocal mutuality between experience (affection) and understanding, for instance, Edwards used the following illustration: A person may know that honey is sweet, but no one can know what "sweet" means until they taste the honey. Edwards used this example many times over. Edwards, The Religious Affections, 272.

59 Spohn, "Finding God in All Things," 252.

son's experiences; it evokes new affections which are unlike any the person has experienced before. Spohn summarizes Edwards' concept of affection as a principle of discernment as follows. Affection and its object [the quality of God and Christ] stand in reciprocal relationship since the object is the objective correlative for the affection, and the affection is the subjective correlative to the object. This correlation of qualities provides the basis for discerning the nature of religious affections and making the crucial judgment about whether genuine conversion has occurred. From the qualities of God made known in Scripture one can infer the appropriate or fitting affective responses in the true Christian. By examining our own affections, we can judge whether they actually tend toward God.[60]

The reciprocity between affection and divine characteristics is recognized by affirming that they are interdependent. Thus, affection is the principle by which humans discern God. This idea provides the epistemological foundation for the twelve principal signs of *Religious Affections*.[61]

2. Affective Discernment for Korean Christians

This research sets its presupposition that the absence of a holistic consideration of religious emotions has solidified the dualistic view

---

60 Ibid.

61 See Jonathan Edwards, *A Treatise Concerning Religious Affections*, Part II & III. In Part II (pp.125-190), "Shewing What Are No Certain Signs that Religious Affections Are Truly Gracious, or that They Are Not," Edwards enlists the twelve negative signs. And in Part III (pp.191-461), "Shewing What Are Distinguishing Signs of Truly Gracious and Holy Affections," he enumerates a set of "twelve positive signs" that help in discerning those influences that can only be accomplished through the saving work of the Spirit.

of emotion and reason among Korean Protestants, as has the Church's negative attitude towards emotion. For contemporary Korean Protestants, however, who acknowledge the insightful work on human nature being done by neuroscientists, especially the research showing the reciprocal mutuality between reasoning and emotion, affections are no longer an object to subdue or subjugate when one approaches God. Rather, as neuroscience has demonstrated, affections can be the decisive path for discerning the movement of the Spirit as well as the critical locus for realizing the authentic nature of human beings. The focus of contemporary Korean Protestants has shifted to examining how to facilitate and handle the affections in order to nurture people's spiritual lives. The neuroscientific view on the affections may play a bridge role for Korean Protestants who look back and reevaluate the spirituality of Jonathan Edwards. As discussed above, Jonathan Edwards was seriously engaged with the affections and considered them the main tool for discerning God's will.[62]

For Edwards, "the true religion, in great part, consists in the affections."[63] Authentic religious experiences should be accompanied by holy and gracious affections. Without a sophisticated observation of the affections as the manifestation of the Spirit, no legitimate dis-

---

62 My research in Korean Protestant literature leads me to pay attention to the fact that Jonathan Edwards has been introduced to Koreans exclusively as a Calvinist and fundamental evangelist. Korean Protestants seems to take advantage of Jonathan Edwards' theology by using his writings to partially justify their fundamental evangelical theology. Reintroducing and reevaluating Edwards through his understanding of the affections, as I have done in this study, would significantly contribute to a more balanced perspective among Koreans on the role of the affections in religious practices.

63 Edwards, *The Religious Affections*, 99.

cernment process can take place. It is remarkable to note that no discrepancy is identified between two disciplinary understanding on emotion/affection between Jonathan Edwards' and Neuroscience. Rather, neuroscience validates Jonathan Edwards' understanding of the affections by affirming that emotion plays a central role in human nature. Therefore, involvement of the affections in the discernment process is indispensable.

This idea creates the space for practicing spiritual discernment in the Korean context. First, a balanced view on the affections will help Korean Protestants overcome a disintegrated worldview. Second, the holistic view of human nature advanced by neuroscience contributes to a shift in the definition and role of the affections in discernment, overcoming the dualistic view of human nature. The integrated view of the affections from neuroscience corresponds with Jonathan Edwards' eighteenth-century understanding; in both cases, the affections are viewed as the central locus for discerning the will and movements of God. Edwards' understanding of religious affections also can definitely help the Korean Church regard affection as a co-agent of human nature, along with reason. This idea also promotes an integrative worldview over the existing multifaceted view in the Korean Church.

Consequently, Jonathan Edwards' conception of and theological analysis of the religious affections could be the bedrock for establishing a vibrant discernment practice in the Korean context, one in which affections, the deep emotional dispositions of the heart, are the center of religious transformation and the principal source of evidence for judgments of discernment. Edwards' theological view on the affections could be used in introducing an affective discernment process in the Korean Protestant context. This could be done because religious affections are regarded as the media of God's inspiration. In addition, Edwards' view on the affections might change Koreans' view of emotion from something to subdue to a source of transformation. This new view also sheds light on the discernment environment, encouraging a less dualistic worldview. This would critically invite some Korean Protestants to facilitate the spiritual discernment to making a critical decision, and further to turn to prayer so as to deepen their spiritual relationship with God. In the end, by fostering the individual's response to God and to the call that flows from each person's relationship with God, affective discernment will be able to offer a turning point for spiritual growth and transformation in the Korean Protestant Church.

V. Conclusion

This research made endeavor to address the centrality of affection in authentic spiritual discernment in the Christian tradition. It began with recognition that the alienated location of the affections in the Korean Protestant churches due to dualistic views on reason and emotion, which have elicited an obstacle to introducing holistic feature of spiritual discernment. At next, the research describes how an innovative understanding of the relationship between reason and emotion, drawn from neuroscience, will play a pivotal role, both implicitly and explicitly, in overcoming the dominant dualistic view of human nature, as well as in promoting spiritual discernment. The term of "Affection" is proposed as "reasoning heart," where both the cognitive and emotive elements of human brain capacity are interwoven without clear distinction but are boosted by their reciprocal mutuality and interdependence. Thirdly, this chapter examines Jonathan Edwards' ideas concerning the religious affections and their relevancy and implications for the discernment process. It is critical to note that the findings of neuroscience about the nature of affection are not discrepancy with the core concept of Jonathan Edwards' affection. Lastly, it presents the way in which the Christian discernment could be applicable as holistic strategy of spiritual formation for Korean protestant church as constructive or integrative ways. The neuroscientific lens turns out to assist us to discover its relevancy of affection for spiritual discernment in the contemporary Korean protestant spirituality.

Potential contribution of this research would be discovered in the fact that the academic endeavor to prompt the constructive conversation and experimental dialogue between neuroscience and spiritual discernment initially took place. I wish this research would be steppingstone to cultivate constructive discourse and academic research between neuroscience and theological reflection via interdisciplinary research method. The comprehensive role of affection in various forms of spiritual practices such as Lectio Divina, Contemplative prayer, Centering Prayer would further be worthwhile to investigating from now on.

Bibliography

Au, Wilkie, and Noreen Cannon Au. *The Discerning Heart: Exploring the Christian Path*. New York: Paulist Press, 2006.

Beauregard, Mario, and Denyse O'Leary. *The Spiritual Brain: A Neuroscientist's Case for the Existence of the Soul*. 1st ed. New York: HarperOne, 2007

Cho, Seongho. "Against Dualistic view of Christian Spirituality in Korea." *Korean Journal of Christian Studies* 97 (2015): 189-208.

Damasio, Antonio R. *Looking for Spinoza: Joy, Sorrow, and the Feeling Brain*. 1st ed. Orlando, FL: Harcourt, 2003.

Dreitcer, Andrew, and Michael Spezio. "Agent-Relational Contemplative Studies of Practices in Christian Communities." In *Mind and Life Summer Research Institute 2012*. Garrison, NY: Garrison Institute, 2012.

Edwards, Jonathan. *Religious Affections*. New Haven: Yale University Press, 1959.

Guelzo, Allen C. "Freedom of the Will." In *The Princeton Companion to Jonathan Edwards*, edited by Sang Hyun Lee, 115-29. Princeton, NJ: Princeton University Press, 2005.

Howard, Evan B. *Affirming the Touch of God: A Psychological and Philosophical Exploration of Christian Discernment*. Lanham, MD: University Press of America, 2000.

Ignatius, and George E. Ganss. *Ignatius of Loyola: The Spiritual Exercises and Selected Works*. The Classics of Western Spirituality. New York: Paulist Press, 1991.

LeDoux, Joseph E. *The Emotional Brain: The Mysterious Underpinnings of Emotional Life*. New York: Simon & Schuster, 1996.

————. *Synaptic Self: How Our Brains Become Who We Are*. New York: Viking, 2002.

Liebert, Elizabeth. *Changing Life Patterns: Adult Development in Spiritual Direction*. New York: Paulist Press, 1992.

————. *The Way of Discernment: Spiritual Practices for Decision Making*. 1st ed. Louisville, KY: Westminster John Knox Press, 2008.

McDermott, Gerald R. *Seeing God: Twelve Reliable Signs of True Spirituality*. Downers Grove, IL: InterVarsity Press, 1995.

Miller, Perry. *Jonathan Edwards*. The American Men of Letters Series. New York: W. Sloane Associates, 1949.

Newberg, Andrew and Mark Robert Waldman. *How God Changes Your Brain: Breakthrough Findings from a Leading Neuroscientist*. New York: Ballantine Books, 2009.

Panksepp, Jaak. *Affective Neuroscience: The Foundations of Human and Animal Emotions*. Series in Affective Science. New York: Oxford University Press, 1998.

Seybold, Kevin S. *Explorations in Neuroscience, Psychology, and Religion*. Ashgate Science and Religion Series. Aldershot, England: Ashgate Publishing, 2007.

Smith, John E. "Religious Affections and the 'Sense of the Heart.'" In *Princeton Companion to Jonathan Edwards*, edited by Sang Hyun Lee, 103-14. Princeton, NJ: Princeton University Press, 2005.

Spohn, William C. "Finding God in All Things: Jonathan Edwards and Ignatius Loyola." In *Finding God in All Things: Essays in Honor of Michael J. Beckley S.J.*, edited by Michael J. Himes and Stephen J. Pope. New York: Crossroad Publishing Co., 1996.

Yoo, Kyung-Dong. "A Study on the Ethical Community over the Problems of the Brain Function and the Brain Consciousness," *Korean Journal of Christian Studies* 96 (2015): 36-66.

6

The Contemplative Desires as Constitutive for Spiritual Discernment

I. Introduction

Desire is the essence of Christian spirituality.[1] Despite the negative views on human nature in the Protestant theological milieu,[2] there seems to be a growing consensus that human desire is so profound that it is what makes a human a human. Philip Sheldrake remarks, "Desires are best understood as our most honest experiences of ourselves, in all our complexity and depth, as we relate to people and things around us."[3] Desires are not some kind of impersonal power "out there" that

---

1 Christian spirituality refers to the lived experience of the relationship between the human spirit and the Spirit of God. It happens in moments of transcendence of self into God, which is embodied not by just a single event or encounter, but by an ongoing process. Sandra Schneiders, "The Study of Christian Spirituality: Contours and Dynamics of a Discipline," *Minding the Spirit*, ed. by Elizabeth A. Dreyer & Mark S. Burrows (Baltimore, Maryland: The Johns Hopkins University Press, 2005), 5-7.

2 For more details, see David F Wells, "The Protestant Perspective on Human Nature," in *The Human Condition in the Jewish and Christian Tradition*, ed. by Frederick E. Greenspahn (Hoboken, NJ: KTAV Publishing House, Inc., 1986).

3 Philip Sheldrake, *Befriending Our Desires* (London: Novalis and Darton, 2001), 18.

controls us whether we like it or not. Thus, they are different from instincts. Even though it is undeniable that desires have sometimes had bad press, being more or less reduced to the domain of the instinctual, they in fact involve unique human qualities, qualities that are intrinsic to humans and grounded in the physical senses.

Human desires as the innermost profound essence of human nature and an intrinsic grounded quality of humans are fundamentally characterized as follows: First, they identify themselves in *what is* rather than in *what ought to be*.[4] Desires could not be placed in a world of duties or ethics. Hence, any ideal that attempts to overcome desire and replace it with reason is both inhuman and unattainable. Second, since desire has a grounded quality, it is inevitably linked to our physical senses that in turn connect us to the world of time and space. In a way, therefore, all desire is sensual; it is associated with our senses.

Beyond the fear of losing control over our inner life to the senses and our concern about failing to obey Church ethical norms as we face our desires, we have the fundamental Christian belief that the human being is *Imago Dei*. This theological understanding crucially enables us to say that our desires are apparently associated with God's. In human desire, God's desire is reflected.[5] Without connecting with God's desire, human desire could not authentically be fulfilled. In other words, discovering our authentic desires — "What do I want or need?"— should be preceded by a deeper awareness of our essential selves: "Who am I?" Over time, a pattern of what a person wants in

---

4 Ibid., 19.

5 Janet K. Ruffing, *Spiritual Direction: Beyond the Beginnings* (Mahwah, N.J.: Paulist Press, 2000), 12-14.

and from life emerges and thus provides one of the best clues to the true self. If our desires reveal who we are, then one value of attending to them is that this helps us gradually not only to see our true self behind the masks we wear but also to encounter the image of God within the ourselves as an individual human being. Desires, therefore, can be considered the essence of Christian spirituality.

The above discussion also indicates the significance of spiritual discernment. Spiritual discernment is defined as an essential spiritual practice for Christians since it is a substantially holistic (affective-cognitive) process of an individual or a community, in which one can notice the movements of spirits in the lived experiences of everyday life, make the best decision based on Christian faith, and act in accord to God's will.[6] In his *Spiritual Exercises*, long considered the primary systematically organized text for spiritual discernment practice, Ignatius of Loyola invites readers to "ask God our Lord for what I want and desire" at the beginning of every period of prayer. This implies that prayer should include reflection on our desires, and then it should facilitate spiritual discernment. To discern our deepest desire and need must be presupposed to making the best decision and acting according to God's will.

The main concern this paper engages with begins with the fact that few Korean Protestant Christians have considered human desire as the essential element not only of Christian spirituality but also of spiritual discernment. For them, it is a rather familiar notion that the Judeo-

---

6 Elizabeth Liebert, The Process of Change in Spiritual Direction: A Structural-Developmental Perceptive (Michigan: UMI, 1986), 21-22. I modified the definition from the way Liebert defines through her expressions.

Christian God is exclusively the transcendent other who speaks to human beings who have lost any ability to approach Him for or by themselves. Due to the strong influence of Calvin's view of human nature, Korean Christians do not intend to believe that any innate resources of human beings could lead them to nurture or enhance their spiritual relationship with God. In addition, according to Korean indigenous psychology, the Korean self is unlikely to harness desire for individual spiritual practices or spiritual discernment.

Given that, this chapter will verify the thesis that the *apophatic* view on desire presented in Gregory of Nyssa's homilies on the Song of Songs sheds crucial light on renewing and transforming the understanding and experiences of Korean desires, which are mostly evaded or distorted by the cultural and psychological consciousness and by Pentecostal evangelism. This new understanding of contemplative desire will ready Korean Protestant Christians to practice genuinely spiritual discernment for spiritual life. This study will first describe the cultural collective consciousness (*woori* consciousness) as an obstacle to look into Korean desires in the Korean self. It will prove that collectivism impedes the accessing of desire as the creative resource for discernment. Next, the work of Gregory of Nyssa will be addressed, particularly his expounding of an apophatic view on human desires in nurturing spiritual relationship with God in his homily on the Song of Songs. Its contemplative perspective on desire will be introduced to foster and rehabilitate the Korean Christian understanding of desire. Lastly, the vital interaction or mutual reciprocity between contemplative desire and spiritual discernment will be suggested as crucial for Korean Protestant spirituality. Specifically, it will encourage Korean

Protestants to awaken to a contemplative perspective on desire, which will lead to an enhancement and transformation of their spiritual discernment process.[7] Consequently, this chapter aims at transforming Korean Christian spirituality by contemplative understanding of human desire so that Korean Christians will be able to nurture their authentic spiritual discernment practice.

II. Evaded and Corrupted Desires

1. The Korean Self and Desires

The eminent Korean indigenous psychologist Sang-Chin Choi elaborates to elucidate the distinctiveness of the Korean self substantially different from the western self.[8] As the first distinctive feature, he notes that the western self pursues individuation of each person focusing on uniqueness, independence, and subjectivity. The Korean self, however, has been formed through internalizing and practicing the social ethical norm, idealized in the value systems appreciated by the society.[9] For Koreans it is a priority to master the societal standards, to assimilate them until the ideal self the society commends is embodied in each Korean self. For example, the notion of "self-reflection" would be comprehended as repentance or regret for one's actions

---

7 The author is aware that one of the appropriate ways to equip Korean Protestants with the contemplative desire is to introduce and engage with it in spiritual practices context.

8 Sang Chin Choi, *Psychology of the Korean People* (Seoul, Korea: Joong-Ang University Press, 2000), 121-139.

9 Ibid., 128.

or thoughts which are objected to by the social norm or the ideal self, rather than as a way reflecting upon the integration of the self. Most important for Koreans is the task of controlling or managing their own minds, emotion, desires, and thoughts to conform to the social norms and standards.

The second characteristic of the Korean self is its "social-cultural contextualism," which positively evaluates persons who adjust and tune their thoughts and behaviors into the situations and the subjects with which they are engaged.[10] Choi states that this contextualism frequently causes westerners to feel embarrassed by Korean hypocritical tendency, since some Korean behaviors lack coherence and consistency. Several researches have indicated that Koreans tend to react differently depending on the specific relationship or psychological mind-set. In other words, while Koreans may open up their minds to people close to them, they are inclined to take formal actions in front of those who are more distant. This implies that the Korean self puts much weight upon adaptability and versatility in individual situations.

The relationship-oriented society has something to do with the third feature of the Korean self. Contrary to the western self pursuing the accomplishment of self-transcendence through constant reflecting on one's self, the Korean self within the relationship-oriented society pays attention to developing cultural-social skills that facilitate comprehending and reading others' minds, thoughts, desires and emotions.[11] Because one's personal authenticity would not be justified by

---

10 Ibid., 129.

11 Ibid., 131.

self-discipline or self-transcendence but by social norms and evaluations, the Korean self has evolved various skills to satisfy others' minds and emotions. Interestingly enough, these social norms and evaluations also play a bridge role in identifying each person's mind and emotions. In the end, the Korean self has an interest in sharing or communicating one's mind and emotions — the so-called "felt mind," which is essentially the core of the Korean self — rather than expressing one's unique quality or self-potentiality. Self-realization for the Korean self, therefore, develops according to the ideal self which Korean society commends. The Korean self takes into serious consideration the question, "What ought I to do?" instead of "Who am I?"

With this understanding of Korean cultural psychology as background, I will now enumerate the several distinctive features of Korean desire. First, the Korean self consists of the interpersonal-oriented structure and lacks an intrapersonal orientation. This is a critical point, since without frequent access to the inner person, desire cannot easily be satisfied or even recognized. Secondly, the Korean appreciation of adaptability and versatility hinders the capacity to observe the deepest desire of the Korean self. While the Korean is accustomed to satisfy others' desire and social needs, they are awkward in reflecting on and satisfying their own needs and desires. Lastly, the Korean self is highly likely to generate deceptive or abusive self-images. Koreans often feel justified in manipulating or torturing themselves to meet social norms rather than to meet their own desires and needs. Consequently, the Koreans are apt to develop a distorted image of them, and perhaps even personality disorders through the conflict between the self with unmet desires and the self that attempts to meet the social standards. It enables us to presume that desire, the innermost profound essence of human nature and an intrinsic grounded quality of humans, is evaded and disregarded in the Korean self. In terms of cultural psychology, Korean people are not good at being conscious of their desires. Then we can ask a critical question: in what ways has Korean Christianity played in affecting the formation of Korean desire?

2. Korean Pentecostal Evangelism[12] and Its Distorted Desires

It is well known among scholars of Korean Christianity that Pentecostal evangelism predominates in Korean Protestantism and contributes to the remarkable growth of Christianity in this country with an only short history of exposure to Christianity.[13] As a good exemplar, the Youido Full Gospel Church in Seoul with more than 800,000 members, symbolizes church growth in Korea.[14] The Rev. David Yonggi Cho, the founder and senior pastor of the church, represents the strong desire for mega-church in Korea. He says, "Church growth has become

---

12 Evangelism is broadly defined here to include movements more specifically known as Fundamentalism and Pentecostalism—as species of Protestantism characterized by a literalist bent in biblical interpretation, a soteriology that values the individual over society, fervent advocacy of evangelism, and the piety that emphasizes the conversion experience and personal relationship between God and believer, relegating rituals such as baptism and communion to a secondary place. In evangelism, salvation is typically achieved through conversion, wherein one accepts Jesus Christ as personal savior and resolves to live in accordance with the Gospel.

13 The most relevant articles recently published are Byong-Suh Kim, "Modernization and the Explosive Growth and Decline of Korean Protestant Religiosity," and Timothy S. Lee, "Beleaguered Success: Korean Evangelicalism in the Last Decade of the Twentieth Century," in Christianity in Korea eds. by Robert E. Buswell Jr. & Timothy S. Lee (Honolulu: University of Hawaii Press, 2006).

14 Chung Soon Lee, "The Pentecostal Face of Korean Protestantism: A Critical Understanding," in Asia Journal of Theology 20 (October, 2006), 406.

one of the most noteworthy subjects in Christianity today."[15] Needless to say, church growth in Korea is propelled and spurred by such Pentecostal and Evangelical theology which exclusively functions only for individual salvation and church growth. Due to this vigorous church growth, about 25 percent of the entire population of South Korea was Christians, counting both Catholics and Protestants. Christianity specifically with Pentecostal Evangelism, the foreign religion now exists as one of the main religions in Korea. In other words, "Christianity has been considered as a Korean people's religion."[16]

In the meantime, Tong-Shick Ryu, a Korean theologian, insists on the critical role and influence of Shamanism over the explosive growth of the Korean churches.[17] He lists a couple of features that reveal how Korean Pentecostal evangelism has learned from shamanism in Korea.[18] First, Shamanism enables Koreans to easily accept God and the Christian spiritual world based on the traditional dualistic worldview of the physical and spiritual realms. Secondly, Koreans understand Christianity as a this-worldly practical religion from the shamanistic perspectives. Thus, whenever people are faced with diseases, sufferings and disasters, they simply pray to God to overcome these. Thirdly, shamanism enables Korean Christianity to shape a dependent and fee-

---

15 Ibid., 408. This is quoted from Yonggi Cho, "The Secret behind the World's Biggest Church," in Azusa Street and Beyond, ed. by L. Grant McClung (New Jersey: Bridge Publishing INC: 1986), 99.

16 Donald N. Clark, Christianity in Modern Korea (Lanham, Maryland: University Press of America, 1986) 36.

17 Tong-Shick Ryu, The Christian Faith Encounters the Religions of Korea (Seoul: The Christian Literature Society of Korea, 1962), 13.

18 Ibid., 37-38.

ble faith by convincing them that belief in God without action is only prerequisite the earthly blessing. It brings about the lack of consciousness of ethical responsibility. Harvey Cox, supporting Ryu, states that "one of the key reasons for Korean Pentecostalism's extraordinary growth is its unerring ability to absorb huge chunks of indigenous Korean shamanism and demon possession into its worship."[19]

It is my contention that such Korean Pentecostal evangelistic theology affected by the shamanistic worldview plays a manipulative or distorting role in Koreans' ability to access or to reflect on their desires. First of all, the negative view of human nature has been so dominant that it is scarcely possible to look inside the Korean mind and uncover its desires. Human desires do definitely lose any capacity to embrace divine features. Second, as long as success is defined as "the attainment of wealth, position, honors, or the like," desires in Korean Christianity are becoming misdirected in the pursuit of material prosperity, the manipulated image of the blessing of salvation. Pentecostal evangelism tends to distort the gospel message that desires are fully met when material prosperity and physical health are achieved. This results thirdly and conclusively in the impossibility of considering that desires can be a locus for encountering God or the pivotal tool for transforming one's spirituality. Korean desires turn out to be manipulated and deviated in Korean Christian spirituality; despite its empowering potential to profound experiences of God, reflection on desires has not been considered constructively as an authentic path to God.

---

19 Harvey Cox, Fire From Heaven: The Rise of Pentecostal Spirituality and the Reshaping of Religion in 21st Century (Reading, MA: Addison-Wesley Publishing Company, 1995), 222.

This investigation of Korean cultural psychology and Korean Pentecostal Evangelism suggests that Korean desires are not recognized properly and that they are even suppressed by the church's dogmatic teachings. But it also fails to facilitate spiritual enhancement or growth because of the shamanistic preference for a dualistic worldview and anthropology. Without a transformation of Korean desires, no authentic discernment process is available in Korean Christianity, since transforming desire is a non-negotiable prerequisite for spiritual discernment.

Wendy Farley's assertion that "Desire must be contemplative"[20] nourishes our discourse. She convincingly remarks that contemplative desires "awaken us to the unity of the love of God and neighbor."[21] In this regard, the contemplative notion of desire found in the theology of Gregory of Nyssa, the ancient Greek theologian, is worthwhile to explore since it provides us with crucial clue to cultivate spiritual sense of desires. His *homily on the Song of Songs* will effectively help us extend our perspective enough to reintroduce the contemplative aspect of desires, which is pivotal for spiritual discernment.

III. The Christian Contemplative Heritage on Human Desire

St. Gregory of Nyssa (ca. 335-ca. 394) is one of the three great Cappadocian Fathers, along with St. Basil the Great and St. Gregory

---

20 Wendy Farley, The Wounding and Healing of Desire: Weaving Heaven and Earth (Louisville, Kentucky: Westminster John Knox Press, 2005), 121.

21 Ibid., 122.

of Nazianzus. Although they all lived in the same area of what is today central Turkey, they were steeped in the best Hellenistic culture of their age and used modes of expression current in contemporary Greek philosophy and literature in conceptualizing and expressing their Christian faith. Gregory of Nyssa inherited the task of completing his older brother Basil's various theological and ecclesiastical projects. His subsequent activities included mediating Episcopal elections, attending the court of the emperor Theodosius, and playing a major role in the Second Ecumenical Council, which met at Constantinople in 381.[22] However, his many literary activities are of greater relevance to our present concern. Among other things, he continued Basil's theological controversy with the Neo-Arian Eunomius and wrote a number of important treaties and exegetical works aimed at fostering and enriching the life of the ascetical communities which his brother had organized. His *Homilies on Song of Songs* was composed found in the middle of his theological journey.[23]

1. Gregory of Nyssa's the *Homilies on Song of Songs*[24] and Union with God

"For all the Scripture are holy, but the Song of Songs is the Holy of Holies."[25] This eulogy of Rabbi Akiva resonates throughout the Chris-

---

22 Verna E.F. Harrison, *Grace and Human Freedom According to Gregory of Nyssa* (Lewiston, N.Y.: E. Mellen Press, 1992), 8.

23 Jean Daielou, "Introduction," in H. Musurillo, ed., From *Glory to Glory* (Crestwood, NY: St. Vladimir's Seminary Press, 1995), 3-10. Verna E. F. Harrison, 5-6.

24 The *Homilies* is usually dated between 385 and 392.

25 Rabbi Akiva, *Tosefta Sanhedrin 12*, 10. It is quoted in Marvin H. Pope, *Song of Songs: A New Translation with Introduction and Commentary*, The Anchor Bible 7C (Garden City, NY: Dou-

tian tradition including Gregory of Nyssa, the fourth-century Greek theologian. In Gregory's view,[26] the primary purpose of the Song of Songs is to guide the soul to union with God.[27] The soul, however, must first be properly trained before it is ready for what the Song has to teach. This is precisely the role of Proverbs and Ecclesiastes: to prepare the soul for the training found in the Song of Songs. Proverbs trains the soul to desire virtue, and it accomplishes this by praising the beauty of Wisdom's body. Ecclesiastes trains desire to long for spiritual beauty; it "elevates the loving movement of our soul towards invisible beauty." Having been trained by Christ (Solomon is for Gregory a type of Christ) through Proverbs and Ecclesiastes, the soul is made ready for the Song of Songs.[28]

1) "I am Wounded by Love"

Since Gregory of Nyssa has told us that the purpose of the Song of Songs is to lead the soul to union with God, it is not surprising that union is a pervasive theme. Notably, Gregory prefers to use vari-

---

bleday, 1977), 19.

26 Gregory of Nyssa is clearly heir to the Judeo-Christian exegetical tradition, like Akiva and Origen before him, of seeing in the Solomonic literature a well-defined pedagogy of desire. In his own prologue to his Homilies on the Song of Songs, Gregory acknowledges a clear debt to Origen. See Martin Laird, "Under Solomon's Tutelage: The Education of Desire in the Homilies on the Song of Songs," in *Modern Theology* 18 (October 2002), 510.

27 Throughout the Homilies on the Song of Songs, the bride can signify either the soul or the Church. On occasion, the bride can be understood as referring to both the soul and the church at the same time.

28 Martin Laird, "The Fountain of His Lips: Desire and Divine Union in Gregory of Nyssa's Homilies on the Song of Songs, *Spiritus* 7 (2007): 41. The quote is from "Homily One," 47 (22, 14-15).

ous imageries for the union without direct use of the word. Through linguistic metaphors he signifies union; he employs, for example, the marriage bed as a symbol of "the union of the soul with God."[29] It is not unfair to say that he believed it is precisely the imagery of union, more than the actual use of technical terminology of union, which yields the deeper insight into the provocative and dynamic understanding of divine union.

The image of the wound has a certain prominence in the *Homilies on the Song of Songs*.[30] The most sustained and moving treatments of Gregory of Nyssa's notion of divine union is found in his treatment of the wound. In the course of Homily Four, Gregory turns to Song 2:4, "I am wounded by love." He says the bride utters these words in praise of the archer's fine marksmanship. Further, he situates this wound of love in a Trinitarian context: the archer is love, the arrow is the only begotten Son, and the triple-pointed tip of the arrow has been dipped in the Holy Spirit. Intriguingly, he says the tip of the arrow that has been moistened in the Holy Spirit is faith: "The tip of the arrow is faith, and by it God introduces the archer into the heart along with the arrow."[31] The Trinity has wounded and indwells the bride, but far from complaining that this arrow has wounded her, she begins to sing in boastful praise that she has been wounded: "'I am wounded by love. O beautiful wound and sweet blow by which life penetrates within!' the arrow's penetration opens up, as it were, a door and entrance for

---

29 Gregory of Nyssa, "Homily Four," 94 (109, 1) in *Commentary of Song of Songs*, trans. with an introduction by Casimir McCambley (Brookline, MA: Hellenic College Press, 1987).

30 Martin Laird, "The Fountain of His Lips," 44.

31 Homily Four, 103 (127, 14-16).

love."[32]

Afterward, as a result of having been pierced to the heart by the arrow that is the Son, the bride herself becomes the arrow: "she now sees herself as the arrow in the archer's hand."[33] This characterizes many of Gregory's descriptions of the bride's union with God; she takes on qualities ascribed to the divine.

The most prevailing significance is found in Gregory's use of oxymorons, such as "beautiful wound" which is a favorite linguistic expression of the Cappadocian *Homilies*.[34] It is key literary expression of his apophatic theology, which can serve to point to a union beyond the grasp of discursive reason. Here the union is expressed in the language of the indwelling of the Trinity. These oxymoronic expressions indicate that the indwelling Trinity and union with God are apophatic states, as are the desires. The bride's desire to union with God is heading for apophatic union. After all, the wounds created by the arrow are beautiful and desirable and inflame yet more vehement desire.[35]

2) "The Divine Night"

In Homily Four we saw Gregory ascribe to faith a precise and intriguing role: the arrow tip of faith mediated divine presence. Gregory has at times a rather exalted notion of faith. Above and beyond the

---

32 Homily Four, 103 (128, 1-5).

33 Homily Four, 103 (128, 13).

34 Martin Laird, "The Fountain of His Lips," 45. Martin points out that Gregory of Nyssa's Homilies of Song of Songs faithfully follows the main features of Cappadocian theological terminology and imageries.

35 Martin Laird, "Under Solomon's Tutelage," 518.

understanding of faith as something to which one gives creedal ascent, Gregory will sometimes use the term faith as a faculty of apophatic union.[36] This understanding of faith as a faculty of union is tied most closely to one of Gregory's signature themes, "the divine darkness." Homily Six provides the clearest example of this, where the bride unites with the bridegroom by "the grasp of faith."[37]

For Gregory the faculty of desire is placed in the soul to create longing.[38] The spiritual pedagogy of the Song of Songs is designed precisely to train the soul by showing it provocative images so that it might long for union with God, who is beyond all concepts and images.[39] Gregory remarks in Homily Six, "I am embraced by the divine night, and I seek him hidden in the cloud. Then did I love my desired one even though he escaped my thoughts."[40] This passage designates the important apophatic idea that the letting go of knowledge based on thoughts and feelings does not bring an end to the bride's desire for the bridegroom; indeed it liberates her desire to love the bridegroom more, even though the bridegroom cannot be grasped by thoughts and feelings. Gregory is highly likely to say that desire goes deeper than thoughts and feeling can go. That is, forsaking all manner of knowledge can only guarantee that the bride moves to a depth of realization she has not previously known. The bride finally realizes that the be-

---

36 Martin Laird, "The Fountain of His Lips," 46.

37 Homily Six, 131 (183, 9).

38 Homily Four, 99 (119, 5-6).

39 Martin Laird, "Under Solomon's Tutelage," 517.

40 Homily Six, 131 (181, 12-16).

loved is know only in unknowing.[41] Laird confirms that it is important to note the apophatic character of the text of the divine night. Darkness is nearly always used by Gregory of Nyssa as a technical term to indicate divine incomprehensibility.[42] Gregory sees thoughts as the obstacle to entering the Song of Songs to commune with God.

2. The Contemplative Desires

The recent studies about Gregory have paid attention more to his understanding on human desire.[43] The dominant view on desire has shift from a bifurcated anthropology (reason here, desire there) into an intrinsically unified, subtly multileveled, and dynamic anthropology. If the human being is to attain union with God, the former view requires that desire be rooted out. The second view, however, sees desire as ineluctable for the divine union, for desire is "part of how mind realizes itself."[44]

Gregory has clearly demonstrated at the outset of the *Homilies on the Song of Songs* that desire should be educated rather than eradicated: "Through the words of the Song the soul is escorted to an incorporeal, spiritual, and undefiled union with God."[45] What is happening to desire in the text of Song of Songs is that it is being transfigured by

---

41 Martin Larid, "The Fountain of His Lips," 47.

42 Martin Laird, "Under Solomon's Tutelage," 514.

43 Enumerating four different studies on Gregory of Nyssa's anthropology, Martin Laird points out in the first part of the article, "Under Solomon's Tutelage," that the recent studies contribute to reevaluating the stance of human desire in the theology of Gregory of Nyssa. Martin Laird, "Under Solomon's Tutelage," 507-510.

44 Laird, "Under Solomon's Tutelage," 509.

45 Homily One, 15 (13-15).

its education and brought to the threshold of the transcendent. While capable of being attracted and attached to material things, the same desire is also capable of being attracted to God.[46] And the erotic beauty of the Word in scripture attracts desire that is excited and inflamed by the Spirit. By the apophatic arrangement which renders desire into the threshold of the transcendent, the desire is led to "a state of dispassionate passion."[47] This paradox constitutes not only the threshold of apophatic desire, but also indicates that the dichotomy between reason and desire does overcome. It implies an ascent to union beyond all images and concepts.

The other distinctive feature of Gregory's spirituality of desire can be found in the term "epectasy" which was coined by Jean Danielou.[48] He notes that Gregory's desire does not ended with the experience of God, but expands in perpetual self-forgetfulness and longs for God ever more deeply.[49] Gregory does not consider spiritual perfection as arriving but as becoming. Therefore, union with God does not bring an end to desire, but it does free desire from its compulsion of grasp; it allows it to expand perpetually in self-forgetful love. It enables the finite human desire to participate in divine infinity. The more the soul participates in it, the more she recognizes that it transcends her as much as before. The soul's awareness of transcendence is not the awareness of

---

46 Laird, "Under Solomon's Tutelage," 515.

47 Ibid.

48 Martin Laird, "The Fountain of His Lips," 47-48.

49 Martin Laird, "The Fountain of His Lips," 47. This is originated from Jean Danielou, *Platonisme et theologie mystique*, 291-307.

an object, but an awareness of perpetual and vast newness.[50]

The above exploration of Gregory of Nyssa's *Homilies on Song of Songs* characterizes several valuable insights on contemplative desire. First of all, for Gregory to be human is to be grounded in paradox. To be human is to be finite and at the same time to participate in the transcendent. This paradoxical perspective with its oxymoronic expression on human nature makes it possible to signify desire as essential to participate in the divine infinity and come to union with Christ. Without facilitating desires, no human being could possibly participate in the divine infinity. Secondly, educated by Proverbs and Ecclessiates, and attracted and inflamed by the erotic imagery in Song of Songs, human desires will be transformed into the qualitatively different dimension accessing the threshold of the transcendent. And third, human desire after an encounter with God is not extinguished but rather expands perpetually in self-forgetful love. That is, the desire is not limited to playing a bridge role in participating in divine infinity, but increases itself as much as before. This reveals the fact that the human desires can perpetually experience vast newness and enormous freshness. This is called contemplative desire.

The research is convinced that Gregory's concept of contemplative desire relevantly challenges the Koreans, and has tremendous potential to influence Korean understanding of human desire and Korean Protestant spirituality. First, contemplative desire confronts the Korean self with a new perspective on human desires. Without taking serious consideration of desires, any efforts and attempt to cultivate the Korean

---

50 Ibid., 51.

self will be meaningless. Reflecting on desires in a contemplative way prevents Korean desires from being evaded or dismissed. Contemplative desire will shed light on healthy ways to rehabilitate and nourish the Korean self.

Secondly, Korean Protestants must take contemplative desire into serious consideration since it overcomes the dualistic view of human nature which has been a rudimentary obstacle for pursuing spiritual development and transformation. The theologically negative view of human nature from the shamanistic cultural influence has blocked to constructive considerations of the Korean mind and desires. In addition, Korean Protestant desire has been tainted by Pentecostal evangelism's distortion of the gospel as a tool for appreciating this-world blessings and the material prosperity. The apophatic view of desire will help Korean Protestants regard desire as the vital locus for encountering God as well as for participating in divine infinity.

IV. Contemplative Desires and Spiritual Discernment

1. Desires in Ignatian Discernment

In Christian spiritual journey, a central and never-ending question is, "How do I know if I am moving towards God, doing what God wants me to do?" The classical phrase implies "seeking the will of God," and the process of attempting to answer that question is the discernment. One of the most artfully encapsulating texts in the discernment tradition is in the *Spiritual Exercises* of Ignatius of Loyola. For Ignatius, as we reflect upon desires as the basis for our discernment, we may spend much time trying to work out where such desires come from or what inspires them. So, discernment is all about recognizing the desires that drive us. While he suggests that all desires and feelings have a direction, some desires are indicated as life-giving and others are ultimately destructive. The former is called consolation, and the latter desolation.[51]

Ignatius articulates two basic kinds of affective experience which he calls consolation and desolation, and he describes how to act appropriately in relation to each (nos. 313-336).[52] On the one hand, the elementary characteristics of consolation (no. 316) are summarized as such: an increase of love of God as well as a deepening of human love, an increase of hope and faith, an interior joy, an attraction towards the spiritual, and a deep tranquility and peace. Ignatius does not indicate that consolation just consists of good feelings and thoughts. On the other hand, desolation (no. 317) may initially be accompanied by feelings that are quite pleasant and attractive. However, whether on the surface or deep down, desolation ultimately reveals itself as drawing us in destructive directions. These tend to be manifested by the following: decrease of faith or hope or the capacity to love truly, inner turmoil and confusion, tendency towards impulsive behavior in the direction of emotional or physical self-indulgence, listlessness, tepidity, unhappiness, and a sense of separation from God.

What needs to be carefully kept in mind is that what makes consolation the consolation is whether the desires lead in a direction toward

---

51 Philip Sheldrake, *Befriending Our Desires* (London: Novalis and Darton, 2001), 110-114.

52 I use the original text from George E. Ganss, ed., *Ignatius of Loyola: Spiritual Exercises and Selected Works* (Nahwah, NJ: Paulist Press, 1991).

God or not (no. 331-332). Despite positive feelings, desires that do not move toward God or to union with God are not considered as consolation. This verifies Ignatius' emphasis on God's initiation of desires: it is God who alone puts proper order into our desires. The reason that good feelings could not consistently be thought of as consolation is that the authentic desires must be originated from God, and we may be capable only of desiring to have the desire. My reading of the *Spiritual Exercises* strongly convinces me that a truly authentic desire is a desire consonant with the fundamental Spirit-given desire for God — called, herein, the "contemplative desires," and only this type of desire is an authentic resource for spiritual discernment.

Consequently, the spiritual discernment process can be authenticated by attentiveness to the contemplative desires. Meanwhile, only through discernment can we distinguish between the positive, fruitful and love-suffused pain never quite absent from any authentic desire, and the fruitless frustration by which we destroy ourselves and others. Desire is powerful, for it is the energy which moves us towards God and the doing of the will of God; at the same time, it can enslave when it is directed to anything other than God. In discernment, the power of desire and the purification of desire meet. Asking oneself, "How does this desire reflect God's desire for fullness of life?" is to accept the need for the continual refinement of desire so that one's desires become ever more congruent with God's desires. Desire and discernment are interdependent and reciprocal. Without one, the other could not exist. Authentic desire and discernment presuppose mutually interconnected and interrelation in Christian spirituality.

2. Contemplative Desire for Korean Christian Discernment

The investigation we have explored demonstrates that searching for our authentic desires has reciprocal mutuality with searching for spiritual discernment via our authentic identity. The more honestly we try to identify our authentic desire, the more we can identify who we truly are. At this level the questions "Who am I?" and "What do I want?" touch intimately upon each other. The more authentic our desires, the more they touch upon our identities and also upon the reality of God at the heart of ourselves, since our most authentic desires spring ultimately from the deep wells of our being where the longing for God runs freely. Our contemplative desires, therefore, to some degree move us beyond self-centeredness to transcending individualism and to self-giving. This enables us to say that our desires begin to reflect God's own desires, God's longing for the world as well as for each of us particularly. The more profoundly we reach into ourselves, the more we experience that the boundary between God's desire and our own becomes blurred. This can be regarded as the authentic moment of spiritual discernment.

Contemplative desire is the most essential element for spiritual discernment. The process of discernment can be understood as a way of moving from the surface of our lives, the place of many desires, to our center, our soul or our true self. Thus, the journey of desire moves us beyond a sense of seeking to conform to an understanding of the "will of God" to an awareness that "God's desiring in us is expressed in and through what we come to see as our deepest desires."[53] God's

---

53 Sheldrake, 117.

desires for us are in accord with our best interests, or our deepest and true self. Sheldrake asks the profound question, "Can we always trust our experience of desire?" He answers, "We can," only by befriending and testing our desire; we can gradually learn how to distinguish deep desires from surface wants and needs.[54]

Given this argument, I will suggest three characteristics of our authentic desires which can be the decisive elements and partners of the Korean spiritual discernment process.[55] First, the place of contemplative desire is one where we know that we are touching a deep well of peace and truthfulness that speaks of infinity — even if we have passed through disturbance and pain on the way. The place of the contemplative desire, our center, is not necessarily an emotionally intense experience. But, it is recognizable as an encounter with our own spirit and God's spirit. Second, that contemplative desire is located metaphorically in the center of our being does not mean it is self-centered. It involves a movement away from isolation and introspection towards harmony or union within us, with God, and with all people and things. So, the deepest desires in discernment urge us to pursue integrity and harmony in our lives. The third feature of contemplative desires is their empowering us to be free so as to make decisions authentically, clearly, and with integrity, moving away from being imprisoned or overly enraptured by the multitude of apparently desirable things.

In conclusion, the Korean self should not hide, suppress, evade and distort its own desires any more, since it is verified that integration

---

54 Ibid.

55 This suggestion is based on Sheldrake, 118-121.

of the Korean self results from fostering and rehabilitating the vital role of desires at the center of the Korean self. For Korean Protestants, facilitating the contemplative desires through Christian spiritual practice is crucially significant not only because it will overcome the dualistic view of human nature which is attributed culturally from the shamanistic worldview, but also because it will prevent Korean Pentecostal evangelism from manipulating or distorting Korean desires. As discussed above, Korean contemplative desires can be proclaimed as essential for seeking or doing God's will (spiritual discernment). Without being appropriately equipped with contemplative desires, Korean Christian discernment cannot be considered authentic. Without harnessing these new perspectives on Korean desires and discernment, any transformation of Korean Protestants spirituality will not be authentically nurtured or enhanced.[56]

V. Conclusion

This research has articulated several critical points on desires and discernment. The apophatic understanding of the desires addressed in the Gregory of Nyssa's *Homilies on Song of Songs* is able to play a significant part in renewing, reshaping and transforming Korean Protestant spirituality and specifically the spiritual discernment process by

---

56 It does not imply that once the contemplative dimension of desire is equipped, no further cultivation process is need. It could not be taken its perfect form so that the consistent endeavor to cultivate and enhance contemplative desire for the life should be guided within spiritual practice and direction context.

taking the desires of individuals into serious consideration. For Gregory, desires are considered essential for humans to be able to participate in divine infinity. Only through contemplative desires, such as those attracted and purified by the erotic words in the Song of Songs, can human nature reach the threshold of self-transcendence and union with God. Gregory was strongly convinced not only that the human-divine encounter and loving relationship is beyond the human rational dimension, but also that the contemplative dimension of desires which are excited and inflamed by the Spirit enable a paradoxical state of dispassionate passion, in which the divine desires are manifested. Gregory's contemplative desire is the pivotal locus for transforming Christian spirituality; it is essential in the divine-human experience.

In addition, this paper has verified the inevitably intimate relationship between contemplative desires and the Christian discernment process. The desires are fundamental elements for discerning God's will since the desires excited and attracted by Holy Spirit can become manifesting resources of the divine desires. The discernment process is also crucial because purifying and distilling the divine desires from human desires that lead to destructiveness is key. They are mutually reciprocal, interdependent and intimately interconnected.

This paper contributes practical suggestions for enhancing Korean Protestant spirituality and spiritual discernment. It strongly urges Korean Protestants to locate their desires in the center of their theological consideration for renewing and transforming their spirituality. The views presented on contemplative desires and their close relationship with spiritual discernment challenges the Korean self to accept and reflect on their desires without evading or disregarding them. These views also challenge Korean Pentecostal evangelism to stop manipulating or distorting human desires. This discourse demonstrates that contemplative desires can play a pivotal role in transforming Korean Protestant spirituality by showing the indispensable connection between desires and discernment.

Neither the contemplative desires nor spiritual discernment has been introduced properly in Korean Christianity to date means that much still remains to be studied. Most of all, however, it will be worthwhile to do in-depth research on the way in which contemplative desires could be beneficial in various form of the spiritual practices in the Korean Protestant context, such as in spiritual direction, *lectio divina*, the Centering Prayer, Jesus Prayer, and so on.

Bibliography

Choi, Sang Chin. *Psychology of the Korean People*. Seoul, Korea: Joong-Ang University Press, 2000.

Clark, Donald N. *Christianity in Modern Korea*. Lanham, Maryland: University Press of America, 1986.

Cox, Harvey. *Fire From Heaven*. Reading. MA: Addison-Wesley Publishing Company, 1995.

Farley, Wendy. *The Wounding and Healing of Desire: Weaving Heaven and Earth*. Louisville, Kentucky: Westminster John Knox Press, 2005.

Ganss, George E. ed. *Ignatius of Loyola: Spiritual Exercises and Selected Works*. Nahwah, NJ: Paulist Press, 1991.

Gregory of Nyssa. *Commentary of the Song of Songs*. Translated with an Introduction by Casimir McCambley. Brookline, MA: Hellenic College Press, 1987.

Halligan, Fredrica R. & John J. Shea. eds. *The Fires of Desire: Erotic Energies and the Spiritual Quest*. New York: the Crossroad Publishing Company, 1992.

Harrison, Verna E.F. *Grace and Human Freedom According to Gregory of Nyssa*. Lewiston, NY: E. Mellen Press, 1992.

Kim, Byong-Suh. "Modernization and the Explosive Growth and Decline of Korean Protestant Religiosity," in *Christianity in Korea*. Edited by Robert E. Buswell Jr. & Timothy S. Lee. Honolulu: University of Hawaii Press, 2006.

Laird, Martin. "The Fountain of His Lips: Desire and Divine Union in Gregory of Nyssa's Homilies on the Song of Songs," *Spiritus* 7 (2007): 40-57.

_____. "Under Solomon's Tutelage: The Education of Desire in the Homilies on the Song of Songs," *Modern Theology* 18 (October 2002): 507-525.

Lee, Chung Soon. "The Pentecostal Face of Korean Protestantism: A Critical Understanding," *Asia Journal of Theology* 20 (October, 2006): 399-417.

Lee, Timothy S. "Beleaguered Success: Korean Evangelicalism in the Last Decade of the Twentieth Century," in *Christianity in Korea*. Edited by Robert E. Buswell Jr. & Timothy S. Lee. Honolulu: University of Hawaii Press, 2006.

Lieberts, Elizabeth. *The Process of Change in Spiritual Direction: A Structural-Developmental Perspective*. Michigan: UMI, 1986.

O'Murchu, Diarmuid. *The Transformation of Desire: How Desire Became Corrupted and How We Can Reclaim It*. Maryknoll, NY: Orbis Books, 2007.

Pope, Marvin H. *Song of Songs: A New Translation with Introduction and Commentary*, The Anchor Bible 7C. Garden City, NY: Doubleday, 1977.

Schneiders, Sandra. "The Study of Christian Spirituality: Contours and Dynamics of a Discipline," *Minding the Spirit*. Edited by Elizabeth A. Dreyer & Mark S. Burrows. Baltimore, Maryland: Johns Hopkins University Press, 2005, 5-24.

Sheldrake, Philip. *Befriending Our Desires*. London: Novalis and Darton, 2001.

Ruffing, Janet K. *Spiritual Direction: Beyond the Beginnings*. Mahwah, N.J.: Paulist Press, 2000.

Ryu, Tong-Shick. *The Christian Faith Encounters the Religions of Korea*. Seoul: The Christian Literature Society of Korea, 1962.

Wells, David F. "The Protestant Perspective on Human Nature," in *The Human Condition in the Jewish and Christian Tradition*. Edited by Frederick E. Greenspahn. Hoboken, NJ: KTAV Publishing House, Inc., 1986.

7

The Communal Discernment
for Pastoral Leadership in Korean Church

I. Introduction

It is a well-known fact that Korean churches are characterized by rapid numerical growth and great spiritual fervor. A lesser known but equally true fact however is that Korean church life is also characterized by intense internal conflict and widespread institutional schism. Many Korean churches and their congregations have come into existence as splinter groups due to bitter fighting and unresolved interpersonal conflicts among church members, often revolving around the question of pastoral leadership. As a Korean minister, my first-hand experiences with parish leaders among Korean churches lead me to believe that the hierarchical and patriarchal style of leadership and decision making has consistently discouraged congregational life so as to lead members to leave their original Korean churches and establish new ones.[1]

---

1 I have engaged with several Korean American churches mostly in California metropolitan areas for more than a decade (from the year of 2001 to 2015). My various ministerial expe-

My argument in this study will first explore the leadership style based on *formalistic authoritarianism* and claims its negative influence on Korean pastoral leadership as the main clue to the inner conflicts and splits among Korean churches.[2] Then, the contemporary ideas of leadership theory for renewing the concept of authority and pastoral leadership will help develop the main argument. Lastly, I attempt to introduce the practice of communal discernment that originated in the Ignatian spiritual tradition as a legitimate decision-making process which has the potential to contribute in critical ways to transforming Korean pastoral leadership. In conclusion, I demonstrate that, to aid in the maturing of Korean church leadership whose authoritarianism has severely aggravated the crisis in Korean churches, reorientation of the theological foundations of the church along with a church leadership that embraces the paradoxical nature of the world must be established.

Then, I will argue that communal discernment should be adopted as pastoral leadership tactic in the church decision-making process. Communal discernment is a method of coming to decisions in an inclusive manner, based on the theological conviction that God's will is paradoxically revealed among people. In this chapter, I attempt to verify that the concept of communal discernment that includes congregation members, lay leaders, and ordained and non-ordained staff is useful

---

riences assist fairly the general assumption that the church conflicts have strongly related with the leadership style.

2 The detailed description and comprehensive survey on the leadership style in Korean churches is well examined in Jrugen Hendricks, 김성욱, "한국교회 성장을 위한 리더쉽 연구," 『신학지남』 73/3 (2006): 230-251.

in pastoral ministry in that it helps all pay more attention to ways to implicitly embrace interconnectedness and mutual interdependence in religious communities, in this case Korean protestant churches.

II. The Leadership Crisis in the Korean Church

My understanding of the *formalistic authoritarianism* in the Korean church, which is culturally grounded with hierarchical and patriarchic style of leadership, is characterized best as following the pyramid paradigm. The pyramid paradigm speaks of a "strong authority" and of the "power play" of the pastor in dealing with his or her church members. Euntae Jo elaborately puts, "power play means that a pastor can control his church members, who are accustomed to obeying their pastor."[3] Most critically, all decision-making belongs to the pastor alone. He is the only person to make decision for the whole church. This causes both the church and the pastor to be in a very vulnerable situation.

First, this top-down leadership in general could not discern and meet comprehensively the spiritual or religious needs of the congregation. Second, the absence of accepting the voice of the lay people in the decision-making process easily engenders exclusion of people and an atmosphere of disregard among church members. It usually leads to loss of membership in the church, including especially the new and

---

3 Euntae Jo, *Korean-American and Church Growth* (Seoul, Korea: Cross-Culture Ministry Institute, 1994), 110.

young generation members of the congregation. Third, under the pyramid paradigm and formalistic authoritarianism all responsibility for a decision must be taken by one person, the senior pastor, which makes the leadership vulnerable in a conflict situation. So, it is readily found in the Korean church that whenever conflict is detected, Koreans think that the pastor leaving the church is the best solution. The situation described above indicates that the authoritarian pastoral leadership style common in Korean churches is easily dismissed and even unacceptable to those who have become familiar with a more democratically oriented society. It is necessary to reconsider from a broad perspective the nature and concept of the leadership in religious institutions.[4]

Recognition of the leadership crisis with the formalistic authoritarianism leads us to ask questions: what kind of the leadership formation will be healthy to Christian community in Korean context? In what ways will the Korean church be able to overcome existing maladies aroused from formalistic authoritarianism and establish fully fledged leadership? What is most appropriate way to integrate between what they believe in church leadership and what they actually practice it in Korean context? Drawing on old wisdom and new insights following will help cultivate and completely reshape the landscape of Korean pastoral leadership.

---

4 The writer however is beware of generalization of this assumption since many christian pastors or ministers have endeavored to be conformed with the servant leadership of Jesus Christ.

III. Renewing the Pastoral Leadership
by Embracing Paradox

1. Overcoming Authoritarianism with Authentic Authority

Leadership theorist Ronald Heifetz challenges the common perception that equates leadership with authority. "We routinely call leaders those who achieve high positions of authority, even though we readily acknowledge their frequent misuse of leadership."[5] This perception mainly fails to distinguish true leadership from authority. By equating leadership with authority, we fail to see the obstacles to leadership that come with authority itself.[6] Heifetz defines authority as the conferral of power to perform a service, rather than as conferred power to dominate others.[7] Moreover, he also suggests two changes in authority leadership: first, the awareness that authority is given and can be taken away; and second, the understanding that authority is conferred as part of an exchange which implies flexibility in obtaining and losing one's authority.[8]

Heifetz's definition of authority deliberately eliminates the dominance-oriented leadership style. This helps us to take a creative new

---

5 Ronald A. Heifetz, *Leadership Without Easy Answers* (Cambridge, Massachusetts: Harvard University Press, 1999), 48.

6 I do not imply there is possibility of leadership without authority. Heifetz also explicates authentic understanding of authority fully enables leadership to be legitimate. Authority is the constitutive element for leadership formation in any place. The bottom line is that authentic leadership must come with the right notion of authority, the conferral of power to perform a service.

7 Heifetz, *Leadership Without Easy Answers*, 49.

8 Ibid., 57.

direction in conceptualizing Korean pastoral leadership in several aspects. First, we need to have a new idea of the role of authority in leadership. Awareness of authority as conferred power to perform a service confronts the Korean formalistic authoritarianism that tends to result in leaders taking the power to dominate church members. And second, Heifetz encourages us to create flexible leadership by exchanging authority among members. This shift will play a significant role in preventing leadership not only from being addicted to or abusing their power and authority but also from the temptation to dominate community members with a top-down communication style. The third benefit from this kind of the authority is a type of leadership which is easily accessible to any member of the community so that the decision-making process will be more sensitive to and inclusive of various groups of people in the community. In the end, this form of leadership is likely to accomplish Calvin's idea of the church, that of a mutually reciprocal and interdependent community. This new concept of authority and church readily enables us to create a new concept of pastoral leadership as leadership thriving within paradox.

2. Pastoral Leadership within Paradoxical Milieu

It is not totally unreasonable to say that living in the age of pluralism and postmodernism implies "embracing paradox and ambiguity." Anderson and Miller-McLemore persuasively assert that ambiguity does not refer to contradictions; it is "inherent in human nature, in human community, in the circumstances of life, and in our theology."[9]

---

9 Anderson & Miller-McLemore, *Faith's Wisdom for Daily Living* (Minneapolis, Minnesota:

Most of all, they effectively remind us that human nature is also paradoxical itself, since humans have the ability to transcend their limitations with a symbolic thought even though at the same time they will eventually die.[10] Employing a similar argument about paradox, Reformed theology states that the Christian is simultaneously righteous and sinful before God. These paradoxes are not regarded as untrue; rather, they address very deep truths. Any effort to choose either part of a paradox will not lead to truth, since paradox is "a self-contradictory statement or proposition that on further investigation may nonetheless be true."[11] Thus, the task of a religious leader living in the pluralistic world is to hold the paradox without choosing one side or the other.

Newton H. Malony comments that religious leadership is easily trapped in conflict because leaders fail to adopt the paradoxical mindset.[12] He correctly presupposes that any religious enterprise willingly sets its foundation in paradox: it is based on otherworldly concerns and yet must function in this world. So, it would be natural for the leadership to exist in this paradox. He maintains that religious leadership requires double vision. It asks leaders to move beyond "either/or" to "both/and." To become a leader with double vision means "to hold two opposed ideas in the mind at the same time, and still retain the ability to function." As applied in Christianity, both human and divine should be considered at the same time. To affirm either the human or

---

Augsburg Fortress, 2008), 16.

10 Ibid., 18.

11 Ibid., 17.

12 Newton Malony, *Living with Paradox: Religious Leadership and the Genius of Double Vision* (San Francisco: Jossey-Bass Publishers, 1998), 6-8.

the divine side of the paradox to the exclusion of the other would be to engage in denial and artificiality.

A classical view about the christian church has confirmed the paradoxical feature of the faith community. The Religious reformer, John Calvin has been regarded as the most influential theologians in the Korean Protestant context. His theology has shed tremendous light upon the theological creeds and confessions characterizing Korean Presbyterian churches, which includes more than 60% of Korean churches. Among the Reformers, Calvin was the one who gave the most attention to the doctrine of the church.[13] He sees the church as the people whom in every age God has called out from the world to serve him. He believed the church was the elect people of God called out of this world to proclaim God's Word.

Meanwhile, Calvin's understanding of church is apparently paradoxical, since the high calling of the church goes hand-in-hand with the humility of the church. The church is a human institution at the same time that it is a holy communion. We have these treasures in earthen vessels, as the apostle Paul made so clear (2 Cor. 4:7).[14] This implies that the leaders of the church can and often do err. The church is a field of grain in which tares all too often have been sown, but this is no excuse to separate ourselves from the church, for it is God's field.[15] Beside that, we need each other. To none of us has God given

---

13 See more details in John T. McNeill, "The Church in Sixteenth Century Reformed Theology," in *Major Themes in the Reformed Tradition*, ed. Donald K. McKim (Grand Rapids, Michigan: Wm. B. Eerdmans Publishing Co., 1992).

14 John Calvin, *Institutes of the Christian Religion*, 4.3.1, trans. Ford Lewis Battles (Philadelphia: Westminster Press, 1960), 1054.

15 Ibid., 4.1.17-22, 1031-36.

all the spiritual gifts. It is through each other in the church where God has seen fit to bless us. In the wisdom of God, it is in this way that the Christian commonwealth is bound together. God's blessings come through the hands of our brothers and sisters in Christ. We need each other, both in material things and in spiritual things.

A pastoral leader equipped with the paradoxical perspective is well aware that most decisions in a church are supposed to be made following prayers so that such decisions will be attuned with God's will. However, leaders also realize that the decision-making process has to take into serious consideration congregational needs and expectations. Noting several occasions in which a pastoral leader might not have an all-embracing mind, Molony states that an exclusive decision-making process tarnishes the most important truth in Christianity: practicing loving one another.[16] It results in the congregation's withdrawal from the church since the limited communication, they believe, does not cherish people and, furthermore, their self-interest is neither satisfied nor considered. Therefore, Malony believes that sharing decision-making with a transparent process is a prerequisite to healthy and authentic leadership in the paradoxical milieu.[17] In this way, we can ensure that the paradox between divine and human is taken into account in the church decision-making process.

The fruits of sharing decisions in religious organizations are as follows. First, church members feel profoundly accepted and understood when they participate in communications and decision-making.

---

16 Ibid., 98-99.

17 Ibid., 99-100.

Second, church leaders do not treat congregation members as employers with growing awareness that the religious organization has to be sustained by members' volunteers, yet at the same time they advocate acceptance, support, and good relationships among members and staff. Third, shared decision-making can prevent pastoral leaders from the vulnerable situation of having to take sole responsibility for every decision they make. The last benefit is derived from the first three - the faith community can participate in the authentic spiritual practice of loving each other. These results of shared decision-making demonstrate that an inclusive approach to making decisions is essential to church leadership in the paradoxical world and would be greatly beneficial to Korean pastoral leaders and congregations. After all, the fruits of sharing decision enable us to present the potentials to resolve the leadership crisis detected in the Korean churches unveiled as formalistic authoritarianism. It seems to be inevitable to accommodate the sharing decision-making process in Korean church since the process prompts feeling of acceptance, enhances security among the leadership, nurtures good sense of mutual accountability, and practices love, the ultimate value of the Christian community.

Now, we will discuss a specific method that facilitates both the authentic concept of authority and the sharing of decisions in the church setting. The method of communal discernment developed long ago by Ignatius of Loyola is invaluable for my argument for renewal and transformation within the Korean church.

IV. Communal Discernment
for Transforming Pastoral Leadership

1. Communal Discernment as Christian Heritage

Decision making is inherent to human nature. We all face momentous decisions as we quite literally become who we are. The Christian tradition has long recognized the importance of decision making.[18] As Elizabeth Liebert notes, "Because our identity is formed in part though our decision, the making of decision is actually a privileged moment for growing in discipleship."[19] Through our choices, we can become the person God is calling us to be. Because our decisions are so central to our identity as persons and as Christians, we can look to the Christian tradition for help in the process of decision making. That help is called discernment. Liebert succinctly defines discernment as "the process of intentionally becoming aware of how God is present, and calling us as individuals and communities so that we can respond with increasingly greater faithfulness."[20] In decision making, self-determination and group identity come manifestly together with God's call.

Community discernment, based on Liebert's work, can be defined

---

18 Joohyung Lee, "The Contemplative Desires as Constitutive for Spiritual Discernment: Centered within Greogry of Nyssa's Homilies on the Song of Songs," *Theological Forum*, vol. 86 (2016): 127-159; Joohyung Lee, "Christian Discernment through the Neuroscientific Lens: Within Jonathan Edwards' Religious Affection," *Korean Journal of Christian Studies*, vol. 101 (2016): 201-225.

19 Elizabeth Liebert, *The Way of Discernment: Spiritual Practice for Decision Making* (Louisville, Kentucky: Westminster John Knox Press, 2008), 8.

20 Ibid.

as the group process of becoming aware of how God is present and of finding God's will through recognizing the initiative movements of the Holy Spirit among the inner being of the community. The participants in communal discernment are entering into a mystery where, simultaneously, we wait on God to show us how we ought to proceed, while using our minds and hearts and the best strategies at our disposal to help us grow spiritually as a group, in order to make decisions together in a faith context.[21]

The practice of communal discernment itself is not new in the Church; a careful reading of the acts of the Apostolic Council of Jerusalem (Acts 15:1-35) reveals all of its essential elements. The apostolic Council of Jerusalem was concerned with great religious issues involving the future of the whole church: were the Gentiles asking for baptism obliged to be circumcised as Jews were? In other words, does salvation come through the law and its practices, as the party of the Pharisees contended, or does it come through the grace of the Lord Jesus alone, as Paul claimed? My focus in reading this passage is on the discerning process of the Church. The apostles gathered together with the elders and disciples. The core of the assembly was the small group which prayed together in the upper room when the Spirit of the Lord was poured out on them. No doubt as they met to deliberate, they were united in prayer again as only they could be.[22] In our contemporary terms, they put themselves into the right disposition before God, or

---

21 Virginia Varley, "Fostering the Process of Discerning Together," *The Way Supplement* 85 (Spring 1996): 84.

22 For more details, see Luke Timothy Jonhson, *Scripture and Discernment: Decision Making in the Church* (Nashville, Tennessee: Abingdon Press, 1996).

they made themselves "indifferent" or impartial. More correctly, they allowed God to dispose their hearts for the truth.[23]

The biblical precedent gives us a broader horizon for considering communal discernment. We acknowledge that we are not joining a movement of dubious origins. We follow a route traced by the apostles. Such historical awareness helps us to realize that ever since the Council of Jerusalem, communal discernment has been practiced in the Church whenever men and women graced by God came together and set out to search for those high thoughts and ways of the Lord that no person can know through his or her own efforts alone.

2. Ignatian Communal Discernment as a Historical Model

Although communal discernment is ancient in the church, the historical precedent for the form to which I refer is the experience of St. Ignatius of Loyola and his first companions in their deliberations about the founding of the Jesuit order. As a group they worked through specific questions of community in the midst of the discerning process, a process well documented in the *Deliberation Primorum Patrum (Deliberation of the First Fathers)*.[24] The document includes the way in which the first fathers of the Society of Jesus reached a decision concerning two issues: the need for a vow of obedience and the procedures for sending their members out to do apostolic works.

Father Schemel and Sister Judith briefly and concisely delineate

---

23 Ladislas Orsy, S.J. *Probing the Spirit: A Theological Evaluation of Communal Discernment* (Denville, New Jersey: Dimension Books, Inc., 1976), 16.

24 John Carroll Futrell, S.J., *Making an Apostolic Community of Love* (St. Louis, Missouri: Institute of Jesuit Socurces, 1970), 187-194.

how the most characteristic of the procedures presented in *Deliberation of the First Fathers* is "the insistence on separating the pro and
con sides of a question at issue, requiring that each person prayerfully
consider and speak to both."[25] Despite the existence of contradictory
opinions, the document shows precisely how the communal discerning
process allowed for an unfolding of comprehensive perspectives on
the issues without dominance by any one individual. More than that,
it also shows how sincerely they engaged in the decision process with
intentional devotional preparation. First, they devoted themselves to
prayers, sacrifices, and meditations, making every effort to find joy and
peace in the Holy Spirit concerning obedience which disposes humans
to glorify God and praise His majesty. The second preparation of the
soul was the communal agreement that no one would persuade another
or incline them more in favor of obeying or of not obeying. They eval-
uated equally each autonomous idea that arose from individual prayer
and meditation. Third, each participant was not supposed to promote
their own opinions and judgments, but they were to freely propose their
ideas. After months of prayer and discussion, these "pilgrim priests"
decided to form a permanent union, and the Society of Jesus was born.
Their authentic use of the communal discernment process has been
demonstrated repeatedly over the centuries since.

The other two resources from the Ignatian tradition concerning
communal discernment can be discovered within the *Spiritual Exercises*.[26] The first is the practice of personal discernment, codified in the

---

25 George Schemel, S.J. & Sister Judith Roemer, "Communal Discernment," *Review for Religious* 40 (November-December., 1981), 825.

26 Andrew Hamilton, "Correct Weight for Communal Discernment," *The Way Supplement* 85

"Rules of the Discernment of Spirit,"[27] which directs the retreatant to reflect on the significant movements of the heart. An individual seeks to recognize the kind of movements taking place within him or her and to grasp the meaning of the consolation and desolation so that he or she can follow the lead of the Spirit. The second source for communal discernment is derived from the *Election* in the *Spiritual Exercises*.[28] Within the Exercises, a retreatant is directed towards choice and practical renewal within a context of prayer. Then, the process of decision-making culminates in the *Election* in that emphasis is placed on the movement of the heart. Even though these two resources were originally designed for use by individuals, both could serve also as

---

(Spring 1996): 19. "The 'Spiritual Exercise' blends not only Ignatius's personal mysticism and spirituality but also his pastoral experience. The exercises can be called the school of prayer created for, and taught by, the Society of Jesus. Ignatius composed them as a manual for the person giving them. They are to be experienced, not read or studied, by the one making them." Harvey D. Egan, S.J. "Ignatian Spirituality," in *the New Dictionary of Catholic Spirituality*, ed. Michael Downey (Collegeville, Minnesota: The Liturgical Press, 1993), 522.

27 In the *Spiritual Exercises*, Ignatius of Loyola outlines "Rules for the Discernment of Spirits," which function critically as the exercitants attempts to respond to the influence of God directing her or his life. The rules unite all of the factors that previous traditions included: good and evil spirits, personal and preternatural influences, thoughts and imagination, and states of affectivity, consolation and desolation.

28 The term *Election* in the Ignatian tradition indicates that each human being is created for a purpose, which is, 'to praise, reverence and serve God our Lord and by so doing to save his or her soul' (*Spiritual Exercises* 22). "Ignatius likewise held that, since human well-being and good order are rooted in consistency between that ultimate purpose and the choices which men and women make in particular circumstances, then if human beings are to flourish, those choices need to be consciously related to that purpose." David Lonsdale, "Ignatian Election," in *The New Westminster Dictionary of Christian Spirituality*, ed. Philp Sheldrake (Louisville, Kentucky: Westminster John Knox Press, 2005), 268; Joohyung Lee, "Centrality of Imagination in Election within Spiritual Exercises," in *Theology and Praxis* 50 (2016): 159-187.

resources for communal discernment, since individual discernment is the fundament resource for group discernment.[29] When an individual comes to a decision, this decision is considered tentative or provisional until confirmed objectively by the person's community. Meanwhile, in communal discernment there often is a higher authority with whom the group has to be in dialogue for objective confirmation. And so this same principle for objective confirmation applies. Therefore, the methods of the Spiritual Exercises which were designed for the individual could be extended to communal reflection and choice.[30]

The *Constitutions* for the Society of Jesus should be taken into account since the constitution implicitly and explicitly is embedded in the key values for communal discernment.[31] Firstly, Ignatius is primarily concerned that decisions among the Society should be made in spiritual freedom, the freedom in which people are as open as possible to Christ. To enable this sense of spiritual freedom, the gathering allows each member's authentic participation with an invitation to anyone to speak regardless of their age or position. The second key value here is the group's unity. Ignatius seems at least to envisage consensual resolutions. For him, God's Spirit is not arbitrary. As a group of people are sharing life vocation and opening to God, the divine wisdom will be reflected in all decisions.

I have been exploring so far the Ignatian experience of communal

---

29 Andrew Hamilton, "Correct Weight for Communal Discernment," 19.

30 Virginia Varley, "Fostering the Process of Discerning Together," *The Way Supplement* 85 (Spring 1996), 85.

31 Philip Endean, "The Draughthorse's Bloodlines: Discerning Together in the Ignatian Constitutions," *The Way Supplement* 85 (Spring 1996), 73-76.

discernment using a couple of historical resources. Even if those three documents represent different styles of discernment, any Ignatian approach to communal discernment will seem to cohere with these approaches.[32] Their basic concerns consist of four aspects. The first concern is that a decision must be made based on an accurate account of all relevant information. Second, the decision should be taken in faith rather than in fear, out of a gospel understanding of the self rather than a constricting self-image. Third, general rules cannot impede people's freedom to do what a situation requires. Fourth, realistic allowance must be made for human limitations. For additional help in coming to a good decision, Ignatius sets forth indifference as a prerequisite for good discernment.

What is the initial implication of Ignatian Communal Discernment for Korean pastoral leadership stuck firmly in formalistic authoritarianism? It is significant for Koreans that Communal Discernment seems to represent a form of participation which is an alternative to the authoritarianism prevalent among Roman Catholics before Vatican II. Communal discernment was rediscovered as a historical reaction against a rigid conception of obedience right after Vatican II. Before the Vatican Council, the old-style obedience and communal discernment was preoccupied with the question of who, in the end, has the power to make the decision. However, the historical transitions of catholic landscape by the Vatican Council caused reevaluation of its significance and the revival of Ignatian communal discernment since Vatican II shook the stubborn foundation of authoritarianism. Its legitimation by Roman

---

32 Ibid., 78-79.

Catholics demonstrated the probability and adaptability of "discerning together," even though it was in a different context from Protestant Korean churches.[33]

3. The Practical Procedure of Communal Discernment

Communal discernment is an instrument offering different agenda for developing true Christian community. It should be confessional not only in that the faith community has embodied the love of God and love is the primary motive in decision making. In addition, it is based on the premise that there can be individual discernment without a relationship to the total faith community, which means no communal discernment is possible without consideration of individual discernment. Its methods set out the presupposition that each individual has the capacity to discern God's will but, even so, each individual's discernment becomes finally authenticated through the process of communal discernment. Drawing on several resources which have reformulated the practical methods and processes of communal discernment for contemporary use, I will here present practical processes and guidelines for Korean communal discernment in the context of Korean pastoral leadership in the parish ministry.[34]

---

33 Philip Endean, "The Draughthorse's Bloodlines: Discerning Together in the Ignatian Constitutions," 79-81.

34 George Schemel, S.J. & Sister Judith Roemer, "Communal Discernment," *Review for Religious* 40 (Nov. Dec., 1981): 825-836; Ladislas Orsy, S.J. *Probing The Spirit: A Theological Evaluation of Communal Discernment* (Denville, New Jersey: Dimension Books, Inc., 1976); Virginia Varley, "Fostering the Process of Discerning Together," *The Way Supplement* 85 (Spring 1996): 84-96; William Barry, "Toward Communal Discernment: Some Practical Suggestions," *The Way Supplement* 58 (Spring 1987): 104-112; Mary Benet McKinney, "Discerning Community Leadership," *Review for Religious* 58 (July-August 1999): 424-428; Pa-

Before beginning a group discernment process there should always be a period of '**readying**.' This is the time of dispositional readiness, which is a matter of the heart. Among the signs of readiness are the following. First is the ability of the members to enter into serious conversation without prejudice and bias with each other. Second, the members are open to prayer, as an essential element for obtaining knowledge not so much by human effort as through God's gracious gift; this knowledge is akin to the "intimate understanding and relish of the truth" which Ignatius speaks of in his *Exercises* #2. The third sign of readiness includes the capacity to trust the discerning process and the facilitator, even when the process is perceived to be out of tune with the group's spirit or agenda. Fourth, the members of the group should have the capacity and the patience to stay with the process to the end.

The discernment process itself is composed of five phases. Phase one is called "**experience**," in which a history or timeline of the church is presented to the members. This can be an instrument for inclusion of new members and of reconciliation and healing among existing relationships. It also can be the vehicle for discerning the presence of God through the historical events of the community. While tracing the historical events from the present back in time, the group eventually comes back to its beginning where the initiating vision took form.

tricia Wittberg, "Community and Obedience: Musings on Two Ambiguities," *Review for Religious* 59, no. 5 (September-October 2000): 526-536. This research is well aware that the adoption of the catholic spiritual tradition without comprehensive consideration about the Korean context would bear undesirable or unintended fruits. The extensive understanding and constructive criticism about the Ignatian tradition should be proceeded before its direct application in Korean church.

Then, the act of storytelling of history becomes a chance to articulate the vision of the group, and the shared vision evokes a sense of commonality that permeates the community and gives coherence to diverse activities.

Once the history line has been recounted, the members are asked to **reflect** on their experience and to understand the movement of spirit in their interior lives (phase two). Helpful questions at this stage to ponder include: *What is the significance of this event? What is it saying?* Then, each person makes a personal assessment of meanings: *Our history says to me that…* After this, all are invited to state their interpretation of the events as follows: *Because our history is what it is, there is a need to….* This praying over the church's history profoundly assists the group to interpret and view its history from the point of view of the main Christian narratives.

After each person has shared their reflections, each person is encouraged to speak about what they have heard (phase three). When everyone has spoken, the group returns to silence to reflect on what they have heard from each other. The **articulation** of each one's experience in prayer places the individual in the communal context and helps the group to become more objective in its understanding of the experience. It also enables trust to grow in the group by sharing some in-depth experiences, which is a way to learn how to be aware of God's work among them. In the fourth phase, everyone is involved in an **interpreting** activity in which people realize the significance of the interior movements of spirits. This action of interpretation is often begun by the simple question, *What does this experience of ours mean?* It is here that the insights about the spiritual discernment process found in Ignatius of Loyola's writings can be very helpful. Interpreting the movement of the heart, group direction, interior moods, feelings or affections, and tendencies have to be seriously and inclusively considered. There are times when the moods or judgments of members of a group can cause discouragement and communal desolation. However, it is at these times that it is important for the group to pause and ask, *What is happening to us? Where did this discouragement originate?* When a group is able to monitor itself in this way, a great deal of growth in spiritual maturity can be expected.

When confidence in the process, and spiritual maturity, and a consensus about the right timing have all been reached among members, the practical **decision-making** process begins as the fifth phase. The first four steps of this phase consist of "initially walking around the issue, gathering all relevant data and posting it on flipchart paper for all to see; second, checking assumptions and determining criteria for choice; third, brainstorming, prioritizing, examining the advantages and disadvantages, making a composite of the groups' list of advantages and disadvantages and taking the matter to prayer, seeking God's help in coming to a provisional decision; lastly seeking confirmation for the decision reached."[35] Diligent monitoring of participants' inner dynamics including mostly affectivity will be the decisive indicator whether the decision making process takes right track. The assured process then prompts all to accept the decision.

In concluding the discernment process, seeking consensus and

---

35 Virginia Varley, "Fostering the Process of Discerning Together," *The Way Supplement* 85 (Spring 1996), 94.

confirmation is so vital since it means something more than the simple words imply. Consensus brings about unity, and it may even lead to an experience of a special sense of wholeness. Finally, the experience of wholeness through the consensus prompts each member to recognize that he or she has been involved in a mystery which has touched the life of each person present: it is God who has worked this change in them.

4. The Communal Discernment as Pastoral Leadership in Korean Church[36]

Attempt to foster communal discernment into the Korean churches and its leadership formation is one of the inevitable endeavors to envision the aim of the practical theology in Korean context through integrating between what churches believe in and how they live out.[37] My hope is that a focus on communal discernment will provoke at least three transformations in the Korean church leadership. The first relates to indifference, the intrinsic prerequisite of discernment. Indifference (or detachment) is generally defined as a willingness to give up any

---

36 One of the legitimate challenges on this research topic would be related with the interreligious approach asking the way in which the catholic traditional methods could effectively applicable in protestant church contexts. As forementioned, it is therefore important to acknowledge the historical or contextual understanding of Ignatian spirituality for authentic procedure or desirable outcomes. However, it is also meaningful to facilitate important spiritual heritage within christian spiritual traditions if it would accommodate the enhancement and nourishment for our contemporary faith community.

37 Don Browning's methodology and understanding of practical theology and Christian church as of living out their faith offer the milestone of this argument. Don Browning, *A Fundamental Practical Theology: Descriptive and Strategic Proposals* (Minneapolis: Fortress Press, 1991), 9-10.

worldly value for the sake of a higher spiritual good, such as seeking, following and decision-making to God's will.[38] Specifically, Ignatius of Loyola states in his legacy work, *Spiritual Exercises* that indifference is preparatory to a choice to live a life that wants what God wants [*Spiritual Exercises*, 23].[39] Anyone authentically seeking to discern God's will is supposed to practice indifference in order to ready mind and soul to make a choice conformity with God's will along the way, we are to abandon preoccupation with worldly value systems. The features of the formalistic authoritarianism as cultural consciousness do not originate from the Christian value system but attached with the worldly value system. The aim of indifference is to liberate community members from mundane or physical desires which distort participant's intention or attention to the decision-making process. I believe indifference also liberates the members from the culturally embedded consciousness, which is the initiative benefit and contribution of the communal discernment in Korean church.

Second gift from practicing communal discernment in Korean church stems from realization that discernment itself is not static, but process; any decision made is not permanent but tentative. Authentic discernment challenges assumptions of evidence and certainty by admitting human incapability to discern decisive God's will because it is

---

38 George E. Ganss, S.J. "Detachment (Indifference)" in *The New Dictionary of Catholic Spirituality*, edited by Downey, Michael (Collegeville, Minnesota: The Litergical Press, 1993), 269-270.

39 Ignatius of Loloya, "Principle and Foundation," in *Spiritual Exercises and Selected Works*, edited by George E. Ganss with the collaboration of Parmananda Divarkar, Edward J. Malatesta, and Martin E. Palmer, preface by John W. Padberg (New York: Paulist Press, 1991).

in part hidden and remains a mystery to human being. To discern the partly mysterious but partly revealed will of God leads us inescapably to embrace of uncertainty and ambiguity.[40] Since the will of God is perceived as hidden and simultaneously revealed, the discernment itself is still process in-between. The will of God is already discerned but not yet totally—paradoxical. It helps us clearly to conceive the identity of the church, the discerning subject, inevitably as paradoxical—a human institution as well as Holy Communion. In the end, practicing communal discernment is confessional by itself, in that the church is paradoxical community to the extent that its discerning process will be paradoxical. The Communal discernment hence emphasizes upon awakening all that the will of God is not exclusively known by one person in a church such as a senior pastor, but by the whole community. The will of God is revealed to ordinary people and to taste the next advantage of the communal discernment.

Lastly, facilitating communal discernment will constructively shifts the concept of authority from being tarnished, deformed, and distorted by the formalistic authoritarianism to being flexibly shared among the constitutive members; from as conferred power to dominate group members to as the conferral of power to perform a service. The primary challenge for the Korean church leadership under the authoritarianism is to embrace lay people as partners to discern the will of God unveiled indiscriminately in the mundane human nature. As above noted, however, communal discernment takes transparency for

---

40 Herbert Anderson and Bonnie Miller-McLemore, *Faith's Wisdom for Daily Living* (Minneapolis: Augsburg Fortress, 2008), 16.

granted in the communication process and it considers all discerners as divine vehicles to perceive the will of God regardless of their ages, social class, gender, position, etc. The radical methods of the communal discernment establish that authority is given to the community, any attempt to dominate others with top-down leadership excludes lay people and distorts the intention for the church.

I eagerly vindicates, I believe that the communal discernment is a genuine spiritual practice that will overcome the leadership crisis of Korean churches that are trapped by formalistic authoritarianism. Adopting the communal discernment is well renew leadership formation since it negatively prevents Korean churches from being split or conflicted through accepting the voice of the lay people in the decision-making process. It also keeps church members actively from becoming vulnerable sacrifices by scapegoat-like by inner conflicts.

Most of all, what makes the communal discernment the most legitimate spiritual practice in Korean church leadership is that the communal decision-making process embodies practice of ultimate will of God, loving each other. The discerning process described above deepens the intimate understanding each other through listening, accepting, and understanding among the members. In communal discernment process tremendously does surly enhance awareness of God's loving presence and does definitely foster confessional affirmation of the communal discernment as 'the shared divine wisdom," where the will of God is revealed among the community.

The endeavors to vindicate necessity of communal discernment in Korean church and to apply it for Korean context leave at least three tasks for future research. First, the way in which Korean Presbyterian churches comprehend community as paradoxical should explicitly be delineated. There is plausible suspicion whether Calvin's understanding of church as paradoxical is authentically accepted to Korean church or not. Second remaining task will relate with the practical concerns that the model of the communal discernment presented herein stems from the catholic tradition: Ignatian tradition. Even if we examined discernment as Christian spiritual practice by noting the biblical foundation, it is mostly predictable to have reluctance or resistance from Korean protestant church due to its catholic roots. The question, then, arise, "how can the communal discernment be introduced to the Korean protestant churches that have prejudice or bias of the catholic churches and its spiritual tradition?" Lastly, the communal discernment is presupposed with personal discernment, since the individual discerning process becomes the most significant resources for the communal discernment. Thus, introducing and internalizing the personal discernment should be concurrent with the way in which both methods can be integrated in discerning and seeking the will of God.

V. Conclusion

This chapter has taken an experimental journey to explain the legitimacy of communal discernment as spiritual practice and its implications in the Korean pastoral context. First, Korean pastoral leadership is restricted by its cultural inheritance of formalistic authoritarianism, a leadership style that undermines the fundamental ground of the church's unity and minimizes the congregational spiritual and religious needs, leading to increasing vulnerability of the leadership in conflict situations. Second, Calvin's theology of the church, points out the paradoxical identity of the church, and Heifetz's elaboration of flexibility in the relation between authority and leadership expands the landscape of the church leadership by showing its potential adaptability in the milieu of ambiguity and paradox. We can acknowledge with Malony's support that pastoral leadership that serves truth must resonate primarily with paradox. And thirdly, the practice of communal discernment stemming from the Ignatian spiritual tradition has been re-discovered and re-introduced as a legitimate decision-making process in pastoral leadership which could critically contribute to transform Korean pastoral leadership in the context of the paradoxical world.

Bibliography

Anderson, Herbert and Bonnie J. Miller-McLemore. *Faith's Wisdom for Daily Living*. Minneapolis, Minnesota: Augsburg Fortress, 2008.

Barry, William. "Toward Communal Discernment: Some Practical Suggestions." *The Way Supplement* 58 (Spring 1987): 104-112.

Browning, Don. *A Fundamental Practical Theology: Descriptive and Strategic Proposals*. Minneapolis: Fortress Press, 1991.

Calvin, John. *Institutes of the Christian Religion*. Translated by Ford Lewis Battles. Philadelphia: Westminster Press, 1960.

Egan, Harvey D. "Ignatian Spirituality." *The New Dictionary of Catholic Spirituality*, ed. Michael Downey. Collegeville, Minnesota: The Liturgical Press, 1993, 521-529.

Endean, Philip. "The Draughthorse's Bloodlines: Discerning Together in the Ignatian Constitutions." *The Way Supplement* 85 (Spring 1996): 73-83.

Futrell, John Carroll. S.J. *Making an Apostolic Community of Love*. St. Louis, Missouri: Institute of Jesuit Sources, 1970.

Ganss, George E. S.J. "Detachment." *The New Dictionary of Catholic Spirituality*. Edited by Michael Downey. Collegeville, Minnesota: The Litergical Press, 1993, 269-270

Hamilton, Andrew. "Correct Weight for Communal Discernment." *The Way Supplement* 85 (Spring 1996):17-27.

Heifetz, Ronald A. *Leadership Without Easy Answers*. Cambridge, Massachusetts: Harvard University Press, 1999.

Ignatius of Loloya. *Spiritual Exercises and Selected Works*. Edited by George E. Ganss with the collaboration of Parmananda Divarkar, Edward J. Malatesta, and Martin E. Palmer. Preface by John W. Padberg. New York: Paulist Press, 1991.

Jo, Euntae. *Korean-American and Church Growth*. Seoul, Korea: Cross-Culture Ministry Institute, 1994.

Johnson, Luke Timothy. *Scripture and Discernment: Decision Making in the Church*. Nashville, Tennessee: Abingdon Press, 1996.

Joohyung Lee. "Centrality of Imagination in Election within Spiritual Exercises." *Theology and Praxis*, Vol. 50 (2016), 159-187.

_____. "The Contemplative Desires as Constitutive for Spiritual Discernment: Centered within Greogry of Nyssa's Homilies on the Song of Songs," *Theological Forum*, vol. 86 (2016), 127-159;

_____. "Christian Discernment through the Neuroscientific Lens: Within Jonathan Edwards' Religious Affection," *Korean Journal of Christian Studies*, vol. 101 (2016), 201-225.

Liebert, Elizabeth. *The Way of Discernment: Spiritual Practice for Decision Making*. Louisville, Kentucky: Westminster John Knox Press, 2008.

Lonsdale, David. "Ignatian Election." *The New Westminster Dictionary of Christian Spirituality*. Edited by Philp Sheldrake. Louisville, Kentucky: Westminster John Knox Press, 2005, 268-269.

Malony, H. Newton. *Living with Paradox: Religious Leadership and the Genius of Double Vision*. San Francisco: Jossey-Bass Publishers, 1998.

McKinney, Mary Benet. "Discerning Community Leadership." *Review for Religious* 58, (July-August 1999), 424-428.

McNeill, John T. "The Church in Sixteenth Century Reformed Theology." *Major Themes in the Reformed Tradition*. Edited by Donald K. McKim. Grand Rapids: Wm. B. Eerdmans Publishing Co., 1992.

Orsy, Ladislas. S.J. *Probing the Spirit: A Theological Evaluation of Communal Discernment*. Denville, New Jersey: Dimension Books, Inc., 1976.

Schemel, George, S.J. & Sister Judith Roemer. "Communal Discernment." *Review for Religious* 40 (November-December, 1981), 825-836.

Varley, Virginia. "Fostering the Process of Discerning Together." *The Way Supplement* 85 (Spring 1996), 84-96.

Wittberg, Patricia. "Community and Obedience: Musings on Two Ambiguities," *Review for Religious* 59 (September-October 2000), 526-536.

III.
Spiritual Formation
for Next Generation

8

Sacred Encounters:

Spirituality in College Education

I. Introduction

According to the Organization for Economic Co-operation and Development (OECD), South Korea currently has the highest suicide rate (33 deaths per 100,000 people) in the world.[1] With the exponentially rising number of Korean suicides, this stunning fact released by the Korean government awakened the college and the higher educational enterprises a few years ago. The suicide rate of college students has been higher than that of high school students.[2] There has been a shared societal awareness about the emotional depression among high school students who have been pressured by the severe competition involved

---

1 Organization for Economic Co-operation and Development, "Suicide," *OECD Factbook*, 2010, http://www.oecd-ilibrary.org/sites/factbook-2010en/11/03/01/index.html?contentType=/ns/ StatisticalPublication,/ns/Chapter&itemId=/content/chapter/factbook-2010-90- en&containerItemId=/content/serial/18147364&accessItemIds=&mimeType=text/html, accessed April 23, 2016.

2 정지웅, 장예진, "대학생을 자살케 하는 나라에서 대학생으로 살기," 경향신문, 2011년 9월 28일자, http:// news.khan.co.kr/kh_news/khan_art_view.html?artid=201109280944112&code=900312, accessed April 10, 2016.

Korean SAT exam preparation. Since the higher suicide rate of college students was not previously socially recognized, it must be an alarm bell to those engaged in college or higher or adult education areas, such as the professors, the practitioners, the lecturers, and the administrators. The news article reported that, based on the government's data, the primary cause of college students to "feel suicidal" is related to financial struggles associated with the high tuition. The second cause is indicated to be "the stress of the competition in searching for jobs or occupations."[3]

These data point to a couple of the societal wounds discovered in Korean society. It is deplorable that plenty of college students have been struggling with a shortage of financial resources to sustain themselves during the college years. Rather than making earnest efforts to seek professional knowledge and classical wisdom, the students are often spending the college years preparing to be competitive so that they would obtain desired jobs with prestigious companies such as Samsung or Hyundai. On the other hand, the college education providers might be pressured to organize their curricula in order to sufficiently equip the students with practical skills—pragmatic but somewhat shallow knowledge.[4] This, however, is far from the original purpose and function of higher or college education. It is fair to say that one of the primary goals of college education is to cultivate and nurture the students' concepts of who they are and what kinds of talents they as

---

3 김남석, "대학선교와 기독교 영성교육: 표층교육을 넘어 심층 교육으로," 『대학과 선교』 21 (2011), 86.

4 Yong Hun Jo delineates how the college students' value system has been affected by certain life goal and shaped for the characters. 조용훈, "기독교대학선교와 대학생의 가치관에 대한 한 연구," 『대학과 선교』 19 (2010), 149-174.

individuals are endowed with. Based upon the developmental psychological framework devised by Erik Erikson, one of the primary purposes of college education or young adult education should be to pay attention to nourishing the students' sense of identity by discovering their life vocation as well as to cultivating the sense of intimacy for the sake of constructing healthy relationships in the interpersonal dimension.[5] That is, the individual young adult in the college setting should be engaged in an appropriate self-development or self-realizing process by integrating their college education with their given life situation. However, Alexander Astin from UCLA mentions the "ironic" fact that the core of a liberal education is grounded in the maxim "know thyself," based upon the classic literary and philosophical tradition, but contemporary college education has paid relatively little attention to the student's "inner development."[6] This seems to deeply resonate with Korean situation regarding the high suicide rate among college students.

This research is raised out of the awareness that the social wounds from the high college suicide rate and the implicit problems within the Korean educational system require reexamining and reformulating the pedagogical methods and theoretical approaches. How can college education pertinently respond to the painful situation of the college students? How could the more relevant pedagogical theories and prac-

---

5 This research assumes that identity issues are still in question in the college years so that college students are highly likely to discover their identity by synthesizing academic knowledge with vocational occupation. See Erik Erikson, *Childhood and Society* (New York: Norton, 1950).

6 Arthur W. Chickering, Forward, in *Encouraging Authenticity and Spirituality in Higher Education*, ed. Alexander Astin (San Francisco: Jossey-Bass, 2006), vii.

tices prompt the transformation of college students in Korean context? What would it be the best way to take a look at the interior lives of today's students? In an effort to answer these questions, this study will first describe two different theoretical pedagogical approaches devised by Paulo Freire: the banking model and the problem-posing model. The former will be illuminated by the current pedagogy of Korean college education, and the latter will be presented as the theoretical foundation for reconstructing the pedagogical frame for college education. Next, the necessity or significance of spirituality in higher education will be introduced. The theoretical construction of the concept of sacred encounters in college education will be delineated with the assistance of insightful theorists such as Parker Palmer, Howard Garner, Thomas Merton, etc. Last, the practical implications of sacred encounters will be exemplified using the model of class formation. This research is therefore arguing that sacred encounters related to spirituality can prompt life-transformative learning and experiences for higher and colleges education in Korea.

II. Embracing Lived Experiences

During the last couple of decades, Paulo Freire's theory about liberatory education in *Pedagogy of the Oppressed* has inspired many educators to renew their pedagogy and educational context. This study assumes that Freire's pedagogical concepts are still relevant and legitimate in renewing Korean college education. By reviewing the contrasts between the banking model and the problem-posing model, this study seeks alternative ways for the current Korean educational systems.

Freire sets the premise that the banking model is based on the assumption of a dichotomy between humans and the world: humans are merely in the world, not with the world or with others; humans are spectator, not re-creator. In this view, humans are not a conscious being, but the possessor of a consciousness. So the empty mind of the humans is supposed to open passively to receive the deposits of reality from the world outside. In this model, the primary role of the educator is to regulate the way the world "enters into" the students.[7] The teacher's task is to fill the student's passive consciousness by making deposits of information that the teacher considers constituting true knowledge. In the dichotomous world, the teacher becomes the subject who obtains authority or control over the information and knowledge of the world. Teachers are the only active agents; they possess all the resources of knowledge and deposit knowledge nuggets into the students as investments for future dividends. The designed response of the students as the object of this model of education is to memorize, repeat, and passively absorb the transferred information and knowledge. This model describes how eventually the teacher consolidates the subordination of the social position of the students into the dominant social power and authority.

For Freire, one of the critical aims of all education is to bring about *conscientization* of the students, awaking all people into the ontological vocation of being a subject in the world.[8] Calling a person into be-

---

7 Paulo Freire, *Pedagogy of the Oppressed*, (New York: Continuum, 2010), 62.

8 Ibid., 35-36. *Conscientization* is the ability to perceive social, political, economic, and cultural contradictions and take action against their oppressive elements.

ing a subject is the process of conscientization, and the primary role of education is to initiate the process within individuals. Such conscientization is what makes us distinct from animals; it is truly living as opposed to merely existing. Thus, it is regarded as a new birth, a transformation from a naive consciousness in which one assumes the world is fated to be structured as it is; bestows magical power to authorities and oppressors; and remains passively and powerlessly submerged within reality as it is. Rather, as a subject, an individual is asked to perceive the contradictions of reality and to claims his or her power to act as an agent of culture and liberation.[9]

Korean college classes are invited by Freire's idea to embrace the social contexts in which experiences are generated. Freire challenges students to reflect fully and comprehensively on their experiences within the social contexts since the social contexts are imposed on some problems that can be objectified, engaged, and transformed. So, students are called to bring their experiences into the class and to discover the problems and contradictions binding or enfettering the human consciousness and eventually to liberate human beings from the social structures. This is called the "problem-posing" model of teaching and liberatory education.[10]

With the historical influences of liberation theology and his existential experiences with unjust situations and unlawful treatment of

---

9 Sung Joo Oh elaborately proposes the way in which the concept of conscientization could relevantly be employed and it could prompt to transform the situations of dehumanization in Korean educational systems. 오성주, "한국 청소년 교육을 위한 포스트 파울러 프레이리의 의식화 교육론에 관한 소고," 『기독교교육논총』 37 (2014), 115-144.

10 Freire, *Pedagogy of the Oppressed*, 65.

farmers, Freire was convinced that liberation must be praxis, not an ideal. Education is to call upon students to be liberated from social or structural oppressions. Distancing from subject-object relations, Freire maintains that liberatory education consists first in dialogical relations between teacher and student; the role of the educator is to create, together with the students, the conditions under which knowledge cannot be controlled by certain people and is transferred into the learners. Even the students in the class can be generators of new knowledge based upon reflection on their experiences in social contexts. Freire understands human beings not as abstract, isolated, independent, and unattached to the world; humans are able to perceive critically the way they exist in the world with which and in which they find themselves.

Liberatory education facilitates students to identify the generative themes within a community and to pose these themes as objectified codes that can be discerned, discussed, and engaged. And students are prompted to reflect critically upon these codes and themes to expose and illuminate the social dynamics, practices, systems, and structures that perpetuate their oppressive dimensions. Since the educator in problem-posing models comes to see the world not as a static reality, but as a reality in process and in transformation, the educational skills and tools are focused on empowering strategic action for social transformation. Thus, the role of the teacher in this model is described as an animator, provocateur, co-investigator, co-creator, and co-actor who persistently empowers the students to illuminate oppressive cultural realities and helps them act for their own and others' liberation.

Freire characterizes the problem-posing education as opposed to the banking model as follows: demythologizing the reality; dialogue as an indispensable act in the human cognitive process; critical thinking; intentionality of consciousness; based on creativity and true reflection upon reality. In brief, "banking theory and practice, as immobilizing and fixating forces, fail to acknowledge men as historical beings; problem-posing theory and practice take man's historicity as their starting point."[11]

The two different models of education from Freire's criticism are highly relevant not only to the current situation but also to the effort to find new ways of pedagogy within the Korean college education context. While the banking model sheds light upon the current pedagogy and its limitations, the problem-posing model can be suggested as an alternative to the Korean context to reformulate college education and class formation. Even if a direct connection or causal relationship is not discovered between the higher suicide rates of Korean college students and the banking model in Korea, it would not be unreasonable to note that the Korean college education needs to take into serious consideration or profound reflection the pedagogical approaches from Freire's framework. The banking model is not a relevant pedagogy model that embraces the life situation of college students so it would be less likely to help students to reshape or foster their life initiatives. The banking model could prevent students in danger or in trouble from engaging actively with or responding to their life issues, since the students would not nurture their capacity to integrate their experiences with appropriate knowledge. Considering the problem-posing model as a plausible

---

11 Freire, *Pedagogy of the Oppressed*, 71.

option, how would this work? This inquiry will engage next with an exploration of the value of spirituality as the foundation for constructing the theoretical development of Korean college education.

III. Spirituality in Higher Education

Given that the problem-posing model of pedagogy is here presented as an alternative for Korean college education, what types of pedagogical models would be applicable to the model? Elizabeth Tisdell, a higher education professor, claims spirituality should be accounted for as a constitutive component in academia because it prompts a genuine learning process in the higher education context.[12] Defining spirituality as "one of the ways people constructs knowledge and meaning,"[13] she is convinced that spirituality can be a critical component in constituting knowledge and meanings in college education. She is not discussing about religion, defined as a shared system of beliefs, principles, and doctrines related to an organized community of faith. Instead, she defines spirituality as how people construct knowledge through meaning-making and awareness of wholeness and the interconnectedness of all things, including unconscious and symbolic processes.[14]

---

12 The necessity of spirituality in higher and college education has been communally claimed and actively discussed within scholars since the first decade of 21st c. cf) Sherry L. Hoppe & Bruce W. Speck, eds. *Searching for Spirituality in Higher Education* (New York: Peter Lang Publishing, Inc., 2007).

13 Elizabeth Tisdell, *Exploring Spirituality and Culture in Adult and Higher Education* (San Francisco: Jossey-Bass, 2003), 20.

14 Ibid., 28-29.

Discussing spirituality in the academy often involves transformative learning. This learning process considers "what students know, who they are, what their values and behavior patterns are, and how they see themselves contributing to and participating in the world in which they live."[15] Based upon this, the college education encourages intentional, engaged, and empowered learners who integrate knowledge, skills, and experiences to make meaning throughout their lives. Consequently, spirituality can direct daily living that consistently exemplifies self-integration, which is holistic, involving physical, psychological, and social aspects of the individual, bringing all aspects of life together in relation to others in his or her world.

Then, what would the possible benefits be of involving spirituality in college education? According to the theory of spiritual development by Love and Talbot, spiritually relevant education can consistently support student development, so that it could be considered as a pedagogical theory, which advocates integrating all aspects of student life with the learning.[16] Students' histories, social interactions, families, religions, values, and so forth provide the framework to make meaning of newly acquired information. Tisdell also argues that integrating life experiences and developing a critical reflective process of self

15 Richard, P. Keeling, *Learning Reconsidered: a campus-wide focus on the student experiences* (Washington, D.C.: American College Personnel Association and National Association of Student Personnel Administrators, 2004), 10.

16 Jennifer Capeheart-Meningall, "Role of Spirituality and Spiritual Development in Student Life Outside the Classroom," in *Spirituality in Higher Education*, eds. Sherry L. Hoppe and Bruce W. Speck (San Francisco: Jossey-Bass, 2005), 32. This theory originated with P. Love, and D, Talbot, "Defining Spiritual Development: A Missing Consideration for Student Affairs." *NASPA Journal* 37, no. 1 (1999): 361-375.

will facilitate knowledge construction in both students and educators. In brief, a spiritually relevant college education will not only prompt the integration of information acquired with the lived experiences of students, but will also trigger mutual reflective learning for both students and college educators. This study has demonstrated the necessity of spiritually relevant education in the Korean college context. Now, given the theoretical foundation, it will endeavor to reconstruct the concept or ideal of education within the spirituality sphere. What would a new concept of education related to spirituality look like in college or higher education?

IV. Reshaping the College Education Landscape

In constructing a theological framework, this research is immensely indebted to Thomas Merton because his words concretely incarnate the philosophy of education: self and the world is the great subject of education and transformation and truth the great goals. He claims that the purpose of education is "to show a person how to define himself authentically and spontaneously in relation to his world—not to impose a prefabricated definition of the world, still less an arbitrary definition of the individual himself."[17] This definition of education has firmly convinced me that creating authentic and spontaneous relations between the self and the world is only possible when education is spiritual or prayerful; it must be centered on transcendence. Transcendence

---

17 Thomas Merton, *Love and Living* (New York: Farrar, Straus & Giroux, 1979), 3.

is characterized as a breathing of the Spirit of love into the heart of our existence, an inspiration that allows us to regard ourselves and our world with greater trust and hope. To experience transcendence means not only to be liberated from self and world but also to open the self to participate in the world. So an education in transcendence engages us with the Spirit of love in the self and the world, enabling authentic and spontaneous relations between the self and the world.

1. Education as Spiritual Formation: Truth and Knowledge as Relational

In the Christian tradition, truth is not a constructed fact that can be systematically measured or scientifically observed; truth is embodied in personal terms, the terms of the one who said, "I am the way, the truth, and the life."[18] While conventional education deals with abstract and impersonal facts and theories, an education shaped by Christian spirituality draws us toward incarnate and personal truth. In this education, we come to know the world not simply as an objectified system of empirical objects in logical connection with each other, but as an organic body of personal relations and responses, a living and evolving community of creativity and compassion.

This brings out the relational nature of knowledge. Obtaining knowledge means entering into a relationship with something or someone. In a metaphorical sense, to know something or someone in truth is to enter into a covenant relationship with the known.[19] On the one

---

18 "The Word became flesh and dwelt among us, full of grace and truth." (John 1:14)

19 Parker J. Palmer, *To Know As We Are Known: A Spirituality of Education* (San Francisco: Harper & Row, 1983), 6-16.

hand, to know in truth is to become betrothed, to engage the known with one's whole self, an engagement one enters with attentiveness, care, and good will. On the other hand, to know in truth is to allow one's self to be known as well, to be vulnerable to the challenges and changes that any true relationship brings. To know in truth is to enter into the life of that which we know and to allow it to enter into ours. Truthful knowing weds the knower and the known. If we believe that knowing requires a personal relation between the knower and the known, then the student is invited to learn by interacting with the world, not by viewing it from afar. The classroom will be regarded as an integral, interactive part of reality, not a place apart. Then what will the class be like? What types of dynamics will we look forward to in the classroom?

2. Transforming via Encounters

Education can be illustrated metaphorically as a spiritual journey of transformation via three scared encounters that are described in the next section. The ultimate purpose of educating or teaching a human being lies primarily in transforming the person's life, essentially changing his or her life into a better or more advanced life. The concept of transformation has several basic presuppositions. First, human transformation happens not through an individual moment or a onetime event but through a repetitive series of transforming experiences, a process. Second, the process consists of three different types of encounters in the triangle of dynamics among the text, the teacher, and the student. And last, a person's transformation can be brought about by internalizing the encounters, which will be discussed below in more detail.

As a Christian educator, I am firmly convinced that these ideas concerning the spirituality of education can be epitomized by "three scared encounters." These encounters may be considered "sacred" since each encounter happens in the most inner and mysterious but essential locus of a person, ultimately shaping the present life of oneself. This conceptualization also regards the classroom as similar to a delivery room in that it is the place where a person is most likely to experience transformative moments.

3. The Journey of the Sacred Encounters

The first scared encounter is implicitly or explicitly held between the teacher and the student. More specifically, it is the encounter between the inner selves of each life. Overcoming the physical meaning of the classroom, a space to transmit a collection of information and knowledge, the class process is comprehensively shaped to accommodate the encounter of the inner selves between the teacher and the learners. When the lecturer does not hold on to his or her initiative in conveying information or knowledge, a mutually influential relation can be embodied through interacting with the students. By listening to the life stories that flow from the students' experiences and the way the students interact with the knowledge or information (especially via spiritual practices and small group discussion), the teacher will encounter the sacred place located in the deepest heart and soul of the students, which might initiate transformation in the inner life of the teacher. As part of the same path, the student might encounter the most sacred place of the teacher, where the humbleness of the teacher is evident in the lecturer's putting aside the biases or prejudices generated from his/her worldview or perspectives. This encounter creatively challenges the inner self of the student to engage with the knowledge for his or her transformation. This encounter between the inner journeys of the students and teacher is the most important resource that allows both to reach out to sacred transformation at the most profound level.[20]

The second sacred encounter is discovered or perceived within the student's intrapersonal or spiritual level, the innermost place. Through reading, researching, sharing experiences with classmates and listening to lectures, the student is encountering the new milieu where his or her life might find crucial momentum for the spiritual journey. Interacting with the literature, pondering his or her own experiences of the practices, and contemplating new knowledge, the student might meet a different kind of him/herself, others, the world, and God, challenging the existing system of knowledge. This journey is liberating if the existing worldview or perspectives that act as stumbling blocks can be overcome and the students find themselves at a pivotal point to take new steps in their life journeys. Ultimately, the students will begin to be aware that they are not just the objects of the learning process; they are the subjects of their destiny. This can be called "a sacred encounter" in that the students may be able to start off on a new phase of their life journey; this encounter of the students and their innermost

---

20 The key concepts are extracted from two literatures. Judith Berling, "Getting Out of the Way: A Strategy for Engaging Students in Collaborative Learning," *Teaching Theology and Religion* 1, no.1 (1998): 31-35; Parker Palmer, *Courage to Teach: Exploring the Inner Landscape of Teacher's Life* (San Francisco: Jossey-Bass, 2007).

place may be a crux experience for their life vocation. To create this atmosphere, the class will facilitate diverse learning paths ranging from spatial, linguistic, and bodily-kinesthetic to musical and visual ways, providing opportunities for the students to use and develop all the different types of intelligence. The various pedagogies assist students to discover their own uniqueness as well as to develop the strengths and talents in which they may discover their vocation.[21]

The third sacred encounter is explored within the teacher's inner journey. The above two encounters require the lecturer to recognize that the teacher is a co-participant in the class process. The teacher is a mediator between the knower and the known, between the learner and the subject to be learned. A teacher, not some theory, is the living link in the epistemological chain. The way a teacher plays the mediator role conveys an epistemology to the student, both an approach to knowing and an approach to living. As a co-facilitator, the teacher might be able to bear witness to the leaf that sprouts from new seeds and to the plants that will grow and be reaped later.

This journey can be called sacred since the teacher can play a "midwife" role in accompanying or being present in a crucial process or moment when new fruits or outcomes are borne through painful reflection or contemplation with tears of joy. It is sacred in that the teacher cannot anticipate the outcomes of the student's inner journey. The experience as a midwife may be transformative for the lecturer, since interactions with the students can authentically or spontaneously

---

21 This idea is constructed based upon Howard Gardner and Paulo Freire. Howard Gardner, *Multiple Intelligences: New Horizon in Theory and Practices* (New York: BasicBook, 2006),,; Paulo Freire, *Pedagogy of the Oppressed* (New York: Continuum, 2010).

create a more mature or improved understanding of the self as well as of the world. The sacred experience establishes the groundwork for the educational formation for the teacher in the next journey of the three sacred encounters with different students.

V. Practical Implications of the Sacred Encounters

Given the problem-posing model of Paulo Freire and the constructed idea of the sacred encounters, I will delineate a class model which can be applicable in Korean college education.[22] This class is in a college setting, and the students would preferably be juniors and seniors who are seriously concerned about their life vocation and professional occupation after graduation. The developmental psychological theories for this class will be grounded with Perry's scheme of the development of discursive maturity among college students.[23] This class is designed partially to assist those college students who are experiencing puzzlement or uncertainty due to the multiplicity and relativism of value systems and worldviews. Its target audience or participants will be college students seeking a safe space on campus to share their painful or despairing experiences and situations and to face the deci-

---

22 The main concept is derived partially from several spiritual practices of the Christian tradition and partially from the "Seeking Peace Poetry and Meditation" workshop of Street Poets Inc. which is a poetry-based peace-making organization located in L.A. (USA) and dedicated to the creative process as a force for individual and community transformation.

23 William G. Perry, *Forms of Intellectual and Ethical Development in the College Years* (New York: Holt, Rinehart & Winston, 1970).

sion-making process about their life direction, such as job searching, financial affordability, or identity crises.

The classroom is decorated with a water altar surrounded by chairs in a circle. At the first class, the students come into the classroom and are invited to introduce themselves with their name in a clockwise direction. As soon as the name is heard, the class is asked to repeat loudly the person's name as an echo. This is intended to confirm or affirm their presence in this group. Echoing one's name is a symbolic collective action that sends the message of acceptance of the person's life. Next, a 20-minute meditation or contemplation is held with a guided direction. The meditation or contemplation will be introduced in the first meeting, explaining that it is not derived from any specific religious tradition; it is designed as a simple spiritual practice. The class will take advantage of the centering moment of the contemplation with a sense of presence that is a critical component in the class's formation.

Next, the lecturer introduces the students to the method of writing a poem collectively. They are asked to write the title and the first line of the poem and pass it to the next person. The next person is invited to compose a line of the poem, which therefore contains as many lines as there are participants. The collective work of composing a poem inclusively joins each participant as co-author or co-creator. The process of writing the poem is very empowering and critical since it prompts the sense of creating art, which is considered as one of the appropriate ways to tender the hardened mind and soul. Participation in creating art is considered crucial in embodying thoughts or ideas as well as in venting inner feelings. A significant concept is embedded in the form of collective artworks: interdependence or interrelatedness is inherent in human beings. The collective work of composing the poem intrinsically teaches the participants that human nature and human activities are interdependent, interrelated, and interconnected. This realization can be extended into the realization that violence or the perpetration of a crime is undesirable but is an inherent part of human nature or society. This recognition does not lead to a skeptical or negative view of the human capacity. Instead, it can call upon us to gaze at violence or perpetration of a crime as reflecting the human potential, since all human beings are supposed to take care of destructiveness or cruelty. This calls out human solidarity against destructive violence.

This concept of human solidarity is more embodied and practiced in the next step of the class. The participants are asked to grab a small stone located under the altar and drop them in the water bowl at the altar. I believe this step is the crux of the class in terms of eliciting social awareness, prompting a contemplative response, creating a safe space, and educating the mind to be nonviolent. The students join to share and confess their firsthand experiences of violence, social injustice, brokenness, guilt, suffering, and associated emotions or feelings such as anger, fear, anguish, hatred, sorrow, grief, etc. The sharing process does not lead the students to vent their emotions or thoughts in a destructive or distorted way but educates them to have a simple observer attitude, bearing witness to the social injustice, perpetration of crime, violence, and suffering. Here, the power of the class is found to be spiritually relevant. The process of composing the collective poem has tendered and shifted their perspectives or attitudes, and it helps them establish the framework for constructive or compassionate perspectives or attitudes toward destructiveness or brokenness. At the last session of the class, all students are asked to join in a blessing ceremony with a simple word, song, prayer, in whatever form of spiritual practice they choose.

This class formation and pedagogy embody the three different sacred encounters as described above: the encounter between the students and the teacher; the encounter between the student's mind and the world; and the encounter within the teacher's inner journey. The desired goal of this class formation with spiritual elements is embraced actively in pedagogy skills, as follow. At first, it empowers the college students to use the skills and to speak out in their own voices through enhancing the self-awareness so that they can cultivate constructive ways to encounter themselves and others, discouraging destructive or harmful ways. Second, it inspires the students to facilitate their own experiences with endowed knowledge so that they can nurture the integration of the learning process. Third, it creates a safe space in which all students are welcomed and accepted so they can share the entirety of their experiences, including the despair, pain, and suffering of their daily lives so that their lives will be affirmed and confirmed in collective or communal ways. And lastly, it cultivates the concept of human interdependence, of an interrelated or interconnected reality, so that it empowers the college student to have a sense of human solidarity, which can be a substantial resource for them to rely upon when facing painful or negative experiences.

These types of class model are designed to promote the sacred encounter with the teacher's inner work since as a facilitator, not a simple lecturer, the teacher bears the witness of the painful or agonizing experiences the students bring up in the class. Bearing witness as co-mediator or co-facilitator of the class, the teacher is asked to engage with the lived experiences of the students and to respond appropriately with professional knowledge and epistemological commitments. This could stimulate the self of the teacher to perceive the real lives of the students as well as to be motivated to analyze and to transform it through academic engagement. The inner lived experiences of the teacher are valuable resources for preparing and designing the next class.

This type of class formation spiritually oriented could not equip college students with certain skills or knowledge to discover good job or occupation. It is not plausible in mass-sized classes, which have usually been held in Korean colleges; only 15-25 students could be affordable. This is my conviction however that the class with sacred encounters could contribute not only to prevent them from suicidal attempts and other types of emotional brokenness related to social issues, but also to change their mind or value systems toward their identity, vocation, and value system. This college education harnessed with spiritual practices will cultivate and enhance the pedagogical methods fundamentally with appropriate and relevant approaches toward the college student's lives and their spirituality.

VI. Conclusion

This research was conducted because of the critical awareness that the high suicide rates of Korean college students partially reflect upon the inappropriateness of college class formation and the lack of integration of the information newly gained in class with the lived experiences of the students. In this research, the banking model in pedagogy is criticized as the model for current class formation in the Korean educational context because its limited capacity to embrace the lived experiences of college students has aggravated the problems immensely. In contrast, the problem-posing model from the framework of Paulo Freire is described as more appropriate for spiritually relevant education. The necessity to introduce and facilitate spirituality in higher education and college classrooms is verified using the work of several theorists, and this opens a door to construct a theoretical stepping-stone for the critical concept, the "sacred encounters," in relation to the spirituality of higher education. Three sacred encounters are desired in college education and in pedagogical approaches to college students since they promote transformative experiences and integration in the lives of students facing critical matters such as identity formation related to professional occupation, stress due to financial issues, and vocational struggles. And the idea of the sacred encounters is practically embodied in the model of a college class portrayed in the last section for the sake of verifying its relevancy and applicability in higher education.

One of the potential contributions of this research will be recognized with the fact that it initiates the research on the way in which spirituality could be employed or embodied in pedagogical methods or class formation in college settings. This study also brings up at least couple of research topics as its sequences. First, it may be able to discover how the pedagogy spiritually informed and practiced equipped could affect on reducing the suicidal attempts or destructive symptoms in a psychological sphere of college students. Second, it incurs the questions of how prayer or contemplation could be relevantly employed or used in various settings of class formation.

Bibliography

김남석. "대학선교와 기독교 영성교육: 표층교육을 넘어 심층 교육으로." 『대학과 선교』 21 (2011), 83-108.

오성주. "한국 청소년 교육을 위한 포스트 파울러 프레어리의 의식화 교육론에 관한 소고." 『기독교교육논총』 37 (2014), 115-144

조용훈. "기독교대학선교와 대학생의 가치관에 대한 한 연구." 『대학과 선교』 19 (2010), 149-174.

Berling, Judith. "Getting Out of the Way: A Strategy for Engaging Students in Collaborative Learning." *Teaching Theology and Religion* 1, no.1 (1998): 31-35.

Capeheart-Meningall, Jennifer. "Role of Spirituality and Spiritual Development in Student Life Outside the Classroom." In *Spirituality in Higher Education*. Edited by Sherry L. Hoppe and Bruce W. Speck. San NFrancisco: Jossey-Bass, 2005.

Chickering, Arthur W, Jon C Dalton, and Liesa Stamm. Forward. *Encouraging Authenticity and Spirituality in Higher Education*. Edited by Alexander Astin. San Francisco, Jossey-Bass, 2006.

Erikson, Erik. *Childhood and Society*. New York: Norton, 1950.

Freire, Paulo. *Pedagogy of the Oppressed*, 30th Anniversary edition. New York: Continuum, 2010.

Gardner, Howard. *Multiple Intelligences: New Horizon in Theory and Practices*. New York: BasicBook, 2006.

Hoppe, Sherry L., & Bruce W. Speck, eds. *Searching for Spirituality in Higher Education*. New York: Peter Lang Publishing, Inc., 2007.

Keeling, Richard, P. *Learning Reconsidered: A Campus-wide Focus on the Student Experience*. Washington, DC: American College Personnel Association and National Association of Student Personnel Administrators, 2004.

Merton, Thomas. *Love and Living*. New York: Farrar, Straus & Giroux, 1979.

Palmer, Parker J. *To Know As We Are Known: A Spirituality of Education*. San Francisco: Harper & Row, 1983.

_____. *Courage to Teach: Exploring the Inner Landscape of Teacher's Life*. San Francisco, CA: Jossey-Bass, 2007.

Perry, William G. *Forms of Intellectual and Ethical Development in the College*

Years. New York: Holt, Rinehart & Winston, 1970.

Tisdell, Elizabeth. *Exploring Spirituality and Culture in Adult and Higher Education*. San Francisco: Jossey-Bass, 2003.

Electric resources

정지웅, 장예진. "대학생을 자살케 하는 나라에서 대학생으로 살기." 경향신문, 2011년 9월 28일자 http://news.khan.co.kr/kh_news/khan_art_view.html?artid=201109280944112&code=900312. Accessed April 10, 2016.

Organization for Economic Co-operation Development. "Suicide." In OECD Factbook 2010. http://www.oecd-ilibrary.org/sites/factbook-2010en/11/03 /01/index.html?contentType=/ns/StatisticalPublication,/ns/Chapter&itemId=/ content/capter/factbook-2010-90 en&containerItemId=/content/serial/1814 7364&accessItemIds=&mimeType=text/html. Accessed April 23, 2016.

9

From Choosing to Being Chosen:

Spiritual Formation for Life Vocation of College Students

I. Introduction

Self-Identity and life vocation are named as primary interest or life goal for college or university students.[1] Most college students expect to discover who they are and what they desires to do or to be for their future life. Answering these questions will be one of the primary purposes for college students (or young adults) and the higher educational system exists for assisting them to answer them. The various psychological researches and sociological evidences demonstrated the significance of college years (or young adulthood) in human developmental process. Jeffrey Arnett reported the ground-shaking research that the college students or young adults are still handling identity resolution as main topic in developmental process, which Eick Erikson regarded as characteristics of adolescence in 1960s.[2] Religious sociologists

---

1 This study defines the college or university students who are enrolled in two years or 4 years higher education program including graduate program. Hereafter, the term of "college students" will represent all of those who are categorized within the social context.

2 Jeffrey Jensen Arnett. *Emerging Adulthood: The Winding Road from the Late Teens through the*

also confirm generational difference that identity and vocation issues should be taken into seriously consideration on the basis of the meaning-making procedure at college years.[3]

One of the primary goals in Christian college education is to cultivate the spiritual or inner life of the student to discover the way in which they would grow cognitively and nurture their self comprehensively based upon holistic growth of Jesus' self at young ages.[4] The higher education has originated from Christian values that the psychological growth and spiritual development besides professional knowledge or field skills should be provided based upon Christian conviction that human development is holistic or integrating[5]. The chaplain ministry of the college or universities could be identified as the major system not only to present the students with the Christian teachings and values, but also to provide the spiritual care service. It covers comprehensive components within Christian chaplain ministry works ranging from providing Christian counseling and chapel, Christian classes, to encouraging evangelical groups and facilitating prayer meetings and communal worship service. The chaplain ministry in higher education

Twenties. New York; Oxford: Oxford University Press, 2004.

3 Carolyn McNamara Barry and Mona M. Abo-Zeba, "Seeing the Forest and the Trees: How Emerging Adults Navigate Meaning-Making," in *Emerging Adults' Religiousness and Spirituality: Meaning-Making in an Age of Transition*, eds. by Carolyn M. Barry and Mona M. Abo-Zena, (New York, NY: Oxford University Press, 2014), 3-7.

4 cf. Luke 2:52.

5 Elizabeth J. Tisdell, "Introduction: Culture, Spirituality, and Adult Learning," in *Exploring Spirituality and Culture in Adult and Higher Education* (San Francisco: Jossey-Bass, 2003), 3-23. Yong-Suk Jung delineates core features of the Christian spirituality as embodied experiences of faith emphasizing the integration of all components of human life aspects. 정용석, "기독교영성연구,"『대학과 선교』15 (2008), 11-49.

context should be equipped with spiritual resources for prompting the students into spiritual growth and development.

Several education researches about the spiritual education or formation for young adulthood have been executed in Korean Christian context, and they shared common concern that young adult peoples have shown less interests in the education or formation program held in Korean Churches. Eun-Ha Cho suggests Korean churches that comprehensive approaches, including psychological and sociocultural frames, to developmental understanding of young adults should be equipped within spiritual education.[6] Kwang-Yool Kim also proposes the Protestant spirituality, holistic mature of faith, comprehensive response to various areas of live as new paradigm for Christian spiritual education of young adulthood.[7] They would not however engage with sufficient endeavor to present the way in which the spiritual formation could be practiced and shaped and spiritual practices could influence upon spiritual development or changes of young adults.

This research will claim a college students' life vocation is correlated with self-identity issues, and spiritual practices and direction could offer critical foundation in prompting the spiritual journey to life vocation which will lead into spiritual growth and development in the college student years. This study will make endeavor to demonstrate that a Christian chaplain equipped with spiritual guidance and spiritual practices could effectively assist college students to discover life vocation which entails to spiritual growth and development. It presupposes

---

6 조은하, "청년기를 위한 영성훈련,"『신학과 현장』17 (2007), 241-261.

7 김광률, "청년영성교육을 위한 교회의 과제,"『기독교교육논총』30 (2012), 199-224.

two preliminary assumptions: the first is the strong association between the identity issues and life vocation. That implies, Christian college students' pursuit for life vocation should be grounded in identifying oneself as Christian. And secondly, those who are standing firmly in Christian identity are likely to discover their life vocation.

Given the presuppositions, this research will make effort to answer several questions: how could the spiritual educational program be provided to strengthen Christian identity and vocation in college education? What kinds of spiritual care model would be plausible for college ministry or university chaplain ministry? How could spiritual practices or direction be embodied in practical ministry for college student? In what ways could the spiritual practice and guidance help college students elicit spiritual growing or spiritual development? Then how could the spiritual guidance enhance or facilitate to develop the sense of identity and life vocation?

Three research procedures will be taking place. First, the socio-religious characteristics of the college students will be explored with theoretical evidences from sociology and religious sociological researches. Spiritual education in Christian colleges or university will be surveyed as the way to portray Korean context and its limitation. At next, the spiritual practice will be introduced based upon the spiritual tradition of Ignatius of Loyola focusing mainly on the *examen* prayer and the concept of *Election*. It will provide spiritual resources to build up the spiritual guidance and direction on Christian chaplain ministry and spiritual care for college or university students. At last, an actual account will be presented as an example of how a college student searched for life vocation through the spiritual practices and direction in chaplain ministry context. This will turn out to propose the way in which spiritual practices and directions would play a complementary role in cultivating the spiritual care within college chaplain ministry.

II. College Education and Spiritual Lives: Life Vocation of the Students

1. Current Soil for College Students

The significance of young adulthood in human developmental span has been prominent since Erikson's theory of human identity (1960).[8] Since then, the various researches and diverse disciplinary approaches to the young adults or college students have gained its greater attention from scholarly and professional circles ranging from developmental psychology, neurobiology, education to sociology.[9] The new academic dialogue commonly circled the sociological term, 'emerging adulthood' specifically indicating those of people of age 18 into the third decade of life (twenties), which was coined by Jeffrey Arnett.

Arguing the necessity of new term of the generation in contemporary society, Arnett enumerates four features of the emerging adulthood leaving adolescence and moving into an through their twenties, including college and graduate students.[10] He defines the emerging

---

8 Erik Erikson, Childhood and Society (New York, N.Y.: W.W.Norton & Company, 1963).

9 Larry J. Nelson, "Series Forward," *Emerging Adults' Religiousness and Spirituality: Meaning-Making in an Age of Transition*, eds. by Carolyn M. Barry and Mona M. Abo-Zena, (New York, NY: Oxford University Press, 2014), vii-ix; Barry and Abo-Zena, Introduction, 4.

10 Jeffrey J. Arnett, *Emerging Adulthood: the Winding Road from the Late Teens through the Twenties*.

adulthood as **feeling in-between** as first feature because they do not see themselves as either adolescents or adults. Secondly **identity exploration** is characterized especially in the areas of work, love, and worldview. The emerging adults seek for new experiences related with their life direction and interests. At third, the emerging adults **focus on the self** not as the way to be self-centered, but simply to show lack of obligations to others, and it leads into constructing new relationship outsides family or adolescent friends. **Instability** is featured as fourth evidenced by changes of direction in residential status, relationships, work and education. Arnett claims that despite of transitional difficulties and unstable status, the emerging adults contain full of possibilities with optimism in the potential to steer their lives in any number of desired directions.

The studies of religiousness and spirituality of the emerging adulthood have responded to the sociological descriptions which has embodied with Christian religious society. Barry and Abo-Zena argue that meaning making is most crucial topic in emerging adults especially the third decade of human life span (the twenties).[11] It is noteworthy of their research that for those who have not constructively engaged with meaning making procedure or who have insufficiently emotional and relational supports in emerging adulthood, they are unlikely to have good transition and may result in developmental detriments or disadvantages. It implies it is likely that meaning making process cultivated by relevant resources will lead into good transition in emerging adult

---

11 Barry and Abo-Zena, "Seeing the Forest and the Trees: How Emerging Adults Navigate Meaning Making," 4-6.

years.

Barry and Abo-Zena are questioning however the emerging adults readily tend to pursue psychological division between religion and spirituality. The emerging adults would not intend to separate religiousness from spirituality as much as psychological research mishap.[12] Rather they seek for integrating both components in their various aspect of life such as friendships, family, and faith communities. They seem to argue against Arnett's positive or romantic description of emerging adulthood from the religious perspectives. Without constructive engagement with meaning making procedure during the emerging adulthood, the optimistic or positive prospective would be in vain or meaningless. They state the meaning making procedure should be gone through by integrating their lives all life components during the emerging adulthood. This is part of the reasons college students are getting increased the interest in spirituality not religion.

According to Glanzer, Hill and Ream, it is important to acknowledge first the religious landscape in American colleges and higher education context significantly diverse, multifaceted, and less preferential to religious teaching as exclusive truth.[13] One valuable findings discovered in their research is that junior college students (3rd year-college student) have shown more interest in spiritual lives as a result of college life than the freshmen. At next, evangelical Christian campus are having a greater influence upon the moral and religious

---

12 Ibid., 6.

13 Perry L. Glanzer, Jonathan Hill and Todd C. Ream, "Changing Souls: Higher Education's Influence Upon the Religious Lives of Emerging Adults," in *Emerging Adults' Religiousness and Spirituality*, 162

lives of their students than secular campuses, but not spirituality.[14] The research demonstrates that first that highly Christian students show the lack of internal capacity to integrate their religiousness with spirituality. At third, despite the fact that the inner desire of the college students to search for spirituality is increased, the current religious resources and its approaches of the campus ministry strategy would not effective or fruitful.

It seems to resonate with the studies of Astin et al (2011) that the students at evangelical Christian colleges and universities are often the high-scoring outliers in their studies of spirituality.[15] Focusing on religious teachings would not properly equip the Christian students with holistic or comprehensive perspectives in the life context, rather fragment their spirituality with critical life issue including the endeavor to seek for life vocation. This is empirical evidence that integrating rigid religious teachings and spirituality is uneasy in spiritual care for college student.

2. Centrality of Vocation and Identity for College Students

In what ways the college ministry could then be effectively assisting them to seek for meaning making process so as to take successful transition in college years? And what kinds of spiritual needs should be met for integrating various aspects of young adulthood life within

---

14 Ibid., 161.

15 Alexander W. Austin, Helen S. Austin & Jennifer A. Lindholm, *Cultivating the Spirit: How College Can Enhance Student's Inner Lives* (San Francisco, CA: Jossey-Bass), 110-114. With quantitative research methods, Austin and his fellow scholars surveyed about 15,000 of UCLA college student and their religious or spiritual life for three years.

college ministry in campus? What sort of spiritual care could help the emerging adults to cultivate inner life so that going through meaning making or life vocation?

Worthwhile to pay attention to a research is discovered by Feenstra and Brouwer noting remarkably that "connection between identity development in Christian college students and their understanding of vocation, as well as correlation between vocational understanding, and spiritual development and college adjustment[16]." Employing the Christian Vocation Assessment Scale, a sociological quantitative research method, they collected, analyzed and presented the data and outcomes. Their investigation demonstrates that identity development and development of vocation follow parallel paths. That is, when Christian college students have explored and made commitments to particular identities they also seek for a greater understanding of their Christian identity and of God's purpose for their life. That is, having a greater understanding of one's Christian identity and God's purpose may impact identity development and vocational understanding.

Setran and Kiesling also stresses that vocation should be one of the primary domains in spiritual formation for emerging adults.[17] They convincingly point out that while emerging adults search for a deep sense of purpose in their lives, they fail searching for life vocation by replacing it with a paid occupation. Unless acknowledging the differ-

---

16 Jennifer S. Feenstra and Amanda M. Brouwer, "Christian Vocation: Defining Relations With Identity Status, College Adjustment, and Spirituality," *Journal of Psychology and Theology*, vol.36, no.2 (2008): 83-93.

17 David Setran and Chris Kiesling, *Spiritual Formation in Emerging Adulthood: A Practical Theology for College and Young Adult Ministry* (Grand Rapids, Michigan: Baker Academic, 2013), 111-138.

ence between a paid job with life vocation, they would not take inner journey to discover the deep sense of purpose of their lives. Vocation, they quote, means we are "called by the One who in calling us to be calls us to service."[18] It implies that the vocational discernment for emerging adults should embrace self-identity issues and furthermore it should expand to bigger question, "whose am I?" or "Where am I belong to?" therefore the life vocation discernment is inevitably following with deeper awareness of self-identity and the calling within divine providence.[19] Vocation indicates the primary calling from divine call wherever we are and whatever we do. Therefore, the correct question to ask for emerging adults is not, "what will I do for a career?" but "what will I do with my life?"

3. College Ministry for Vocation and its Limitation

Let us turn to our primary context, the chaplain ministry of Christian colleges or university in Korea. It is not uneasy to discover the scholarly or theoretical endeavor to suggest or devise a new and effective model of spiritual education or formation in Christian college or chaplain ministry.[20] Among them, Mira Han's article has distinctively presented spiritual education model for Christian colleges or universities as one of the most relevant in Korean context.[21] At first she jux-

---

18 Ibid., 119. It is originally quoted from Walter Brueggemann, "Covenanting as Human Vocation," Interpretation 33, no.2 (1979): 125.

19 Ibid., 119-120.

20 김미경, "기독대학생의 기독교 정체성 확립을 위한 삶의 접근요인과 과정 탐색,"『교육과학연구』제43집 제1호 (2011): 211-234; 최윤영, "대학생의 신앙성숙도와 자아정체감에 관한 연구: 기독교 영성프로그램 참여 전후 비교를 중심으로"『신앙과 학문』17(3): 293-317.

21 한미라, "포스트모던시대의 핵심 인재개발을 위한 기독교 영성교육모델: 기독교대학의 위기극복을 위한

taposes the different expectation or understanding between what the global companies seek for and what the Christian leadership purses. And she points out that the difference or discrepancy could elicit critical question or academic direction of Christian colleges drifting education methods between its Christian identification and its effective purpose.

She takes good account of the significance of holistic approaches or methods in educating the students not only to educate comparative leaderships through global standard-embedded education with postmodern method without undermining the core values of Christian leaderships. She proposes five pedagogical methods for spiritual education: building up relationship-eliciting environment, making up own life documentary film, interviewing oneself as significant others, writing his/her own epitaph and mapping life direction. These methods are believed to cultivate the sense of spiritual components in students' live so that it could bring up an integrating model of spiritual education in Christian college education.

Despite of its plausibility and practicality of the model and theoretical reconstruction of Christian identity in college education, I am still questioning about the way in which they would be relevant in nurturing college students with creative and holistic characteristics of spiritual education integrating spiritual lives with rest of the life experiences. Even if they are likely to offer good chance for meaning making procedure, it does not provide any specific direction of the way in which college educators or advisors guide them into new meaning.

대안" 『기독교교육정보』 제35집 69-113.

In addition, it does not give sufficient opportunity to cultivate spiritual sense of identity and to seek for life vocation, which should be primary goal in spiritual formation and education in college chaplain ministry.

This research acknowledges necessity of specific and practical guidelines for college student to experience spiritual sense of identity and vocational discernment. How could it bring up or where could it take place? Spiritual practices or direction in Christian tradition would present complementary or alternative approaches to the primary concern of this research: life vocation for college students or emerging adults. Spiritual practices based upon the concept of Ignatius of Loyola's daily examen prayer and election will be explored as formative method for spiritual formation of life vocation for college students.

III. Spiritual Wisdom for Vocation: Ignatius of Loyola

The *Spiritual Exercise* composed by Ignatius of Loyola has been known as the paramount in Christian spiritual practice tradition since he collected, complied and integrated the diverse methods of spiritual practices within the volume.[22] He facilitated various methods of prayers in Christian spiritual traditions to help the giver or the receiver of the spiritual exercise ranging from examination of conscience, meditation, and contemplation, vocal or mental prayer to imaginative prayer with the Bible. The comprehensive or detail explanation of the

---

22 George E. Ganss, S.J. ed. *Ignatius of Loyola: The Spiritual Exercises and Selected Works* (Mahwah, N.J.: Paulist Press, 1991).

classical text is not primary aim in this research so that it is not productive to make effort to explain when, what where and how the text would work. The primary concern of this research starts with what Ignatius delineates the purpose of the classic text in the introduction: "seek and find God's will in the ordering of our life for the salvation of our soul,"[*Spiritual Exercises*, 1] on the context of life vocation related with Christian identity in college spiritual developmental process.

Ignatius is consistently pointing out in several corner of the classical text that the primary purpose to give or join spiritual retreat or practices is to discover the will of God and to make a decision given to a person.[23] Its significance is revealed by the fact that he made up for spiritual practices for making choice in the Second week [SE, 168-189].[24] Locating it at the end of the Second week in which retreatant and directee are following the journey of Jesus' life in imaginative meditation and contemplation, he implicitly emphasizes that one faces a moment to make a choice or decision to follow the way of Jesus or not.

This research will selectively facilitate two spiritual practices from the Spiritual Exercises for cultivating inner works or reflection which elicits college students to engage with Christian identity and life vocation question. The first spiritual practice is the "examen prayer" introduced as daily spiritual practice for the students. Ignatius introduced a

---

23 It was written taking account of specific context, which is spiritual retreat. Discovering the wills of God for community is not specified in text. Many literatures in the spiritual practice circle however indicate that the practices are also well equipped for community.

24 In Ignatian context, the term 'week' does not indicate the chronological sense; it implies the second stage or next step in which retreatant meditates and contemplates the life story of Jesus.

prayer named "Examination of Conscience" in First week as the crucial way to harness practitioners with scrutinizing the inner parts or examining internal movements. Within spiritual exercise and any other spiritual practices, a desire is considered as the core subject to examine including thoughts, feelings and deeds since Ignatius believed it is the ultimate locus in which human soul is responded to spirit-good or evil. Human inner parts and internal inclinations are affected or embodied actually by desires. That is, when human soul is led by good spirit, it is purified or liberated from physical or materialistic desires. The desire to follow the Jesus' way and the leading of Holy Spirit would be increasing. On the other hand, when the desire is occupied by evil or bad spirit, the desire toward Jesus would be decreasing or reluctant. The former is called consolation, and the latter desolation, which will be dealt detail in *Election* in which spiritual discernment will briefly be utilized.

1. *Examen* Prayer

Ignatius was firmly believe that the Examination of Consciousness (Examen prayer, hereafter) should be initial step in contemplative prayer which leads one's soul to thorough and comprehensive examination of thoughts [33-37], words [38-41], and deeds [42] individual moment of life. It is to be cautious that this prayer is intended not to meditate the literary meaning of thoughts, words, or deeds, but to use them as vehicle to examine where the desire moves or responded to. It results in awakening one's soul by figuring out which spirit, good or evil, influence much on the soul. He also guides detail contents of what procedures should be involved in the examen prayer [43].

The examen prayer starts with gratitude to God and highest grace and everlasting love of Christ. At next petition needs to take place in prayer for taking away one's sins so that a soul is invited to let the desires or attempts go and to stay in spiritual indifference, confessing it is all about something God does. At third step, the internal inclination or consolation and desolation movement is consistently reviewed and monitored. It helps a soul examine which moments are filled with joy, love, hopes, and compassion, or which one with anxieties, fears, resistance and so on. In the fourth, a soul is supposed to ask for forgiveness and restoring the sacred desires with Holy Spirit. At last, a soul is asked to move forward the future wit hope rather than staying in past sins or faults preparing the life of future in reliance upon God's grace.

This spiritual practice prepares college students to reflect their daily life in their prayer as well as to deepen the contemplative aspect of prayer, which cultivates the spiritual awareness of the divine presence, prevailed in their moment of life. The examen prayer helps shape the students' spiritual formation of the way in which he or she identify themselves as Christian fundamentally through which their soul commit in the deeper or meaningful relationship with Jesus.[25] In addition, this prayer could be practiced without spiritual retreat in allotted extra schedule, which can be employed in daily routine life of campus. The legitimacy and appropriateness is stemmed from the nineteenth annotation of Spiritual Exercises in which a person or a student who is

---

25 Ignatius presupposes the examen prayer is accompany with meditating the biblical accounts of Jesus' life and ministry. Following the Ignatian guidance, this study presumes that the spiritual fruits of the examen prayer will be multiplied when a daily meditation of Bible.

involved in public affairs or pressing routine life could perform the exercise everyday [19].

2. *Election*, the Discerned Choice

The next spiritual practice is *Election*, which means making a choice or decision. As aforementioned, a choice making following the wills of God in individual lives is the primary goal of the prayer and embodiment of spiritual practices in daily life. Ignatius notes first spiritual indifference as prerequisite for the prayer of election since otherwise, he or she switch an end with a means. It states for instance making a choice to marriage or to become a minister is not the end to Ignatius, but it should be a means to praise and serve God. Without indifference or spiritual freedom, one could confuse with which is essential or primary purpose of life, not marriage nor ministry, but live by the will of God [169-170].

Making a sound and good election for a soul would take three different ways or procedures according to Ignatius. The first kind of election is the making choice without any hesitation or doubt, but distinctively clear or manifested with God's will [175]. He exemplifies what St. Paul and St. Matthew experienced when they followed Jesus Christ. Michele Ivens commentates it with four features: "1) the experiences has an 'object,' something is shown; 2) the will is moved by God himself to follow the way shown; 3) there is no doubt, or possibility of doubt, on either of the above points; 4) the situation is the same as the vocations of St. Paul and St. Matthew."[26] Iven states precaution in this

---

26 Michele Ivens, *Understanding the Spiritual Exercises Text and Commentary; a Handbook for*

election however that it does not indicate explicitly the dramatic quality of the Damascus road experiences to Paul. It also does not precisely mention consolation: comprehensive understanding is necessary.

The second election is a choice making within the consolation-desolation frame. In the second week of spiritual exercise context, a retreatant or directee have meditated and contemplated imaginatively the biblical accounts and they are asked to follow the Jesus' ways. The spiritual engagement with the contemplation incurs various feelings, thoughts, desires, memories and imagination, through which he or she realize that it is the deep influences of good or bad spirits manifest: consolation and desolation. The role of discernment here is essential for offering guidelines or methods between two internal dynamics. The "rules of the discernment of spirits" [313-336] should be acknowledged, learned and facilitated for both director and directee. Critical is to discern which spirits has affected upon one's inner desires and to be aware of the way in which he or she make a decision or choice based upon discerning God's will. Again, keeping consolation is not the ultimate goal of the discernment, but making a good choice according to God's will.

Last method of election demands more delicate skills or deliberate methods to find out the will of God in making a decision. This type of choice making starts with awareness that the inner movement or internal desires would not be affected distinctively one way or the other. At this time, it is critical to clearly articulate what the choices or decisions would be made through this discernment process: which

---

Retreat Directors (Leominster: Gracewing, 1998), 135-136.

direction would I be take for my life vocation, college or not?; which major should I take in college department, economic or management? What kinds of community service experiences would be helping me to discern my life vocation? When could I marriage, before or after graduation degree?

This articulation of the discerning questions asks for facilitating more cognitive or reasoning capacities in discerning the wills of God to prevent them from being captivated or captured by unclear spirits or desires. It uses with the frame of "pro and con" through which each option or choice would generate advantages or disadvantages, and benefits or loss. It demands therefore deliberate description, comprehensive analysis of the current situation, thorough speculation of outcomes or results followed by each choice or decision. The data or information through the pro and the con will be brought up into contemplative prayer time so that it incurs internal inclination or inner movement to certain direction or option through consolative or desolative dynamics. If one goes through consolation consistently toward specific options regardless of compensating for the cons, it would be safe to make a choice or decision. If the desolative movement might be coming up within one's inner movement, it is improper to make a rush decision and they rather wait for a while until consolation would be gained. Most importantly, the check and balance between the options or directions should be magnified by cognitive or reasoning engagement.

For developed or detail method, Ignatius offers the additional guideline for the third election procedure with three imaginative situations [185-187]. First, a student is asked to imagine a person whom he or she have never seen or known before and he or she would have same situation and context with discernment process. Then ask for imagining what kinds of advices of comments you would give to him or her. At second, one is ask to imaginatively contemplate what sorts of spiritual guides or advices would be given for the decision or choice at "a death bed." Thirdly, one is supposed to imagine oneself standing in the judgment day or final day of the human history, and ask for contemplating what choice or decision could be made. These imaginative contemplations elicit clearer internal movements or desires between consolation and desolation, so that it is not only taking away of the ambiguity within a soul but also helping one's desire to perceive the will of God equipped with indifference and spiritual freedom.

Ignatius clarifies again that these whole procedure should set its purpose not for fulfilling one's desire or oneself, but for the greater glory of God and the greater perfection of his or her soul [185], which is a purified desire and spiritual freedom. Any choices or decision made through the discernment process might make effort to obtain the confirmation of the will of God toward one's life direction, a life vocation, which ultimately glorifies God for the greater.

At next step, we will examine the way in which the two spiritual practices, the examen prayer and election, could be facilitated as prayer method to foster the Christian identity and to discover the life vocation for the college students. The essential guidelines of spiritual direction in prompting spiritual formation will be briefly surveyed with an actual account of a college student's spiritual journey of life vocation. It will also prove the college chaplain could play a critical role in inviting and leading the college student's spiritual journey as spiritual director.

IV. From Choosing to Being Chosen: Spiritual Formation for College Students

This research sets the presumption that college students' effort to discover the life vocation should come together with the identity, especially Christian identity since Christian vocational discernment involves a growing awareness of God's purpose to choose their lives. As Sharon Parks has expressed, those in this age group often miss out on the formation of "big enough" questions and dreams to guide their adult vocational lives.[27] The discernment process for life vocation of emerging adults should be understood in bigger frame than personal interests, specific jobs or occupations. In addition, those who commits with emerging adults should embrace a comprehensive purpose of God toward individual lives that encompasses all of life. A real account will be unfolded below telling the way in which spiritual practices could foster the sense of Christian identity and entail to discover the life vocation in college ministry through spiritual direction.[28]

Y is a female senior college student planning the graduation in next semester. She faced to make decision or choice whether she would apply for the academic graduation degree program in university, or join a social volunteer service and its community which she desire to

---

27 Sharon Daloz Park, *Big Questions, Worthy Dreams: Mentoring Young Adults in Their Search For Meaning, Purpose and Faith* (San Francisco; Jossey-Bass, 2000), 138.

28 This research recognizes that spiritual practices held with some college students could not effectively work in universal sense. Depending on the religious background, historical experiences with church, dogmatic orientation or social standings, the outcomes of this practice would be varies.

engage with for future. Her life vocation seems to be directed readily to become a community organizer who would facilitate community activities through organizing or coordinating the community members and its systems. She expressed excitement about her plan to become a community organizer telling that she has found out the specific job position in the society. She was not sure however when she would engage in the community organizer position because of several realistic obstacles hampering her to make a decision or choice promptly.

First, she admitted that she has gone through little experiences or intern careers on the social field of community organizer except the social community membership during the college years. She did not know where she would start with to become a social organizer. It became the main inner sources for her to feel afraid or hesitant of jumping in the social life right after the college graduation next year. Secondly she acknowledged her desire to study more about the social field in academic program so that she could be more qualified to become a professional organizer for future. At third, she also noticed her parents' expectation for her to get a job which was not related with her intended job, since they thought the social organizer would be a tough job for female in Korean society with lack of reward (little salary). Given the situation, she wanted to discern her life vocation and how much related the community organizer with her life vocation would be.

As a chaplain and spiritual director, beginning the spiritual journey about Y's life vocation I invited her to narrow down choices or options for discernment process. The "narrowing" discernment context provides a solid and consistent locus for careful thought and fruitful labor, helping her avoid fragmenting her diverse gift and passion. She articulated then her discernment question as such: "which route would be better for me to prepare the life vocation, entering an academic graduation program in social works after the college graduation, or joining in a social community to engage readily with the field of social organizer?"

At the first session of spiritual direction, She was oriented with two foundations of the spiritual practices and prayers: daily meditation of Bible and examen prayer. She was led to meditate the gospel of Mark every morning and night followed by the examen prayer. And the spiritual journaling was introduced as complementary but critical tool to record her inner journey or movements, which would become critical resources to discern the wills of God toward her. The weekly spiritual direction sessions for next five weeks were provided not only to guide her spiritual journey, but also to facilitate the election prayer for discerning her life vocation. In every session, her spiritual movement between consolation and desolation was checked. This spiritual journey informed as process was introduced not as a vehicle to make a certain choice or decision, but as a discernment process to know the wills of God, ultimately to dwell in the presence of God within one's given context and life situation.

In the second, discernment of spirits was introduced and assists her to see the inner movements between consolation and desolation. The daily bible meditation and examen prayer was getting settled at her routine life and the spiritual journal was more encouraged. The primary role of spiritual director at this stage is to assist to strengthen the personal relationship with Jesus through the biblical accounts and to figure out the way in which the spirit of Jesus, Holy Spirit has been perceived in her daily life in her examen prayer.

At the third session, she shared her profound experiences of challenging from Jesus' calling to her while meditating the Mark 10:22-27. The biblical accounts portrayed a young rich man asking Jesus of what he should do after observing the laws. Jesus invited him to sell all belongings or properties, follow him. The young rich man went away. Y mentioned about being a real Christian or Jesus' discipline. This challenges prompted her to think of the deeper dimension of being discipline of Jesus in existential or spiritual level. In the conversation with spiritual director, she began realizing that the Jesus' calling to be a disciple asked her not to do something about Jesus, but to engage intimate relationship with Jesus via following his way. The primary role of spiritual director would not lead with certain agenda, but help her see whether her inner desire would be cling to or move toward the wills or the desires of God. The session ended by inviting Y to contemplate what she was newly aware of being a discipline of Jesus as well as doing the works of Jesus or being a follower.

Fourth session was meaningful for Y in terms that she shared her new awareness of the true meaning of the vocation. She told that the matter of vocation was not about what she would do, but about how deeply or genuinely she would engage in the intimate relationship with Jesus and God. And the relationship with Jesus indicated her authentic identity as Christian or Jesus' disciple. The spiritual indifference or freedom was confirmed as good foundation in her spiritual ground. Then, she was asked to detail the description of "pro and con" in each options or choices given, and to discern which options would affect certain inner movements, consolation or desolation, entailed by the

Holy Spirits or Evil Spirits.

The particular questions for discernment based upon the *Election* from Igantius' *Spiritual Exercises* took place at the second half of the session. Y was asked to portray the imaginary situation following the Ignatian guidance: "imagine a person whom you have never seen or known before, and he or she would have same situation and context with discernment process. Then ask for imagining what kinds of advices of comments you would give to him or her." At second, Y was asked to imaginatively contemplate what sorts of spiritual guides or advices would be given for the decision or choice at "her death bed." Thirdly, Y was invited to imagine herself standing in the judgment day or final day of the human history, and ask for contemplating what choice or decision could be made. Unnecessary to answer the questions at the place, she was asked to contemplate repetitively in her meditation and prayer next week. It informed her that it would elicit different inner movement which would be an important resources for discerning the wills of God within her life.

In the fifth session, she shared her new awareness that the life vocation would not cling to what kinds of job or occupation she would be called, but about praising God who choose her to live out the faith and the good news in given life situation. While talking about the discernment, she readily confessed that she understood the life vocation was not choosing something for herself, but about the spiritual realization of God's choice for her life: "from choosing to being chosen." The life vocation was regarded as the spiritual journey to discern where the wills of God would be embedded in her life stories or experiences and to embody it in her given situation. So that she readily confessed that no matter what she would do, how her life would be shaped, her life focus moved from what she desired to discern what God wants her to do in daily life. The inner desires seems to be matched with spiritual indifference, which is holy desire to tune her life with the wills of God. The chaplain invited her to check her inner desire soon after her new awareness, and she confessed the increase of desire to know God's wills and to dwell in the presence of God.

In the second half of the session, Her inner movements via scrutinizing the options had consistently directed to the second option, which was "joining the social community first." Her inner freedom did not swayed or diminished even if her choice would not satisfy her parents' expectation. She made resolution to convince her parents first regarding her choice, but she was encouraged to have conversation with parents as the spiritual way to confirm the wills of God in her choice making process. Important to inform that her discernment could not finalized, but be tentative until the intrinsic will of God would not be confirmed in our actual life context.

The five-week spiritual journey with Y presented critical implications in the research topic. First, it is demonstrated that the strong correlation between the life vocation and Christian identity. Seeking for life vocation is supposed to stand firmly in the self-identity as Christian. It is highly likely that Christian college students who look for life vocation should be grounded in one's inner identity as Christian especially in the individual relationship with Jesus the Lord. Without establishing the Christian identity, colleges' effort to look for life vocation would be vulnerable or fruitless.

At second, the examen prayer method with daily bible meditation is essential requisite for spiritual journey to figure out the inner dynamics, especially in prompting the consolation and desolation dynamics. At third, the three contemplative questions drew out of the election practice could play critical role in discerning the inner movements or desires and in figuring out the way in which holy spirit or evil has affected in Y's soul each. They became the primary data or resources to analyze the desire of Y's soul and discern where the spiritual indifference should be checked. Lastly, it is critical to prove that the spiritual formation of the life vocation for college student could be plausible in chaplain ministry. It could not only enhance the sense of Christian identity of Christian college students, but also to foster the intrinsic capacity of a college student to discern their life vocation through the spiritual practices and prayer methods, which entails into the spiritual formation for college students.

The critical role of the chaplain as spiritual director could not be neglected. The spiritual or ministerial understanding of the spiritual direction could cultivate and empower the ministries of Christian chaplain in college. It is regretful that the limitation of the research scope could not spare to explain the Christian ministry of spiritual direction in more details. But the primary function of spiritual director in the spiritual direction ministry is to walk with an directee and his or her spiritual journey without direct intervention or psycho-analytic approaches. The presence of God is the main foundation for director to rely on, and its primary role should be understood not as the initiator in the relationship, but as spiritual coordinator who would assist a soul to be staying in the presence of God and dwelling in Holy Spirit[29]. The most appropriate metaphor representing the role of spiritual director is a "midwife," who is present with the pain of a mother and assists her to give a birth of baby.

Second prerequisite for the spiritual direction ministry is that it presumes the intimate relationship and truth-based relationship with directee. The model of the relationship thus is "soul mates," or "spiritual companion" rather than teacher-student relationship, which demands for spiritual awareness that Holy Spirit is working and speaking within individual spiritual journey. The last limitation or challenge of the spiritual formation of the life vocation for college students will be found in cultural or religious prejudices or bias about the contemplative prayer. It is undeniable that the contemplation has been still considered as Buddhist spiritual tradition such as Zen in Korean Christian context. Thus, the comprehensive orientation of the contemplation within Christian historical context and spiritual heritage should be preceded and oriented before actual engagement in spiritual practices.

V. Conclusion

This research made endeavor to present the way in which spiritual care could be facilitated in college chaplain ministry in Korean context. The self-identity issues and life vocation has been featured as

---

29 William A. Barry and William J. Connolly, *The Practice of Spiritual Direction* (New York: HarperCollins Publishers, 1986), 3-12.

most important subject of the college student according to the socio-psychological studies. Current religious education or approaches however would not present reliable spiritual resources for college students especially in integrating various aspects of life as well as in helping discover the life vocation. The concept of election in Ignatius' Spiritual Exercises is introduced as spiritual practice to lead college student into the contemplative prayer for seeking for life vocation. The examen prayer, daily bible reading and spiritual journaling are proposed as constitutive components not only in figuring out the inner movements, but also in discerning the wills of God and the movements of spirits. The rules of spiritual discernment by Ignatius are also facilitated in guiding a college student to engage with the intrinsic dynamics between consolation and desolation.

The actual account of spiritual journey with a college student has presented as an example of how the spiritual practices with spiritual direction could cultivate a soul to discover the life vocation by discerning the wills of God specifically toward the life and soul. It is meaningful to verify that the life vocation should come with searching for one's identity. That is, establishing or consolidating a Christian identity should be grounded in finding out one's life vocation, especially the intimate relationship with God. The spiritual practices are critical to cultivate the sense of Christian identity and the calling from God toward the life. It crucially reconstructed the understanding of the vocation as such "from choosing to be chosen" by God in given situation. It also demonstrated the way in which the spiritual practices and direction could nurture the chaplain ministry in Korean context. Despite of several challenges or limitation, this can be effective spiritual care method to foster the sense of spiritual formation of Korean college student regarding Christian identity and the life vocation.

Bibliography

Arnett, Jeffrey Jensen. *Emerging Adulthood: The Winding Road from the Late Teens through the Twenties*. New York; Oxford: Oxford University Press, 2004.

Austin, Alexander W., Helen S. Austin and Jennifer A. Lindholm, *Cultivating the Spirit: How College Can Enhance Student's Inner Lives*. San Francisco, CA: Jossey-Bass, 2011.

Barry, Carolyn McNamara and Mona M. Abo-Zeba. "Seeing the Forest and the Trees: How Emerging Adults Navigate Meaning-Making." *Emerging Adults' Religiousness and Spirituality: Meaning-Making in an Age of Transition*. Edited by Carolyn M. Barry and Mona M. Abo-Zena. New York, NY: Oxford University Press, 2014.

Barry, William A. and William J. Connolly, *The Practice of Spiritual Direction* (New York: HarperCollins Publishers, 1986.

Erikson, Erik. *Childhood and Society*. New York, N.Y.: W.W.Norton & Company, 1963.

Feenstra, Jennifer S. and Amanda M. Brouwer. "Christian Vocation: Defining Relations With Identity Status, College Adjustment, and Spirituality." *Journal of Psychology and Theology*, vol.36, no.2 (2008): 83-93.

Ganss, George E. S.J. ed. *Ignatius of Loyola: The Spiritual Exercises and Selected Works*. Mahwah, N.J.: Paulist Press, 1991.

Glanzer, Perry L., Jonathan Hill and Todd C. Ream. "Changing Souls: Higher Education's Influence Upon the Religious Lives of Emerging Adults." in *Emerging Adults' Religiousness and Spirituality: Meaning-Making in an Age of Transition*. Edited by Carolyn M. Barry and Mona M. Abo-Zena. New York, NY: Oxford University Press, 2014.

Ivens, Michele. *Understanding the Spiritual Exercises Text and Commentary: a Handbook for Retreat Directors*. Leominster: Gracewing, 1998.

Nelson, Larry J. "Series Forward," *Emerging Adults' Religiousness and Spirituality: Making in an Age of Transition*. Edited by Carolyn M. Barry and Mona M. Abo-Zena. New York, NY: Oxford University Press, 2014.

Park, Sharon Daloz. *Big Questions, Worthy Dreams: Mentoring Young Adults in Their Search For Meaning, Purpose and Faith*. San Francisco; Jossey-Bass, 2000.

Setran, David and Chris Kiesling. *Spiritual Formation in Emerging Adulthood: A Practical Theology for College and Young Adult Ministry*. Grand Rapids, Michigan: Baker Academic, 2013.

Tisdell, Elizabeth J. *Exploring Spirituality and Culture in Adult and Higher Education*. San Francisco: Jossey-Bass, 2003.

Wuthnow, Robert. *After The Baby Boomers: How Twenty- and Thirty-Somethings Are Shaping the Future of American Religion*. Princeton, New Jersey: Princeton University Press, 2007.

김미경. "기독대학생의 기독교 정체성 확립을 위한 삶의 접근요인과 과정 탐색." 『교육과학연구』 제43집 제1호 (2011): 211-234.

김광률. "청년영성교육을 위한 교회의 과제." 『기독교교육논총』 제30집 (2012): 199-224.

정용석. "기독교영성연구." 『대학과 선교』 제15집 (2008): 11-49.

조은하. "청년기를 위한 영성교육." 『신학과 현장』 제17집 (2007): 241-261.

최윤영. "대학생의 신앙성숙도와 자아정체감에 관한 연구: 기독교 영성프로그램 참여 전후 비교를 중심으로." 『신앙과 학문』 17(3): 293-317.

한미라. "포스트모던시대의 핵심 인재개발을 위한 기독교 영성교육모델: 기독교 대학의 위기극복을 위한 대안." 『기독교교육정보』 제35집 69-113.

10

Thomas Merton on Christian Nonviolence:

Toward a Social Embodiment of Compassion

I. Introduction

As of April 2017, the political tension and military maneuvering was reaching new heights in the Korean peninsula. Freezing the diplomat conversation and mutual interaction, the North Korean government has executed a nuclear missile test several times ranging to some part of U.S. territory, and the international media have comprehensively delivered aggressive and threatening situations about North Korea's military actions. The South Korean government has eventually closed the joint Korean industrial park in Kaesong, North Korea, in which has played symbolical role in creating peace movement between two governments. Furthermore, the international tension around the Korean peninsula has aggravated among multiple countries, especially U.S.A. and China, regarding the THAAD system, which is allegedly targeting the military structures in the mainland of China as critical portion of the missile system among the military ally of three countries, USA, Japan & Korea. This also increased the political and military tension along the Korean peninsula.

To make it worse, some Korean Protestant ministers have been making claims from church podiums about the inevitability of the use of military power to subdue North Korea's naive aggressiveness in the context of South Korea's political instability facing the unprecedented presidential election process due to the impeachment of the last president, Park Geun-Hye. One of the Old Testament biblical commentaries are employed to support this stance depicting the story of the Israelites entering Canaan, saying that this was about Yahweh's conquering the gentiles or other deities. The conquest story in the book of Joshua is highly likely to be interpreted as a salvific event so that violent actions are still seen as a legitimate way to fulfill the promise of Yahweh. No doubt, this interpretation would implicitly tolerate violent actions within the church and further unconsciously encourage people to engage with violent action or words in the name of God within the Korean church context. Due to my critical awareness of the inappropriateness of messages from the religious community that provoke violence, as well as my belief in that peace-making is one of the primary roles of the church in contemporary times, this research sets the premise that compassion should be the most legitimate spiritual resource in the formulation or reshaping of the social spirituality of Korean Christian churches.

In his metaphysical reconstruction of the theological unfolding of compassion, Oliver Davies asserts that compassion is the heart of the Christian response to God as well as the divine kenotic ontological presence in the relationship with human nature.[1] In his book *Compassion*, Henri Nouwen and his colleagues describe the intimate relationship of God's loving compassion that is interwoven in our humanness. Exploring the spiritual meaning of the Greek, *splangchnizomai*, Nouwen notes that compassion is "such a deep, central, and powerful emotion . . . that it can only be described as a movement of the womb of God."[2] Compassion is a womb-like experience, the innermost triggering from the deepest part of a being. There, humans by divine grace are invited to participate in God's deepest motions in holistic ways—physical, emotional, cognitive, and spiritual—through acts of kindness and consideration, forgiveness and healing to others. By its nature, compassion takes seriously into account the social or moral dimension of human nature since its spiritual quality tends to be embodied in the interpersonal and social sphere.

The spiritual formation of Korean churches has been influenced considerably by the liberation themes of the Israelites' exodus, and this had a comprehensive impact on its social engagement and actions in political persecution and oppression during the Japanese occupation period (1910-1945). For instance, it is well known that in 1919, 16 out of 33 leaders of the March First Independence Movement were identified as Christians. Even though the Christian contribution to engagement in social modernization or political democratization in Korean society has partially been acknowledged during the second half of the

---

1 Oliver Davies, *Theology of Compassion: Metaphysics of Difference and the Renewal of Tradition* (Grand Rapids, MI: William B. Eerdmans Publishing Co., 2001), 232-253.

2 Donald P. McNeill, Douglas A. Morrison, and Henri Nouwen, *Compassion: A Reflection on the Christian Life* (Garden City, NY: Image Books, 1983), 16.

last century, the lack of social consciousness or disintegration of the churches within the society has been blamed on the core loss of the social credibility of Korean churches in first two decades of third millennium. Some theological scholars maintain there is a historical calling of the Korean churches to solidifying social or communal spirituality by reshaping or renewing churches' spiritual formation.[3]

This awareness arouses the following fundamental questions: How should Korean Christians respond to the current situation of increasing tension or potential violence in the Korean peninsula? In what ways is the concept of nonviolence integral to the Christian faith tradition? As a strategic and deliberate way of Christian compassion, how could the nonviolence be used to cultivate social compassion within Korean society throughout the peninsula?

This research will make endeavor to demonstrate in part that for Thomas Merton, contemplation is the fundamental foundation where compassion is later incarnated as a spiritual component of nonviolence, and in part that the authenticity of nonviolence can be verified by the way in which it is incarnated by compassion. It will envision the enhancement of the societal spiritual formation of Korean Christian communities engaging further with practical tactics.

---

3 Cf) 이학준, "한국교회, 패러다임을 바꿔야 산다," (서울: 새물결플러스, 2011); 양희송, "다시, 프로테스탄트," (서울: 복있는 사람들, 2013).

II. Merton's Path toward Compassion

It is beyond doubt that Thomas Merton is one of the spiritual figures in modern history who has had a great influence upon the Christian spiritual life. Since his first book, *The Seven Storey Mountain*, was published in 1948, his writings and spirituality have immensely stimulated or reshaped the spiritual life of contemporary Christians within the western hemisphere, even continuing after his death. It was not accidental that his autobiography was phenomenally popular, since it spelled out his sense of spiritual hunger, bewilderment, outrage, and deep longings of contemporary life after the Second World War. The spiritual journey and writings of this contemplative writer still resonate deeply in all corners of the world among people seeking authentic spiritual lives.

It should initially be noted that Merton was simultaneously renowned as a social critic as well as a writer. Even though he earned his initial fame as a contemplative writer in the Unites States, living in the Abbey of Gethsemani, a Trappist monastery as a monk, his writings and voice not only invited people into the contemplative life but also had an extensive audience concerned about social issues such as the Cold War, nuclear arms, the civil rights movement, poverty, etc. His eager endeavor to raise an international alarm about the destructive power of nuclear weapons and to participate in social action seems to be closely related to his life-long experiences. As Merton commented on the historical context of his life, "in a year of a great war . . . I came into the world"[4]; his lifespan (1915 – 1968) bore witness to the most violent years of human history, ranging from World Wars 1 and 2 to the Korean War, the civil rights movement, and the Vietnam War. He had gradually become aware of the destructive violence that culminated in atomic power, and he also perceived that it created tension, terror, fear, and anxiety, deteriorating human dignity and the spiritual life. And he voiced the concept of nonviolence as a spiritual response to the perpetuation of violence, advocating the way of nonviolence as a means to achieve Christian vocation in contemporary society.[5]

Remarkably, however, Merton's voice of social criticism and his concept of nonviolence did not show up in the early stages of his spiritual journey. Rather, young Merton was more austere and modest to the world, according to his autobiographical account of his conversion to Catholicism and his entrance into the Trappist monastery. But, Merton's spiritual journey was sufficiently mature to turn his attention to the critical situation facing human beings, especially in the 1950s and 1960s. He engaged deeply with nonviolence and introduced it as the Christian spiritual strategy in a violent world. It is actually the crux of the integration of his spiritual journey that had started as a contemplative monk engaged in an *apophatic* quest to be united with God, seeking for the true self, freed from the false, and moving into embracing the world as the crucial locus for integrating contemplation with action. The concept of nonviolence can be considered not only

---

4 Thomas Merton, *the Seven Storey Mountain* (Garden City, NY: Image Books, 1970), 3.

5 The comprehensive survey about Merton's thoughts on nonviolence can be discovered in 오방식, "토마스 머튼의 비폭력에 대한 연구," 『59회 실천신학회 정기학술회 자료집』(2016), 51-70.

as the social embodiment but also as the integrative form of Merton's spirituality.[6]

What does it mean, that nonviolence was a spirituality of compassion for Merton?[7] Little specific argument has been articulated that Merton devised or theologized the concept of compassion as part of his conceptual construction[8]; instead, it permeated his whole spirituality. This research starts with the idea that his social critique was "the fruit of a compassion learned through a life of monastic ascesis and contemplation."[9] I assume that Merton's concept of nonviolence is implicitly embedded in the core of his spirituality of compassion. Surveying Merton's principle ideas concerning topics such as contemplation, self, human nature, and solidarity will uncover the intrinsic value of compassion within the spiritual milieu of Thomas Merton. By doing so, this inquiry will argue that Merton's idea of nonviolence can be considered the maturing embodiment of his spirituality of compas-

---

6 Cf) Shannon indicates that nonviolence for Merton is regarded as "a way of life," and this research agrees fully with the concept. William Shannon, *Passion for Peace: Reflections on War and Nonviolence* (New York: Crossroad Publishing Company, 2006), 4.

7 This study defines the spirituality of compassion as internal awareness or spiritual status quo as one discovers the self and God in contemplation. Contemplation leads into the new awareness of mutual reciprocity and interconnectedness among the self, others, the world within the presence of God. It asks a soul to share the essential experiences ranging from joy, sorrow, suffers, desire, needs, etc. of the peoples, which is a critical vehicle to commit oneself to God in given context. As the same way God would engage with the people and the world, a soul would feel and act in nonviolent way.

8 This research is well aware that Merton's literatures have extrinsically mentioned the indispensable link between action and contemplation. However, the contribution of this research is more weighed upon explicitly articulating its dynamics and association between the spirituality of compassion and the nonviolence in Merton's writings.

9 John Eudes Bamberger, Preface, in Henri Nouwen, *Pray to Live: Thomas Merton: A Contemplative Critic* (Notre Dame: Fides/Claretian, 1972), ix.

sion. I will also argue that integrating Merton's spiritual wisdom in the Korean Protestant context is appropriate for cultivating Christian compassion.

1. Contemplative Life

The reason *The Seven Storey Mountain* moved contemporary readers might stem from Merton's unique journey to explore the meaning of life through his inner journey. Introducing the contemplative life, Merton called upon modern people initially to discover the value of solitude and silence.[10] He characterized American culture as being geared to generate noise so as to distract us from remaining silent. The modern lifestyle encourages us to keep running without allowing us to face ourselves; the noisy life prevents us from facing the depths of our being. This causes us to consistently ignore the inner self, distracting us with the surface that is untrue to our own reality. And this causes the flight from the self and further flight from God. For Merton, the silence is more than a prerequisite for the inner journey in order to take away the superficial, external mask that noisy society wears. The primary function of silence is to protect us from flight from a deep encounter with our true inner self and with the true God. For Merton, silence enables us to get a truer and more balanced perspective on our own lives and enables us to pursue the whole reality by drawing together the scattered and fragmented pieces of reality.

In this sense, solitude is not withdrawal from ordinary life, but it is its constitutive ground in which we reconstruct a simple, holistic

---

10 Thomas Merton, *Love and Living* (New York: Farrar, Straus & Giroux, 1979), 40-43.

but unpretentious inner life structure. Merton is firmly convinced that solitude is a spiritual resource out of which the divine love and grace flows and simultaneously an inner practice to renounce our illusion as well as to cultivate our capacity to stretch out to meet others' needs with genuine compassion.[11]

For Merton, the original purpose of silence and solitude is to invite the reader into the life of contemplation as well as to discover himself and God within. And the life of contemplation features three dimensions. At first, contemplation is defined as a life fully awake, fully aware that it is alive.[12] Contemplation initiates the true encounter with God in which a soul is touched by God, and it seems to sprout the seed, to lead into new awareness or awakening of a soul to the Real within all that is real.

In contemplation, the encounter with God next asks the soul to respond to a call from Him/Her who is the ground of all beings, speak through and for the ground, and let God's unsounded voice resonate in the inmost center of our own being. Contemplation as the encounter and call thus cannot be executed by the external self; only the inner self can respond to the ground of all being.[13] Focusing upon the encounter of the inner self with God, Merton mentions *le point vierge*, literally meaning "the virgin point." This is a metaphor for portraying the place deep within that is the point of our encounter with God and other beings (the world).[14] There exists some place within the innermost where

---

11 Merton, *Loving and Living*, 23-24.

12 Thomas Merton, *New Seeds of Contemplation* (New York: New Directions Book), 1-5.

13 Merton, *New Seeds of Contemplation*, 7.

14 Ibid., 37-39; Thomas Merton, *Conjectures of A Guilty Bystander* (New York: Doubleday,

a contingent being depends upon divine love, and as a soul approaches *le point vierge*, the soul eventually can discover God the same way God discover us. This implies that human nature is inherently made to rely upon divine love, and this reliance is the legitimate response to the call from God. There, God will discover us, and God's discovery of our being brings about a new being and a new mind within the innermost place. This is articulated by Merton's term that the contemplation of the human being is able to participate in the contemplation of God.[15] That is, contemplation for God is to discover Godself in us, and contemplation for the human being is to be discovered by God.

Contemplation facilitates therefore the new establishment of one's identity.[16] Exemplifying a tree glorifying God by being a tree, Merton maintains that God's discovery of a soul asked us to be ourselves, rather than become self-defined or conditioned by an external illusory framework. The way to glorify God is to be what God wants us to be here and now. As God discovers us in contemplation, our finding out our true identity is taking place, and we discover our reality, our own happiness, and our salvation. This feature of contemplation is represented in biblical and theological terms as rebirth.[17] Merton reformulates it with the significant transition from the false (old) self to the true (new) self. To be born again is to be liberated from egoism, beyond selfishness, beyond individuality in Christ. For Merton, contemplation prompts the spiritual awakening of mind and heart so that the false self

---

1989), 158.

15 Ibid., 39.

16 Ibid., 29-36.

17 Merton, *Love and Living*, 192-195.

might be considered as illusion, generated by the external, fragmented, or decentralized perception, and the true self emerges and is aware of the real in Spirit. Remarkably enough, Merton remarks that the rebirth in contemplation is not one-time event, but a continuous dynamic of inner renewal. Rebirth in the Spirit is supposed to happen repeatedly through successive stages of spiritual development.

In fact, Thomas Merton specifically links compassion with contemplation. "Contemplation is out of the question for anyone who does not try to cultivate compassion for other [people]".[18] However, it must not also be ignored that contemplation is the fundamental foundation where compassion is later incarnated as a spiritual component of nonviolence. Rather, the authenticity of contemplation can be verified by the way in which it is incarnated in compassion in engaging further with the world. Merton's contemplative life actually embodied the encouragement of the spirit of compassion in his encounters with the world.

2. Transforming Vision to Compassion

Merton's contemplative life faced a critical opportunity to be changed, was asked to be expanded when he walked around the corner of Fourth and Walnut street in downtown Louisville.[19] He remembered it as an overwhelming realization and new awareness that all the peo-

---

18 William Shannon, Christine Bochen, and Patrick F. O'Connell, *The Thomas Merton Encyclopedia*, (Maryknoll, N.Y.: Orbis Books, 2002), 73. It is originated from Merton, *New Seeds of Contemplation*, 77.

19 Thomas Merton, *Conjectures of a Guilty Bystander* (New York: Image Books, 1968), 153-156.

ple on this street had never met him or personally connected with him, but that these total strangers were not alien. This new awareness or awakening came out of three realizations. First, he had not left behind the world. Merton initially thought he had left behind the world when he entered the monastery. His pursuit of solitude and contemplation implied a distancing of himself from the world. However, this new awareness drew him into the transforming vision that the world is the locus to be embraced in contemplation. And second, he was stunned by the realization that all strangers also belong to God, just as he did. Merton was awakened to the fact that people are not different from each other, that this is actually an illusory perception given by the world of technology, mass media, revolutions, etc. He noted, "liberation from an illusory difference was such a relief and such a joy to me. . . . Thank God, thank God that I am like other men, that I am only a man among others."[20] The third and last realization was that Merton's sense of responsibility for the people and the world was increased once he was convinced that his solitude had a place in the world. By claiming, "there are no strangers!" Merton embraced the people in the world as his brother and sisters.[21] This awareness played a crucial role in constructing his rudimentary ideas about social critics, human solidarity, and the peace movement. He mentioned that contemplative perception is grounded in God's eyes, in a contemplative view upon the people and the world. This led him to speculate about people and about a world without hatred, cruelty, and greed, since he was grounded in

---

20 Merton, *Conjectures of a Guilty Bystander*, 154.

21 Ibid., 155.

God's view, perspective, heart, grace and love.

Here we are able to discover the spiritual component related to compassion in Merton's spirituality. His sense of compassion came out of contemplation, an expanded awakening that all people and their lives can be seen from God's eyes. Contemplation from the perspective of God's eyes and heart assisted Merton to embrace and approach the world and its people with compassion. Contemplative compassion led him to a true awareness that "we have to renounce our selfish and limited self and enter into a whole new kind of existence, discovering an inner center of motivation and love which makes us see ourselves and everything else in an entirely new light."[22] He asserted, therefore, the necessity to engage with contemporary problems or issues around the world, such as Aushwitz, Hiroshima, Vietnam, and Korean peninsula, as an authentic way of contemplative life. He seems to claim that committing himself to international problems is the genuine way to live out the contemplative life. His transforming vision had gradually guided him to see the centrality of the appalling violence that was still being perpetrated in the world. Since the summer of 1961, he was firmly convinced that the primary task of Christian living in a violent world is to work for the total abolition of war.[23] And Merton profoundly delineated the roots of war as fear, human instincts, and affection.

Then, what are the constitutive components of the roots of all war?

---

22 Thomas Merton, *Contemplation in a World of Action* (New York: Doubleday, 1971), 173.

23 Thomas Merton, "The Root of War Is Fear," *Catholic Worker* 29 (October 1961): 11-13. Merton deliberately omitted this concept in his book *New Seeds of Contemplation* (Chapter 16) and published it in a journal in order to evade the censor from his religious community.

Merton identifies distrust as the first characteristic of human nature. He seems to be lamenting the fact that humans do not trust one another— they do not even trust themselves. This distrust originates in disbelief in God, the ground of being. Hatred is named as the second origin of the fear. Merton appears to deplore the human reality that our hatred of ourselves is "too deep and too powerful to be consciously faced,"[24] and it prevents us from identifying our sins and from taking accountability for our sins or sinful behaviors. The fear of facing our own sins results not only in minimizing our own, but also prompts us to accuse others for their faults. Human neglect of our sins or faults turns our attention to finding a suitable enemy, a scapegoat who can take on all human faults. The enemy is the cause of every wrong in this world. The third aspect of fear stems from human dishonesty, from the refusal to accept the reality of the goodness that partially existed in others. The distorted human disposition of seeking for a scapegoat ironically uncovers our own malice, intolerance, lack of realism, and ethical and political naiveté.

What is the antidote for human fear that could prevent violence and war? Merton first calls upon human solidarity to liberate us from any malicious endeavor to isolate others. And humans must attempt to accept ourselves, "whether individually or collectively, not only as perfectly good or perfectly bad, but in our mysterious unaccountable mixture of good and evil."[25] This foundational reality should permeate our mutual recognition of the right of others to be respected. How-

---

24 Merton, *New Seeds*, 112.

25 Merton, *New Seeds*, 117.

ever, Merton well acknowledges the weakness of human nature, noting that mutual respect of one another must be grounded in the mysterious power of the love of God, which alone can protect humans against themselves as well as can turn evil into good. Consequently, the antidote to fear is to love God and love others above all—in other words, humility, the human capacity to recognize one's inherent limitations, and acceptance of the co-existence of good and evil in human nature.

This conceptualization of human nature in the face of war and violence shows us the horizon of how compassion is developed and functions within Merton's spirituality. Human solidarity is the primary context where compassion is embodied. Merton asserts that without compassion, one cannot treat others or neighbors as they are. Compassion for Merton is not only an ultimate resource of human solidarity, but also the prime method for subduing the violent response to each other.[26] He clarifies that the more humans differentiate themselves from others, the more violence is likely since the differentiation tends to regard others as enemy or evil. Compassion is based upon human sameness, in the awareness that "they suffer, they feel somewhat as I do when I suffer."[27] This exploration of Merton's transforming spirituality leads to a discussion of his concept of nonviolence in the following section.

---

26 Ibid., 76-77.

27 Ibid., 76.

III. Merton on Nonviolence

This chapter has explored contemplation as the central vision, along with its social implications, in Thomas Merton's spirituality. It is strongly assumed that, for Merton, the path to nonviolence should be grounded critically within the concept of a contemplative life and human solidarity out of the sacred sense of compassion toward human race.

Merton's idea of nonviolence is substantially articulated in his essay "Blessed Are the Meek," in which we can explore several resources for his theoretical construction.[28] First, he clearly elucidates that Christian nonviolence depends upon God and God's word, as opposed to violence that depends entirely on its own calculations. Merton's description of nonviolence starts with the Sermon on the Mount, indicating that the core of nonviolence is humility and meekness, established in the Christian faith in the saving grace and love of Christ. And the indwelling of the Spirit brings forth the reign of God through human participation in the Spirit. The eschatological qualities of meekness and hope discovered in the martyrs and the apostles are identified as the other Christian soil that nurtures nonviolence. These spiritual virtues help one not only to refrain from violent aggression and self-justification, but also to seek justice in the light of final judgment.

---

28 This article was Merton's response to the request of Hildegard Goss-Mayr of the Fellowship of Reconciliation. It was published in Germany in 1966 and in the U.S. in 1967. Thomas Merton, "Blessed are the Meek: Christian Roots of Nonviolence," *The Nonviolence Alternative* (New York, NY: Farrar, Straus & Giroux, 1980), 208-218.

Without understanding Gandhi's concept of nonviolence, we could not fully understand Merton's. The core of Gandhi's nonviolence can be summarized as follows: first, the deepest part of human beings is peaceful, not aggressive; second, love is more natural to humans than hatred; and third, truth is the law of our being. Reading about Gandhi's Hindu ascetic interpretation of western Christianity, Merton was surely convinced that the traditional Christian doctrine of original sin could be comprehended as optimistic since it does not teach that humans are by nature evil, but rather that evil and hatred are an unnatural disorder.[29] In this way, Merton was possibly able to consolidate this view of human nature and its potentiality for unity, dignity, and trustworthiness.

Thus, Merton enumerates seven qualities and strategies for Christian nonviolence that are fundamentally originated from his spirituality of compassion. **First**, Christian nonviolence is aimed at the transformation of the whole world, not one group or region. **Second**, it should be done not for us, but for others and our neighbors, especially the poor and the oppressed as embodiment of compassion. **Third**, nonviolent tactics should be non-violent, non-judgmental, and compassionate, since our nonviolence is rooted in peacemaking. **Fourth**, the primary goal of Christian nonviolence is to show the world that our humility can be an alternative to the existing systems since it is true and our truth in God brings forth genuine peace. **Fifth**, the methods or task for nonviolence is to dissociate ourselves from dishonest, violent,

---

29 Thomas Merton, "Introduction: Gandhi and the One-Eyed Giant," *Gandhi on Nonviolence* (New York: New Directions, 1965), 8-9, 11-13, 23-27.

and inhuman ways and to ground ourselves in the truth we are trying to prove. **Sixth**, as non-violent resisters, we are supposed to learn from our enemies, admitting that our counterparts are not totally inhuman, wrong, cruel, etc. In other words, we are called to love our enemies and to discover the good values even within the people against us, so as to find God in all kinds of human beings. **Seventh**, Merton asserts, the quality of our nonviolence is "decided largely by the purity of the Christian hope behind it."[30] Regarding eschatological qualities, the true quality of our nonviolence is determined by our hope and humility in faith. The hope could prevent us from aggressiveness or actions based in self-justification or self-assurance. Only meekness and humility will fulfill the last but crucial portion of the nonviolence, based in hope from faith and the grace of Christ.

This survey of the components of compassion in Merton's spirituality shows that compassion was integrally embedded in his practical ideas of nonviolence. It must be noted most of all that his concept of human nature derived from the sympathetic or compassionate understanding that truth, love, and peace are placed inherently in the deepest part of human nature. This theological understanding was the existential fruit of Merton's contemplative life, as seen above. He was contemplatively aware of human connectedness and mutual relatedness, and this enabled him to see the human potential for the good and right, which could not be disappeared by the false self. Next, his spirituality of compassion was most distinctively manifested in humility, being sufficiently humble to learn something from the adversary. Merton

---

30 Merton, "Blessed are the Meek," 215.

persuasively argues that the power of contemplation leads us to see truth in reality and guides us to see strengths as well as vulnerabilities within those who are violent, since this helps us not to be trapped by self-deceptive perspectives on the situation. The spiritual capacity to learn from our enemies leads to liberation from the hatred or anger that occupies our minds and hearts, and allows us to become humble with a nonviolent attitude. And third, the spirituality of compassion enables the strategy of nonviolence, for Merton, by taking into consideration the poor, the oppressed, and the marginalized in the world. Nonviolent resistance is chosen as a tactic out of compassion toward the poor, the humble, and the oppressed.

IV. Korean Protestant Nonviolence

Suppose Merton were still alive and could hear the news of the North Korean threats of using a nuclear weapon and the military actions of surrounded countries, how would he respond to this critical situation in the Korean peninsula? In what ways would Merton invite the South Korean churches to commit to a nonviolent response or action as compassion-based spiritual formation? Based on Merton's spirituality, here is a proposed strategy for Christian nonviolence for Korean Protestant churches.

First, Merton says that the contemplative orientation and approach should be prioritized to introduce Christian nonviolence, since contemplation initiates full awareness or awakening to the real, which is hidden or distorted by the illusory or selfish world. Leading into a genuine encounter with God, contemplation allows one to discover one-self within the divine milieu where the external, false or fragmented self is asked to be centered or reborn into the true self.

Second, Merton would urge Korean Christians to explore the value of communal spirituality in their spiritual formation, distancing themselves from being stuck in the pitfall of individual-oriented spiritual formation. This may also entail being more conscious of the limitations of the prosperity gospel, which is culturally related to the shamanistic spiritual orientation and economically capitalistic materialism in the Korean context.[31] More actively, communal spirituality broadens the spiritual spectrum of Korean people to realize the interdependence or interrelatedness among the creatures and within the world. It also reminds Koreans of the Christian vocation to fulfill justice. **Third**, as referred to above, the biblical interpretation justifying violence should be abstained from since it promotes a violent or aggressive attitude toward North Korea. **Fourth**, eschatological hope must be the theological foundation of the nonviolence because our primary function is not to judge the perpetrators; God will do that for all of us at the end of time!

Merton's nonviolence as the spirituality of compassion culminates in the next three practical tactics. **Fifth**, Korean Christians should be encouraged to discover something worthwhile to learn from the perpetrators of violence, their enemies. This is grounded in the confessional conviction that nobody is fully inhumane or evil, because of *Imago*

---

31 David Chung, *Syncretism: The Religious Context of Christian Beginnings in Korea* (Albany, NY: SUNY, 2001).

Dei, so we are called to discover the good even within the people who are against us.

Sixth, nonviolent tactics based upon compassion cultivate our endeavor to understand the desperateness, helplessness, and hopelessness in which our opponents' wounds or shame are embedded. For instance, the aggressive actions and hostile reactions of North Korea are justified in their media as a way to protect their dignity or national identity; this implies that the North Koreans felt that their precious and valued sense of dignity has been disregarded or ignored unfairly or inappropriately by South Korea and the United States.[32] Compassion-based nonviolent tactics could enable us to see the inner and deepest wounds the perpetrators have undergone. Thus, it could guide us to make an effort to understand how the wounds were generated and became triggers for violence and aggression.

Lastly, Christians who practice nonviolence and compassion should not neglect to reflect upon our own violent dispositions and inner wounds. Walter Wink spells out the core strategy of nonviolence, which is to acknowledge that the enemy is our ally in cultivating our spiritual virtue of love, since their perpetration helps me realize our wounds that need to be healed, attended to, and taken care of.[33] Without being aware and taking care of our inner wounds first, we could neither properly control our violent dispositions nor facilitate nonviolence

---

32 North Korea stated its sense of threat on the occasion of a joint military drill held by the South Korean and U.S. armies (Editorial, "North Korea Threatens U.S. Over Joint Military Drill," *New York Times*, February 24, 2013, http://www.nytimes.com/2013/02/24/world/asia/north-korea-threatens-us-over-military-drill.html, accessed March 5, 2017).

33 Walter Wink, *Engaging the Powers: Discernment and Resistance in a World of Domination* (Minneapolis: Fortress Press, 1992).

as the social embodiment of a compassion-based spirituality. That is, Christian nonviolence leads us to turning back to our inner self, the ground of our being, the genuine encounter with God, and the contemplative life as the impetus of a spirituality based in compassion.

V. Conclusion

This research has examined Thomas Merton's nonviolence in the context of the acceleration of military actions around Korean peninsula aroused by the nuclear weapons threat from North Korea and the THAAD settlement within South Korea. This survey made an endeavor to present Christian nonviolence as a compassion-oriented spirituality that could reshape or renew Korean Christian spiritual formation. Contemplation as being fully awake or aware has been introduced as the substantial foundation of compassion and nonviolence. It facilitates not only the reorientation of one's perspective with God's, but also the initiation of a new identity from the false or old self to the true or new self by evading the illusions and distortions the outer world generates. Merton's insight in which he penetrated the nature of human violence guides us to see the human fear and vulnerability behind the war. It enlightens our comprehension of the interrelated or interconnected features of human nature within the contemplative framework, and further it calls upon Christian vocation and human solidarity to accomplish justice and peacemaking by engaging in nonviolent tactics and strategies. The specific guidelines for the Christian vocation of nonviolence, presented by Merton in his article "Blessed are the Meek," were also explored in this chapter. And lastly, the theological and practical strategies of Korean Christian nonviolence were constructively outlined as the social embodiment of compassion-oriented spirituality. This study has endeavored to demonstrate that Merton's idea of nonviolence is the mature, integrated form of his compassion-oriented spirituality. It is still quite applicable to cultivate this form of Christian nonviolence or peacemaking in Korean Christian churches and its social spirituality, and to initiate social integration and international peace-making movement around Korean peninsular.

Bibliography

Primary

Merton, Thomas. "The Root of War is Fear." *Catholic Worker* 29 (October 1961): 11-13.

_____. *Conjectures of a Guilty Bystander*. 1st ed. Garden City, NY: Doubleday, 1966.

_____. *Faith and Violence: Christian Teaching and Christian Practice*. Notre Dame, IN: University of Notre Dame Press, 1968.

_____. *The Seven Storey Mountain*. New York: Octagon Books, 1978.

_____. *The Nonviolence Alternative*. New York, NY: Farrar, Straus & Giroux, 1980.

_____. *Contemplation in a World of Action*. Gethsemani Studies in Psychological and Religious Anthropology. Notre Dame, IN: University of Notre Dame Press, 1998.

_____. *New Seeds of Contemplation*. New York: New Directions Book, 2007.

Merton, Thomas, and Christine M. Bochen. *Thomas Merton: Essential Writings*. Modern Spiritual Masters Series. Maryknoll, NY: Orbis Books, 2000.

Merton, Thomas, and Lawrence Cunningham. *Thomas Merton, Spiritual Master: The Essential Writings*. New York: Paulist Press, 1992.

Merton, Thomas, Patrick Hart, and Jonathan Montaldo. *The Intimate Merton: His Life from His Journals*. 1st ed. San Francisco: HarperSanFrancisco, 1999.

Merton, Thomas, Naomi Burton Stone, and Patrick Hart. *Love and Living*. New York: Farrar, Straus, and Giroux, 1979.

Secondary

양희송. 『다시 프로테스탄트』 서울: 복있는 사람. 2013.

오방식. "토마스 머튼의 비폭력에 대한 연구," 『59회 실천신학회 정기학술회 자료집』(2016), 51-70

이학준. 『한국교회, 패러다임을 바꿔야 산다』 서울: 새물결플러스. 2011.

Apel, William D. *Signs of Peace: The Interfaith Letters of Thomas Merton*. Maryknoll, NY: Orbis Books, 2006.

Chung, David. *Syncretism: The Religious Context of Christian Beginnings in Korea*. Albany, NY: SUNY, 2001.

Culliton, Joseph T. *Non-Violence—Central to Christian Spirituality: Perspectives from Scripture to the Present*. Vol. 8, Toronto Studies in Theology. New York: Edwin Mellen Press, 1982.

Davies, Oliver. *Theology of Compassion: Metaphysics of Difference and the Renewal of Tradition*. Grand Rapids, MI: William B. Eerdmans Publishing Co., 2001.

Givey, David W. *The Social Thought of Thomas Merton: The Way of Nonviolence and Peace for the Future*. Chicago: Franciscan Herald Press, 1983.

Malits, Elena. *The Solitary Explorer: Thomas Merton's Transforming Journey*. 1st ed. San Francisco: Harper & Row, 1980.

McNeil, Donald P., Douglas A. Morrison, and Henri Nouwen, *Compassion: A Reflection on the Christian Life*. Garden City, NY: Image Books, 1983.

Nouwen, Henri. *Pray to Live: Thomas Merton, Contemplative Critic*. Notre Dame: Fides/Claretian, 1972.

Shannon, William. *Passion for Peace: Reflections on War and Nonviolence*. New York: Crossroad Publishing Company, 2006.

Shannon, William, Christine Bochen, and Patrick F. O'Connell. *The Thomas Merton Encyclopedia*. Maryknoll, NY: Orbis Books, 2002.

Wink, Walter. *Engaging the Powers: Discernment and Resistance in a World of Domination*. Minneapolis: Fortress Press, 1992.

Online Resource

Editorial, "North Korea Threatens U.S. Over Joint Military Drill," *New York Times*, February 24, 2013, http://www.nytimes.com/2013/02/24/world/asia/north-korea-threatens-us-over-military-drill.html, accessed March 5, 2017.

11

Grace in the Divine Milieu:

Re-appreciation of Divine Initiatives in Nature

I. Introduction: Appropriating the Divine Grace

The protestant churches all around the world are considerably celebrating the 5th Centennial the year of 2017 and so does the Korean churches. Martin Luther's reformation spirit has globally been reappreciated or reexamined as the local churches have implicated it in given cultural context or historical situations. One of the spiritual convictions on which the reformers stood was that the Divine Grace would be the ultimate foundation in the salvific works of divine Trinity within human history claiming *"Sola Gratia!"* The centrality of divine grace and its historical implication however has been interpreted or employed explicitly to validate human exploitation over the nature during the last several centuries in western churches. One of the most polemic issues for the Reformation in the western Christian history was about the way which how human beings has been engaged with Divine Grace.[1] The

---

1 Alejandro R. Garcia-Rivera, *A Wounded Innocence: Sketches for a Theology of Art* (Collegeville, MN: The Liturgical Press, 2003), 105.

historical development of the theological idea that Grace extends only to the human species has a little distorted that Grace exists exclusively for the salvation of human beings for ages. This traditional theology has permeated into human history and it has played a significant role in justifying human supremacy over Nature during the last centuries.

The environmental crisis, global warming, and natural resources deplete however incurs to ask the question of the validity of the fundamental belief in our contemporary world. "Does the divine Grace manifest within other creatures in right ways?" "Do creatures besides human beings have any capacity to reflect on divine Grace?" "Is this world the explicit platform for human nature to perceive God's grace?" It proceeds to rethink of the critical question, "Is the human being's understanding of divine grace rightly manifesting in the relationship with Nature? "What on earth is Grace?"

This research stands on the belief that the theological concept of grace should firstly be reformulated or reshaped in the contemporary era when the global world has seriously faced by human exploitive activities and its aftermath, global warming, natural resources crises, etc.[2] Renewing the spirituality of Christian reformed church should begin with theological discourse that divine grace calls human responsibility for salvation of the world.

With the conviction that Grace should be neither anthropocentric nor Christianity-centered,[3] this research will make endeavor not only

---

2 Daniel A. Rober, *Recognizing the Gift: Toward a Renewed Theology of Nature and Grace* (Minneapolis, MN: Fortress Press, 2016), ix.

3 According to Carpenter, several eminent theologians including John Hick and James Gustafson are concerned about the fact that grace has become a monopolistic definition

to redefine Divine Grace in relation with Nature, but also to emphasize the relevance of the new definition of Grace to the Reformed theological tradition.[4] This research stands on the conviction that restoring the originality in the relation between divine grace and Nature would be the most appropriate way to appreciate or celebrate the 5th Centennial of Reformation.

This research is executed within practical theological enterprise out of the practical or pastoral awareness that the limited scope of grace in reformed tradition is not assumably workable in ministerial or missional context. My professional experiences as spiritual director have prudently told that appropriating the concept of grace in contemporary society is prerequisite in initiating spiritual practice. The college context has challenged the religious bigotry that human species is the exclusive subject to acknowledge the divine grace on earth. The current notion of grace seems to fail embracing the new knowledge or information from natural scientific disciplines such as neuroscience, natural science or astrophysics so it turns out to lose its relevancy in cultivating human spiritual sense and in transforming spiritual formation. It is constructive theological study in that generational or cultural components will be employed as constitutive component in enhancing theological legitimacy. This research pursues spiritual formation

of Christianity. They resonate with the idea that grace is a theocentric category which opens potentiality of a global theology. Carpenter's *Mind and Grace: Toward an Integral Perspective*. (New York: Crossroads, 1988), 169-171.

4 This research acknowledges that the theological discourse on grace and nature has not been taking place within protestant community as much as the Catholic Church. One of the reasons would be that the protestant theology inquires comprehensively the matter of nature within the anthropological term of "the free will."

of Reformed Christian tradition in that it orients to formulate new type of spirituality relevant to contemporary Christians.[5]

As a practical theological project pursuing the fusion of horizon, this research will integrate multiple disciplinary approaches to the subject matter since it will enhance its academic credibility and practical relevancy.[6] It will firstly explore new research outcomes from neuroscience, which is regarded as groundbreaking in explaining the human mind from the cutting edged scientific enterprise (descriptive). At next, the relation between mind and nature in Bateson's anthropology and Peirce's ontological philosophy will be investigated as the philosophical insights for this discourse (normative). At third, Grave's system theory will be examined as alternative or integrating frame in the relationship between the mind and the body (analysis). Fourthly, aesthetic methodology from Garcia-Rivera and its key concept, "foregrounding" will be introduced and applied for our given context. As a consequence, this research attempts to propose most relevant definition of Divine Grace in new scientific environments, so that it enhances the validation of the Reformation Spirituality with Nature.

---

5 Spiritual formation pursues to renew or transform the lived experiences of one's spirit in given context. Joohyug Lee, "Sacred Encounters: Spirituality in College Education," *University and Mission* 31 (2016): 317-319.

6 Don Browning, *A Fundamental Practical Theology* (Minneapolis, MN: Augsburg Fortress, 1996).

II. The Limitation of Grace in the Reformed Tradition

According to a prominent theologian James Carpenter, God's initiatives are inherently pursuing to interact with and relate to the creature.[7] The unique and mysterious scheme of God's revelation manifests within the universe with Grace being the center of all divine action. In the Protestant theology, however, Grace seems to be veiled behind the curtain of history's main stage, camouflaged in the name of such doctrines as creation, anthropology, and salvation. Despite this veiling, Grace is precisely the central locus for humans to encounter God. Carpenter asserts that the reason Grace is diminished as a subordinate is that "anthropocentric assertiveness" has become the obstacle to expand understanding of Grace as universal in scope.[8]

The Hebrew Bible, regarded as the most instrumental revelation by the Reformed tradition, depicts abundant resources to indicate that God values and takes delight in all creatures. Further, its writings highlight all creatures as being able to give glory to God, their creator, in some ways. For instance, "The heavens are telling the glory of God; and the firmament proclaims his handiwork." (Psalm 19:1 NRSV). In other words, no absolute right of humanity over nature exists; on the contrary, human beings are entrusted with its care and protection.

Within traditional Reformed circle however Grace has seemed to

---

7 James A. Carpenter, *Nature and Grace: Toward an Integral Perspective* (New York: Crossroads, 1988), 166. He also asserts that the Grace of God operates consciously and unconsciously—and biologically as well.

8 Ibid., 166.

be restricted just for human salvation. Reformed theologians' main concern of Grace focuses heavily on human sinfulness, which is a significant distinguishing point from Catholic theology. Emphasizing God's favor on sinful human nature, Grace for Reformed tradition plays a significant role in leading the whole process from justification to salvation. Human sinfulness lost its capability to take part in the salvific process; therefore, faith is that on which human nature must rely. No talk of works without faith could have validity. And while the image of God did belong to man's being at one time, it had been lost through sin. At present nothing good remained in fallen man; all his/her thoughts, words, and deeds were polluted by sin. After all, during the Reformation the focus was leading toward the concept that human nature turns out to be estranged far from Grace.

As spiritual director or pastoral counselor, I have unceasingly experienced at the first hand that the relatively limited scope of grace within reformed tradition has somewhat hampered Christians to experience profoundly the love of God as well as to heal their wounded-ness in their lives. Especially, the anthropocentric frame or dogmatic tendency of divine grace within reformed tradition has implicitly hindered those who are engaged with spiritual practices not only to build up intimate relationship with God, but also to encounter the divine action outside of human sphere such as environment, nature, or universe. It is critical challenge for spiritual director or practitioners since one of the ultimate purposes of spiritual practice is to integrate what one believe with what one experience in holistic sense. The current theological concept of grace in reformed churches seems not to assist their believers to cultivate the confession of grace, rather it somewhat engenders to be fragmented in their faith journey.

Given that, we could discover the relevant critics from Roger Haight regarding the inherent weakness of Luther or Calvin understands of Grace. Firstly, he contends that the weakness of Reformers' concept of Grace stems historically from his partial interpretation of the biblical languages. Even if they attempted to revise the dogmatic interpretation of the Catholic Church which had resulted in catechism, they seemed not to be liberated or overcome from his historical or cultural frames, "the anthropocentric." If God's salvific will is universal, it could be unlikely to limit God's Grace to human existence by seeing the Bible mediated only through the channel of an explicit knowledge of God's Word.[9] Once Grace would be thought of as universal, it ought to be inclusive to whole creatures, rather than belonging solely to human nature.

The second weakness within the Reformed community is related implicitly with its overemphasis on unmerited Grace. It has solidified the dualistic division so that it has turned out to separate human engagement from Grace. It has recently distracted scholars from dialogue with cutting edged sciences demonstrating the interconnectedness between the mind and body, neurons and human thoughts. It challenged the current understanding on human nature within Christian community so that it has lost its relevance or attraction in contemporary world. Christian anthropology has been confronted especially by neuroscience that connects brain function with mind function. Thus, they persuasively assert that "There is interdependence between what

---

9 Roger Haight, *the Experience and Language of Grace* (New York: Paulist Press, 1979), 101.

is happening at the physical level of brain processes and at the level of cognition and behavior."[10]

III. The Challenge from Cognitive Neuroscience

The feeblest point in the Reformed tradition is found in anthropology exclusively based on substantial dualism. Human beings consist of soul and body; the former as a spiritual substance, and the latter as physical. To be sure, this idea has been prevalent in Christian tradition. The early church set down dualism against Gnostic influence. The Neoplatonic worldview in the Middle Ages strongly affected theological formation of dualism. And modern rationalism also is responsible partly for the firm adherence to the idea that human cognitive ability only proves the existence of a being: *cogito, ergo sum*. In particular, the Cartesian worldview of scientific materialism, which views the cosmos as a vast machine composed of independent and externally related pieces, especially promotes fragmentation in relation of human nature with Nature.

In addition, it is generally accepted presumption is that human beings experience duality on a daily basis.[11] Take dieting, for instance. Human beings realize they need a strong will to combat physical temptation even when they desire to lose weight. The physical desire or in-

---

10 Malcolm Jeeves, "Human Nature: an Integrated Picture." in *What about the Soul? Neuroscience and Christian Anthropology*. Edited by Joel B. Green (Nashville: Abindgon, 2004), 173.

11 Ted Peters, "The Soul of Trans-Humanism" in *Dialog: A Journal of Theology*, Vol. 44, no. 4 (Winter 2005), 386-7.

stinct could mainly be governed by a mind controlling, which validating the common assumption that physical sphere should be spiritual or internal one. The dualistic experience of human nature convinces that this world consists of spiritual and physical nature.

Neuroscientists would say *No* to that assumption. Joseph LeDoux, a cognitive scientist, establishes his work on the materialistic hypothesis that the mind is a product of the brain; accordingly, he attempts to demonstrate how the brain makes the mind possible. Within neuroscientific frame LeDoux investigates to study unconscious brain processes located underneath consciousness by saying "Cognitive neuroscientists have been very successful in relating perception, attention, memory, and thinking to underlying mechanisms in the brain," he emphasizes.[12] For him, "Every brain has billions of neurons that together make trillions of synaptic connections among one another." [13] The way in which information transfers within a single neuron is an electrical process, but at synapses the electrical process is converted into chemical transmitters. Under multiple hierarchical networks of synapses, man's knowledge of the complex circuits form systems with specific functions and basic feelings such as fear, rage, and so forth. For example, connections between the orbito-frontal cortex, the anterior cingulated, and the amygdale along with their interactions enable control of affect and emotion.[14] This is a revolutionary idea contrary to the traditional

---

12 Josepth LeDoux, *Synaptic Self: How Our Brains Become Who We Are* (New York: Penguin Books, 2002), 24.

13 Ibid., 49.

14 Joohyung Lee, "Christian Discernment through the Neuroscientific Lens: within Jonathan Edwards' Religious Affection," *Korean Journal of Christian Studies* Vol.101 (2016): 204-207.

understanding that each brain area takes charge of each function and memory.

Next, LeDoux illustrates the self as the totality of what an organism is physically, biologically, psychologically, socially, and culturally. He states, "The different components of the self reflect the operation of different brain system...while explicit memory is mediated by a single system, there are a variety of brain systems that store information implicitly, allowing for many aspects of the self to coexist."[15] As for the way in which the mind of a human being is formed, it is a case of nature (genes), nurture (environmental stimulus), or both. LeDoux explains that "Genes only shape the broad outline of mental and behavioral function...inheritance may bias us in certain directions, but many other factors dictate how one's genes are expressed."[16] He concludes that nature and nurture are not different things but instead are different ways of doing the same thing—wiring synapses in the brain.[17]

As a consequence, LeDoux's investigation gives us this insight: "You are your synapses. They are who you are."[18] What man previously thought was spiritual, mental, or transcendental here is reduced to what is bodily, physical, and chemical. The conclusion that all spiritual and transcendental experiences can be regarded as different phenomena of synaptic works is threatening to religious enterprise indeed.

---

15 Ibid., 31.

16 Ibid., 66.

17 Ridley stands against LeDoux's reductionism. Ridley contends that nurture is affected by genes just as much as nature is. See Matt Ridley's *Nature Via Nurture: Genes, Experience, and What Makes Us Human* (New York: HarperCollins, 2003), 149.

18 Ibid., 324.

Then, in what ways can Christian theology respond constructively to the scientific findings saying that human lives can simply reduce to synaptic connections? And how can it be constructively implicated for Christian community in this scientific world?

IV. The Philosophical Insights on Relationality

As broadly criticized, LeDoux's point has been criticized as reductionist stance. Ted Peters contends that the science of the brain and the technology of the brain, curiously, are highly likely to be dysfunctional. They are contradictory, at least in part. The tendency of science is toward reductionism, toward reducing our minds and our souls to biological activity.[19] This research is convinced that the reductionist stance of scientist will not be constructive in building up a relevant theological discourse. So now, we move on to the alternative solution asking, "In what way can the existence of human beings avoid biological reductionism?"

Garcia-Rivera convincingly proposes the theological reconstruction of the relational dynamics between nature and mind would be affected as looking into the philosophical insights of Charles S. Pierce. The founding thinker of pragmatism in American history, Peirce was initially convinced that "Both Nature and Mind had been artificially separated and that their necessary connection could be found again

---

19 Ted Peters, "The Soul of Trans-Humanism," in *Dialog: A Journal of Theology*, Vol. 44, no. 4 (Winter 2005), 382.

in a reexamination of the nature of Being."[20] Pierce strongly believes that the concept of *being* must be approached by logic. Pierce first established in his logic three phenomenological categories: quality, fact, and law (habit), acknowledging that all human experience belongs to the three elements. Later he developed these into three corresponding metaphysical categories of *Firstness, Secondness,* and *Thirdness.* Peirce recognized three elements are applicable to every dimension of a being. "The first is a *quality* of feelings. The second is the energy (or *fact*) with which it affects other ideas…the third is the tendencies (or *habit*) of an idea to bring along other ideas with it."[21]

Pierce asserts that human species do not live on the basis of logic by rational materialism, but live on the basis of a new logic by being relational. Pierce recognizes that the new logic would have dealt more with relationships than with substances. That is, the reality is consisting with relation along with the physical and the mental. Then, Pierce devises the third reality since the first two realities could not be perceived independently. For being included as realities, a subject of perception or experiences is required. He names it "independent of the knowing mind" which he calls the *interpretant*.[22] For him, an idea cannot be constituted only thought what people might assume. Rather, a concept or notion is generated by a sign which is interacting activities among the signified, the signifier, and the interpreter (**logic of sign**). For instance, an experience of gratitude (the interpreter) could be gen-

---

20 Alejandro Garcia-Rivera, *the Community of the Beautiful: A Theological Aesthetics* (Collegeville, MN: The Liturgical Press, 1999), 103.

21 Ibid., 104.

22 Ibid., 106.

erated as a sign of gratitude (the signifier) is perceived in the mind of a recipient (the signified).

Given that a reality is relational, Pierce discovers the important role of non-rational forms of thinking such as imagination which enables the advancement from logical to metaphysical thinking. That is, the human mind, in principle, could formulate a virtual infiniteness rather than logic. It draws him to the conclusion that mind and reality have evolved simultaneously and in a relationship of dynamic and formative interaction; moreover, it makes a transition from phenomenology to metaphysics.[23]

Based on the frame, Peirce provides his kernel of the philosophical concept, "the law of mind," which shows that in mental phenomena ideas tend to spread continuously and to affect certain others which stand to them in a peculiar relation of affectability."[24] As an idea would be utilized among the human connection, the transition of the idea cannot just be a cognitive process, but affective components are essentially involved. Herein, Peirce critically contends the human person (self) as a connection of ideas. Pierce is convinced that human beings do not exist in a logical way, but in a *relational* one based on his or her interaction with others.

Pierce comes to the revolutionary conclusion that "matter" in traditional philosophy and science really exemplifies "effete mind." In Peirce's view, however "body" and "mind" are two terms for the same finite. Only two remain: mind and effete mind. The leading concept

---

23 Ibid., 151.
24 Ibid., 156.

here is the "continuity between non-living and living tendencies and between living and conscious tendencies in nature."[25] Namely, nature is "mind-like." Peirce's relational concept of reality leads to overcome dualism of spirit-matter, which is crucially responding to the scientific reductionism. Human mind cannot be just neuronal connections between synapse, but is continuing subject between biological substances and non-biological (transcendent) tendencies. This statement is still applicable in neuroscientific field since the reality of the reductionist findings could not fully explainable in whole human experiences yet. This is the milieu where possibly grace would be found.

It is notable that devising the system theory, Gregory Bateson builds up a more decisive understanding of the relationship between mind and nature based upon Pierce's thoughts. Bateson sees the mental characteristics of mind not just within the man but immanent in the entire circuit of interaction. Thus, the immanent mind is located in the total system. For him, a human mind first is defined as a mass of interacting parts or components. The differences of each part prompt not only changes, but also the transformation of preceding events under a hierarchy of logical types.[26] Corresponding to Pierce, Bateson implies that nature exclusively can exist in relationship with mind. Nature exists as same as the mind does. Namely, nature and human nature do not exist in a separately substantial way, for some sense connection with each other exists. Therefore, resonating with Peirce's theological idea continuity links creature and creator, Bateson considerably

---

25 Ibid., 161.

26 Gregory Bateson, *Mind and Nature: A Necessary Unit* (New Jersey: Hampton Press, 2002), 85-86.

claims nature is extrinsic, the mind is intrinsic, and they cannot exist independently.

Levels of Human Experiences

The concept that reality is relational leads us into the idea that the mind plausibly interpenetrates the whole *being*. Then this research will move onto the next critical question, "Unless dualism is valid, how can a human being exist?"

A Christian theologian pioneering in neuroscience and religious experiences, Mark Graves first agrees with LeDoux's assertion that human nature has a hierarchical system. On the one hand, He critically pinpoints a reductionism fallacy that LeDoux reduces the human system to mere biological level, the synapse. On the other, Graves stands with Bateson's concept that the component of system is shared in every level of the system of *being*. At first, he introduces five levels of the system in nature and they are locating hierarchically: subatomic, physical, biological, psychological, and cultural. Each level is interacting mutually in a hierarchical fashion with the lower levels forming the higher. Graves elucidates to illustrate the way in which each level interacts with and is interdependent upon their relationships through the example of the effect of calcium ion in each level. Since the calcium ion can be transmitted into whole level except cultural. The calcium ion participates in each system and the relationships among the systems do have patterns.[27] He demonstrates that the results show pat-

---

27 Mark Graves, *Mind, Brain, and the Elusive Soul: Human Systems of Cognitive Science and Religion* (New York: Routledge), 63-70.

terns interpenetrating each level, simultaneously playing crucial roles in each level.

Next, Graves acknowledges that cross-cultural interaction brings out a transcendent level. Resonating with Bateson's concept of mind, he states that on perceiving differences between two cultures, they interact with each other and result in changes. Furthermore, transformation or transcendence happens in such a way that one cannot form within its own. Here results the main question: "What are the characteristics of the cross-cultural interaction that bring about transformation?" Significantly, Graves suggests it is loyalty. Borrowing an American philosopher Josiah Royce's definition, Graves defines Loyalty as "a commitment to the principle of commitment and dedication that demonstrates support and obligation to the loyalty of those in opposing cultures to their particular cause."[28] Royce's ethical definition of loyalty, in "loyalty to loyalty . . . one attends to another's loyalty, avoids unnecessary conflict in the interest of harmony."[29] That is, interacting with each other by being loyal-to-loyal plays a decisive role in bringing out transcendence in the levels.

Graves states that Royce believes, the experience of transcendence is not realized by individuals, but communally in the context of relationship. By **interpreting signs**, a human being is able to participate in transcendence as individuals extend their lives into the past, present, and future. But it also emphasizes an isolated individual as a member of a community. Interpreting signs becomes an act of unitive transfor-

---

28 Ibid., 132.

29 Ibid., 137.

mation and redemptive, since it results in *at-one-ment*. In sum, Piece and Royce both establish in their philosophy that a *Being* is **relational** and simultaneously **communal**.

This research is ready to answer the next question: "How can human nature experience divine Grace?" The way a being exists is not rationally logical, but relational and communal. A being can be whole explicitly by the provision of connectedness and interaction with different parts.

V. Toward Aesthetics Dimension of Grace

This research has made endeavor to elucidate the way in which divine grace can exist as the same way a being can. It initially proves that both dualistic division and materialistic reductionism could be overcome. Secondly, the American philosophical frame provides us with theoretical insights that realities are neither composed by substance nor independent way. Rather it is relational and communal. Now, we can return to ultimate question regarding the way in which the divine grace within the reformed Christian circle could be more appropriate in scientific world.

Theological endeavor to integrate grace with nature has been comprehensively made by Thomas Aquinas so it deserves to explore his concept of grace within his theological structures. As well known, Aquinas' theological construction had heavily been grounded in Aristotle's causation in philosophy, which supplies an appropriate tool to overcome dualistic worldview. It is believed to be a critical clue that

Aquinas' concept could be still relevant theological conversant to our contemporary world, where the neuroscientific findings has challenged to the dualism. Rather than exploring whole theological spectrum, we will pay more attention to the fact that Aquinas constructed his concept of Grace out of the concept of *habitus* from Aristotle's philosophical term.

For Thomas Aquinas, the fundamental human problem is that human nature is not sufficient for achieving the supernatural end for which they are intended. Grace, then, becomes that which fulfills or elevates human nature so that it might achieve its supernatural destiny. In Aquinas' thoughts Grace in itself perfects the soul's essence, since it is a certain participatory likeness in the divine nature. Grace accomplishes this elevation of the human soul through its infusion into the human soul as a **habit** (habitus).[30] As Roger Haight indicates, "Since a habit is a specific principle of operation, grace is conceived of as the new nature, the higher principle of activity to a supernatural end."[31] What is apparent from this very brief description is that, ontologically speaking, Grace is a habit, a permanent disposition residing in the human spirit. For Aquinas, **habitual grace** raises human nature so that a human being may be proportionate to his or her transcendent end, which is a new nature. Furthermore, habitual grace residing in the soul gives rise not only to sanctification but also to participation in divine works and His creativity. It is notable the way in which Aquinas' definition of

---

30 This definition in Thomas Aquinas originated from Aristotle's Habitus, meaning to anticipate the **future** based on **past** experiences, and to force **presence** toward setting up physical law. Thus, it indicates that in habit, past, present and future co-exist.

31 Roger Haight, *the Experience and Language of Grace* (New York: Paulist, 1979), 60.

habitual grace would be corresponded to and relevantly familiar with both the **logic of sign** in Pierce and the **interpretation** in Royce. They are all pointing out transcendental experience of human nature. For Aquinas, the habitual grace inherently lead human being into spiritual experiences by perceiving the interconnectedness and mutual reciprocity among the natures. A being acknowledges the divine grace permeated into the whole creatures on earth. The grace habitual, relational and communal invites a soul to see the holistic and integrating aspect of divine grace and creative works. It is the experiences of awe or wonder toward the ultimate beauty. The habitual grace finally prompts human being to experience aesthetic aspect of nature.

Garcia-Rivera contends that the **aesthetic** dimension is critically essential in appreciating divine grace and its creative works. When humans discover aesthetic values, they may ultimately be able to understand what ways human beings exist. Adopting Mukarovsky's semiotic terminology, Garcia-Rivera explains the aesthetic dimension of grace utilizing the concept of being as "foregrounding" along with relational and communal. "Foregrounding" defined "lifts the lowly up" a selected piece of the background to give it value. This helps humanity view a broader horizon of the world and nature. He believes that a Being should be aesthetic even since the divine creation also is created not according to "a logical rule of law, but to the laws of the heart." He convincingly states that "The universe is ordered less by the laws of design than by the laws of the love of difference." Foregrounding leads humans to take a holistic perspective and to acknowledge a being aesthetically, rather than logically.

Garcia-Rivera's aesthetical concept of "foregrounding" provides us with theological insights for human nature to knowing the Being (God). He states that when habitual grace engages with human being, the human path to knowing God cannot be formulated by logical rationalism—but by aesthetic approaching, "foregrounding." Herein, figuring out clearly the specific definition of "knowing" in this context is critical. According to Garcia-Rivera, human beings are inherently given the capacity to facilitate another kind of knowing besides perception and cognition: the spiritual sense. The significance of the spiritual sense, contrary to others, lies in its "fullness" of sensing—that is, the reunion of the "material" and "spiritual" sense." This holistic perception is "inside and outside looking into one another in an encounter which is a struggle, a reciprocal influence."[32]

According to Garcia-River, beauty is **unitive** and **holistic**. The aspect of beauty also is discovered in the sign of logic in Peirce and interpretation in Royce. For him, the aesthetic dimension of a being tends to disclose its nature by answering the critical questions. So he refers to the aesthetic questions and answers it to make the points to holistic views and unitive interaction among any issue. The first aesthetic question is, "Does the aesthetic perception of a being make possible to bring about participation of human nature into the habitual Grace?" Yes, indeed. On realizing a being as the foregrounding, not backgrounding of the nature,[33] it lifts human nature up, giving opportunity to look at nature from the perspective of Grace.

This triggers the second question on necessity of the *Deo*-drama,

---

32 Garcia-River, *the Community of the Beautiful: A Theological Aesthetics*, 173-174.

33 Ibid., 168-169.

"is there *Deo*-drama, not human drama in nature?" he answers yes too since each human story is subordinated in the *Deo*-drama. It is imperative to interpret human experience of any tragedy from the transcendent perspectives. Otherwise, no way to understand the way in which an innocent people have been experiences the inexplicable sufferings in human history. The *Deo*-drama enables human beings to comprehend their suffering from transcendent viewpoints, not from their own nature. However, when human nature enters into relation with Nature, it becomes a vehicle, ironically, to be able to go through transformation and transcendence. In **habitual grace**, human being can see God's story within the universe and equip them to understand how all stories are interwoven and interconnected, affecting each other. Then, one can recognize that as human nature belongs to nature, human tragedy can be solved readily. This is the crucial realization of someone with the foregrounding, the aesthetic dimension of grace.

Therefore, the aesthetic perception is not judgmental—whether it is beauty or not, but about appreciation—whether it is beautiful or ugly. This process of appreciation lifts the lowly up by "foregrounding" so that it prompts transformation or transcendence to a level of a being. Consequently, the meaning of the aesthetic sense in habitual grace is to discern a holistic world and its unitive interaction. Here is the significant locus to renew humanity's understanding of salvation and redemption. Grace sanctifies Nature including human nature. The grace embedded in Nature can interact with human nature. Human nature can neither be superior to, nor separated from Nature. This is the watershed to accommodate the out-of-date Grace into the contemporary world. This is the launching place to rediscover the value of Grace in the post-modern society.

Grace in Divine Milieu

In his remarkable book *The Divine Milieu*, Teilhard de Chardin stresses that creation is not an end, but a process.[34] He convinces us that the mystery of creation is incarnation in which spirit becomes matter since spirit and matter are not separated or isolated, as the same way heaven and earth coexist. How does Grace manifest itself in the Divine Milieu? It is Nature. The grace relational, communal and aesthetical will be manifested in Nature as divine gift.

When I visited the Korean War Memorial in Washington D.C., I felt something compelling comes up in my mind. First of all, I realized the names inscribed in the death list are interconnected with my life, even if I have never met them alive. It incurred my communal consciousness that their death is not just American loss, but the collective sacrifices for human freedom or dignity. The status depicting American soldiers engaging a battle mission in harsh weather condition told me that it is not just their stories; it is my story and our stories. My personal consciousness was expended into the communal and collective consciousness, which is mutually connected. Regardless of the alive or death, the people's stories are interconnected to each other.

At next, the compelling awareness moved into spiritual reflection that an individual story has become constitutive elements of the whole story. My personal narrowed perspectives were confronted by bigger view and it readily led me into new dimension of reality in which dual-

---

34 Pierre Teilhard De Chardin, *The Divine Milieu* (New York: Harper & Row, 1960).

istic worldview is meaningless anymore. The boundaries between the enemy and ally, your country and mine, communism and capitalism, night and day become blurred. It reminded me of the biblical imagination that tiger and lamb share co-exist without compromising tension and conflict, but peaceful indwelling is present. The aesthetic experiences in the war memorial ushered me into new consciousness and spiritual sense, the holistic awareness of relational and communal realities. I felt standing on the highest point and looking down the world where all beings and existence are harmonious and matching without conflicts. It is liberating experiences, redemptive, transformative. It is about the divine grace, which is permeated in divine milieu.

Yes, divine grace manifests itself in Nature. Grace and nature mutually presupposes to each other. Nature is given the capacity to transcend itself through Grace; Divine Grace is incarnated through Nature. no contradiction or denial is allowed. Rather the authentic integration and mysterious harmony manifest in the divine milieu. This is the locus where reformed tradition could be reformulated or reshaped for renewing or transforming their Christian spirituality to regain its relevancy or credibility in our contemporary world.

VI. Conclusion

This research makes endeavor to invite the Christian Reformed tradition to take into serious consideration of reformulating Divine Grace in natural scientific world. The main problem of the Reformed tradition is that, while overemphasizing grace as a divine gift and sinful nature of human, they have generated a deep chasm between nature and human nature. Grace has been stuck within the dualistic world-view, which seriously hampers those theologians in engaging in dia-logue with the natural sciences. Paradoxically, the out-of-date notion of Grace becomes a barrier in seeing God's revelation of Himself in nature. Their isolated Grace may give rise to a narrowing of the posi-tion of God, shrinking the potential area of salvation and redemption in the universe. Therefore, this inquiry is convinced that deliberate effort to engage dialogue with the natural sciences and their information will be threshold to rediscover divine grace.

The practical theological research method of interdisciplinary approaches contributes to enhance the credibility of theological dis-course through engaging with various disciplinary discourses on grace and nature. It initially confronted to the neuroscientific assumption of biological or materialistic reductionism in religious experiences. The philosophical insights are presented as critical vehicle to demonstrate the realities are perceived as mechanical or dualistic ways; rather it is relational and communal. At next, aesthetic experiences encapsulate the way in which divine grace would manifest through nature, and the experiences of beauty give rise to spiritual awareness to interconnected or interpenetrated nature. The holistic perspective leads us to the new awareness that Divine grace will not legitimate human supremacy over nature; rather human nature is inherently connected and related with Nature, the divine milieu. It is a liberating locus not only to renew the spirituality for an intimate relationship with God, but also to join the creative works of the Trinity in given context.

Bibliography

Bateson, Gregory. *Mind and Nature: A Necessary Unit*. New Jersey: Hampton Press, 2002.

Browning, Don. *A Fundamental Practical Theology*. Minneapolis, MN: Augsburg Fortress, 1996.

Carpenter, James. *Nature and Grace: Toward an Integral Perspective*. New York: Crossroads, 1988.

Duffy, Stephen. *The Dynamics of Grace*. Liturgical Press: Michael Glazier, 1993.

Garcia-Rivera, Alejandro R. *A Wounded Innocence: Sketches for a Theology of Art*. Collegeville, MN: The Liturgical Press, 2003.

──────────. *The Community of the Beautiful: A Theological Aesthetics*. Collegeville, MN: The Liturgical Press, 1999.

Grave, Mark. *Mind, Brain, and the Elusive Soul: Emerging Systems of Cognitive Science and Religion*. New York: Ashgate Publishing, 2008.

Haight, Roger. *The Experience and Language of Grace*. New York: Paulist Press, 1979.

Jeeves, Malcolm. "Human Nature: An Integrated Picture," *What About the Soul?: Neuroscience and Christian Anthropology*. Ed. by Joel B. Green, Nashville: Abingdon, 2004.

LeDoux, Joseph. *Synaptic Self: How Our Brains Become Who We Are*. New York: Penguin Books, 2002.

Joohyung Lee. "Christian Discernment through the Neuroscientific Lens: within Jonathan Edwards' Religious Affection," *Korean Journal of Christian Studies* Vol. 101 (2016): 201-225.

────────. "Sacred Encounters: Spirituality in College Education," *University and Mission* 31 (2016): 317-319.

Peters, Ted. "The Soul of Trans-Humanism," in *Dialogue: A Journal of Theology*, Vol. 44, no. 4 (Winter 2005).

Ridley, Matt. *Nature Via Nurture: Genes, Experience, and What Makes Us Human*, N.Y.: HarperCollins, 2003.

Rober, Daniel A. *Recognizing the Gift: Toward a Renewed Theology of Nature and Grace*. Minneapolis, MN: Fortress Press, 2016.